Praise for *Staying Alive* and Vandana Shiva

Staying Alive

Staying Alive

WOMEN, ECOLOGY,

AND

DEVELOPMENT

Vandana Shiva

North Atlantic Books
Berkeley, California

Published by   Cover photo © iStockphoto.com/ferrantraite
North Atlantic Books   Cover design by Jasmine Hromjak
Berkeley, California   Book design by Adept Content Solutions

Printed in the United States of America

Previously published in 1999 by Women Unlimited and in 2010 by South End Press.

Staying Alive: Women, Ecology, and Development is sponsored and published by North Atlantic Books, an educational nonprofit based in Berkeley, California, that collaborates with partners to develop cross-cultural perspectives, nurture holistic views of art, science, the humanities, and healing, and seed personal and global transformation by publishing work on the relationship of body, spirit, and nature.

North Atlantic Books' publications are distributed to the US trade and internationally by Penguin Random House Publishers Services. For further information, visit our website at www.northatlanticbooks.com.

Library of Congress Cataloging-in-Publication Data

Shiva, Vandana.
  Staying alive : women, ecology, and development / Vandana Shiva.
    pages cm
  Includes index.
  First published in India [in 1988] by Kali for Women and Women Unlimited.
  Summary: "Presents a clear case for why our current development paradigm is more accurately characterized as what Vandana Shiva calls 'maldevelopment'—the violation of the integrity of organic, interconnected and interdependent systems that sets in motion a process of exploitation, inequality, violence, and injustice that is dragging the world down a path of self-destruction, threatening survival itself"— Provided by publisher.
  ISBN 978-1-62317-051-6 (Trade paper)—ISBN 978-1-62317-052-3 (E-book)
  1. Women in development—India. 2. Human ecology—India. 3. Patriarchy— India. 4. Environmental policy—India. 5. India—Social policy. 6. Women—India— Social conditions. I. Title.
  HQ1240.5.I4S54 2016
  305.420954—dc23   2015033602

3 4 5 6 7 8 9 KPC 25 24 23 22 21

CONTENTS

ACKNOWLEDGMENTS

This book is a gift to those who made it possible:

- The many women, peasants, and tribals of India who have been my teachers in thinking ecologically.

- Rajni Kothari, who made such learning possible by creating the context for intellectual freedom.

- Jayanto Bandyopadhyay, my ex-husband, who was my partner in learning.

- Rajuji, my father, who first mothered me and then my son.

- Kartikey, my son, for his generous love which allows me to do what I do.

To my late mother
for her legacy of the courage
to think and act differently

The Gendered Politics of Food and the Challenge of Staying Alive

Agriculture, the growing of food, is both the most important source of livelihood for the majority of the world's people, especially women, and the sector related to the most fundamental of economic rights—the right to food and nutrition. Women were the world's original food producers, in terms of the work they do in the food chain, and continue to be central to food production systems in the global South. The worldwide destruction of the feminine knowledge of agriculture evolved over four to five thousand years by a handful of white male scientists in less than two decades has not merely violated women as experts but, since their expertise is modeled on nature's system of renewability, has gone hand in hand with the ecological destruction of nature's processes and the economic destruction of poor people in rural areas. Agriculture has been evolved by women. Most food producers, farmers, in the world are women, and most girls are future farmers; they learn the skills and knowledge of farming in fields and farms. Women also produce more than half the world's food and provide more than 80 percent of the food needs in food-insecure households and regions.

Food security is, therefore, directly linked to women's food producing capacity. Constraints on this lead to erosion of food security, especially for poor households in poor regions. Diversity characterizes women's work, their planting and sowing of foodcrops, and the pattern of their food processing. The dominant systems of economics, science, and technology have conspired against women and girls by conspiring against diversity. From field to kitchen, from seed to food; women's strength is diversity; women's capacities are eroded when this diversity is eroded.

Economics has rendered women's work as food providers invisible. Because women provide for the household, not the market, they have remained invisible as farmers despite their contribution to farming. People fail to see the work they do in agriculture; their production tends to go unrecorded as "work" or is seen as being outside the "production boundary" by economists. There is a conceptual inability on the part of statisticians and researchers to define women's work inside and outside the house (and farming is usually part of both); this non-recognition of what is and is not labor is exacerbated both by the great volume of work that women do and the fact that they do many chores at the same time. Problems of data collection on agricultural work arise not because too few women work, but because too many women do too much work. It is also related to the fact that although women work to sustain their families and communities, most of their work is not measured in wages and is concentrated outside market-related or remunerated work.

Science and technology have rendered women's knowledge and productivity worthless by ignoring the dimension of diversity in agricultural production. According the Food and Agriculture Organization report *Women Feed the World,* women use more plant diversity, both cultivated and uncultivated, than agricultural scientists have knowledge of. Contrasted with the monocultures promoted by western science, in Nigerian home gardens women plant 18 to 57 plant species. In sub-Saharan Africa they cultivate as many as 120 different plants alongside the cash crops managed by men. In Guatemala, home gardens of smaller than 0.1 hectare have more than ten tree and crop species. In one African home garden more than 60 species of food-producing trees were counted. In Thailand, researchers found 230 plant species in home gardens. In India, women use 150 different species of plants for vegetables, fodder, and health care. In West Bengal, 124 "weed" species collected from rice fields have economic importance for farmers. In the España region of Veracruz, Mexico, peasants utilize about 435 wild plant and animal species, of which 229 are eaten. Women are the biodiversity experts of the world.

While women manage and produce diversity, the dominant paradigm of agriculture promotes monoculture on the assumption that monocultures produce more. While biotechnology is projected as increasing food production four times, small ecological farms are hundreds of time more productive than large industrial farms based on conventional farming.

As FAO's (World Food Day, 1998) report on eastern Nigeria found, home gardens occupying only 2 percent of a household farmland accounted for half the farm's total output. In India, Navdanya's studies on biodiversity-based, ecological agriculture indicate that women-run farms produce more food and nutrition than industrial, chemical farms. Clearly, if women's knowledge were not being rendered invisible, the use of the 2 percent of land under polyculture systems would be the path followed for providing food security. Instead, these highly productive systems are being destroyed in the name of producing "more" food.

Just as women's ways of growing food produce more food while conserving more resources, women's ways of processing food conserve nutrition. Hand-pounding or milling rice with a foot-operated mortar and pestle preserves more protein, fat, fiber, and minerals. If the rice is preserved, the nutrients conservation is even more dramatic. Thus, when mechanical hullers replace the hand-pounding—as in Bangladesh, where 700 new mills supplanted the paid work of 100,000 to 140,000 women in one year—women are not only robbed of work and livelihoods, but people are robbed of essential nutrients.

Feeding the world requires producing more food with fewer resources, that is, producing more with less. Women are experts in this and their expertise needs to filter into our institutions of agricultural research and development. Women's lack of property rights is a major constraint on their capacity to feed the world. Property rights include rights to land, as well as rights to common resources like water and biodiversity. New intellectual property rights (IPRs) are alienating women's rights to biodiversity and erasing their innovations in agricultural biodiversity. If the erosion of women's capacity for feeding the world has to be prevented, IPR regimes need to evolve *sui generis* systems that recognize and protect women's collective and informal innovation. While women are being denied their rights to resources, dominant agriculture is increasingly appropriating resources and rights from women in subsistence agriculture as it presents itself as the only alternative for feeding the world.

Women farmers in the Third World are predominantly small farmers. They provide the basis of food security, and they provide food security in partnership with other species. This partnership between women and biodiversity has kept the world fed throughout history, is doing so in the current moment, and will continue to feed the world in the future. It is this partnership that needs to be preserved and promoted to ensure food security.

Agriculture based on diversity, decentralization, and improving small farm productivity through ecological methods is a women-centered, nature-friendly agriculture. In this agriculture, knowledge is shared—other species and plants are kin, not "property"—and sustainability is based on the renewal of the earth's fertility and the renewal and regeneration of biodiversity and species richness on farms. There is no place for monocultures of genetically engineered crops or IPR monopolies on seeds. Monocultures and monopolies symbolize patriarchal agriculture. The war mentality underlying military-industrial agriculture is evident from the names given to the herbicides destroying the economic basis of the survival of the poorest women in the rural areas of the Third World. Roundup, Machete, and Lasso from Monsanto. Pentagon, Prowl, Scepter, Squadron, Cadre, and Avenge from American Home Products, which has merged with Monsanto. The language is of war, not sustainability. The most widespread application of genetic engineering in agriculture is herbicide resistance, that is, the breeding of crops to be resistant to herbicides. (Monsanto's Roundup Ready Soybean and Cotton are examples of this application.) When this technology was introduced into Third World farming systems it led to an increased use of agrochemicals, thus increasing environmental problems. It also destroyed the biodiversity that is the sustenance and livelihood base of rural women: what are weeds for Monsanto are food, fodder, and medicine for Third World women.

While women have maintained the continuity of seed over millennia in spite of war, flood, and famine, the masculinization of agriculture has led to violent technologies ensuring that seeds do not germinate. This has been described as terminator technology. Termination of germination is a means for capital accumulation and market expansion. But the abundance in nature and for farmers shrinks as markets grow for Monsanto. When we sow seed we pray, "May this seed be exhaustless." On the other hand, Monsanto and the U.S. Department of Agriculture (USDA) ask, "Let this seed be terminated so that our profits and monopoly are exhaustless."

The violence intrinsic to the methods and metaphors used by global agribusiness and biotechnology corporations is a violence against nature's biodiversity and women's expertise and productivity. The violence intrinsic to the destruction of diversity through monocultures, and the destruction of the freedom to save and exchange seeds through IPR monopolies, is inconsistent with women's diverse, nonviolent ways of knowing nature and providing food security.

Genetic engineering and IPRs rob women of their creativity, innovation, and decision-making power in agriculture. Corporate globalization, driven by capitalist patriarchy, has transformed food, food production, and food distribution. The control over the entire food chain, from seed to table, is shifting from women's hands to global corporations who are today's "global patriarchs." When corporate-controlled food is no longer food, it becomes a commodity—it doesn't matter whether it ends up as biofuel for driving a car, feed for factory farms, or food for the hungry as long as a profit is made. Not only is food displaced, women's knowledge and work, skills, productivity, and creativity are destroyed. In place of women deciding what is grown in fields and served in kitchens, agriculture based on globalization, genetic engineering, and corporate monopolies on seeds will establish a food system and worldview in which the men who control global corporations also control what is grown in our fields and what we eat. Corporate men investing financial capital in theft and biopiracy will present themselves as creators and owners of life.

Agriculture systems shaped by women have a number of key features. Farming is done on a small scale. Natural resources—soil, water, biodiversity—are conserved and renewed. There is little or no dependence on fossil fuels and chemicals, which is vital in a period of climate change and peak oil. Inputs needed for production such as fertilizers are produced on the farm from compost, green manure, or nitrogen-fixing crops. Diversity and integration are key features and nutrition is a key consideration. Women-run small farms maximize nutrition per acre while they conserve resources.

Women-centered agriculture is the basis of food security for rural communities. When the household and community are food-secure, the girl child is food-secure. When the household and community are food-insecure, it is the girl child who, because of gender discrimination, pays the highest price in terms of malnutrition. When access to food diminishes, the girl child's share is last and least.

The politics of food is gendered at multiple levels.

First the Seed: Globalization and the Gendered Politics of Seed

The seed is the first link in the food chain. For 5,000 years peasants have produced their own seeds, selecting, storing, replanting, and letting nature take its course in the food chain. The conservation of seeds by women in their work in food and grain storage has ensured the preservation of genetic diversity and the self-renewability of food crops. All this changed with the Green Revolution. The Green Revolution commercialized and privatized seeds, removing the control over plant genetic resources from Third World peasant women and giving it over to western male technocrats in the International Maize and Wheat Improvement Center, the International Rice Research Institute, and multinational seed corporations.

Women have acted as custodians of the common genetic heritage through the preservation of grain. A study of rural women of Nepal found that responsibility for seed selection is primarily a female one; in 60.4 percent of the cases, women alone decided which type of seed to use, while men decided in only 20.7 percent of the cases. As to who actually selects the seeds in cases where the family decides to use their own seeds, in 81.2 percent of the households this work is done by women alone, by both sexes in 8 percent, and by men alone in 10.8 percent of households.

Throughout India, even in times of scarcity, grain for seed was conserved in every household so that the cycle of food production was not interrupted. For thousands of years the peasant women of India have carefully maintained the genetic base of food production. This common wealth, evolved over millennia, was defined as "primitive" by the masculinist view of seeds, which saw its own new products as "advanced" varieties.

The destruction of the self-reproducing character and genetic diversity of seeds was the beginning of seeds becoming a source of profits and control. This was an attack on the feminine principle. The hybrid "miracle" seeds are a commercial miracle because farmers are forced to buy new supplies of them every year. Hybrids do not produce seeds that reproduce the same result because hybrids do not pass their traits on to the next generation. With hybridization, seeds could no longer be viewed as a source of plant life; they were now a source of private profit only.

Green revolution varieties of seeds were clearly not the best alternative for increasing food production from the point of view of nature, women, and poor peasants. They were useful for corporations that wanted to increase seed and fertilizer sales, and they were useful for rich farmers wanting to make profits. The same international agencies that financed research on the new seeds also provided the money for their distribution. The challenge of selling a new variety of seed to millions of peasants who could not afford to buy them was solved by the World Bank, UNDP, FAO, and a host of bilateral aid programs, which began to accord high priority to the distribution of high-yielding seed varieties in their aid programs.

Seventy percent of India depends upon traditional systems of production for their survival. Seeds produced and sold by farmers account for over 70 percent of the total seed supply in the country. Similarly, more than 70 percent of India's health-care needs are met by traditional systems of medicine, whose practitioners use over 7,500 varieties of medicinal plants as part of their healing work. In fact, the biodiversity-based traditional health-care system is being kept alive by 360,740 Ayurvedic practitioners, 29,701 Unani experts, and 11,644 Siddha specialists, according to an ethno-botanical survey taken in the late 1990s. In addition, millions of housewives, birth attendants, and herbal healers carry on village-based health traditions.

The sharing and exchange of biological resources and knowledge of their properties and use has been the norm in all indigenous societies, and it continues to be so in most communities today—including modern ones. But sharing and exchange are converted into "piracy" when individuals, organizations, or corporations who receive biodiversity and knowledge from indigenous communities freely convert this gift into private property through IPR claims.

Through IPR claims, seed, the common resource shared and saved by women, becomes the "property" of Monsanto for which royalties must be paid. Seed pirated from communities is now treated as "pirated" if it is saved or shared. The highest human values are converted into a crime; the lowest human traits are elevated to "intellectual property rights."

The Trade-Related Aspects of Intellectual Property Rights (TRIPS) Agreement of the WTO is one aspect of globalization that when combined with the opening up of the seed industry could become the biggest threat to people's food security. The section of TRIPS that most directly affects farmers' rights and agriculture biodiversity is Article 27.5.3(b), which states:

> Parties may exclude from patentability plants and animals other than micro-organisms, and essentially biological processes for the production of plants or animals other than non-biological and micro-biological processes. However, parties shall provide for the protection of plant varieties either by patents or by an effective *sui generis* system or by any combination thereof. This provision shall be reviewed four years after the entry into force of the Agreement establishing the WTO.

The article thus allows two forms of IPRs on plants—patents and a *sui generis* system. The Patent Act and the National Plant Variety legislation drafts are becoming major contests between public and corporate interests. In India, the 1970 Patent Act excluded all methods of agriculture and horticulture. In addition, the exclusion of product patents in the area of agrochemicals was ensured through Section 5a. The Patent (Amendment) Bill, 1995 sought to remove these restrictions in the field of agriculture. Further, since it did not articulate new criteria for exclusion, it allowed for the patenting of plants, plant products, plant characteristics, their genes, bio-pesticides, bio-fertilizers, and the like. The totally unrestricted scope that this bill proposed would have undermined Indian agriculture, threatened Indian farmers, and imperiled food security. It failed to pass in Parliament because of these serious implications.

Over the past decade, through new property rights and new technologies, corporations have hijacked the diversity of life on earth and people's indigenous innovation. Intellectual-property-rights regimes, globalized through the TRIPS agreements of the WTO, have been expanded to cover life forms, thus creating monopoly control over biodiversity. In India, the Biodiversity Act, 2002 should have defended community rights; instead, it facilitated the privatization of biodiversity and indigenous knowledge. This is why the success of movements in forcing Syngenta to back off from pirating of our rice is significant.

In Navdanya, we conserve 2,000 rice varieties in our community seed banks, one of which is basmati, the aromatic rice for which Dehradun is famous. This variety, which farmers in my valley have been growing for centuries, was claimed as "an instant invention of a novel rice line" by a U.S. corporation called RiceTec (patent no. 5663454). After a four-year-long campaign most of RiceTec's patent claims were overturned. Similarly, the use of the neem tree, which our mothers and grandmothers have used for centuries as a pesticide and fungicide, was patented by W.R. Grace, another U.S. corporation. We challenged Grace's patent in the European Parliament and in the European Patent Office. After a fight of more than ten years the patent was revoked.

This phenomenon of biopiracy, through which western corporations are stealing centuries of collective knowledge and innovation from Third World women, is now reaching epidemic proportions. Monsanto is now calling this biopiracy a "partnership" between agribusiness and Third World women. For us, theft cannot be the basis of partnership—partnership implies equality and mutual respect. Partnership with Third World women necessitates changes in the WTO/TRIPS agreement, which protects the pirates and punishes the original innovators. It also requires changes in the U.S. Patent Act, which allows rampant piracy of our biodiversity-related knowledge. These changes are essential to ensure that our collective knowledge and innovation are protected, and that women are recognized and respected as farmers and biodiversity experts.

Raw to Cooked: The Gendered Politics of Food Processing

If patriarchal "intellectual property rights" are used to destroy biodiversity and usurp women's knowledge embodied in breeding seed, "sanitary and phytosanitary" laws—food safety defined from the perspective of capitalist patriarchy—are used to destroy women's expertise in producing quality, healthy, and tasty food and replace it with processed junk food. Food-safety laws are being shaped that deregulate large corporations and overregulate the small-scale, self-organized economy. These laws promote globalized food production at the expense of local food and farmers. The EU, for example, now insists that milking cows be fully mechanized. It also prescribes that only steel machinery and filtered air be used for processing. This is beyond the financial capability of most cattle owners, as they have only one or two milking animals.

Similar measures have been prescribed for agro-processing by global agribusiness to make fresh, locally produced food appear "backward," and stale food clothed in aluminum and plastic appear "modern." Industrial processing and packaging was first applied to edible oils to the benefit of imported soybeans, destroying the livelihood of oil-mill operators and small farmers. An attempt is now being made to take over the wheat economy.

The Indian wheat economy is based on decentralized, small-scale local production, processing, and distribution. While each individual participant is small, wheat and flour provide livelihoods and nutrition to millions of farmers, traders, and local mill operators. The decentralized, small-scale, household-based economy of food production and food processing is huge in aggregate—while ensuring that fresh and wholesome food is available to people at accessible prices. It is estimated that more than 3.5 million family-run kirana shops supply wheat to Indian consumers, and more than 2 million small neighborhood mills produce fresh flour. In addition, flour is produced by millions of women working at the household level. The rolling pin for making rotis has always been a symbol of women's power. Moreover, such production and processing does not have the devastating environmental impact of industrial agriculture.

Of the 15 million tons of atta flour purchased annually, less than 1 percent carries a brand name because Indian consumers trust their own supervision of quality at the local chakki better than a brand name attached to stale, packaged flour. This decentralized, small-scale economy based on millions of producers, processors, and traders works with very little capital and even less infrastructure. However, such a people-centered economy impedes big agribusiness, which is looking to transform the Indian wheat economy into a source of profit.

The destruction of millions of livelihoods, of local decentralized economy, and of people's access to fresh and cheap atta is described as the "modernization of the food chain." In the Third World, packaged food is promoted as the food of the rich, even though the rich in industrialized countries in fact eat fresh food, while the poor are forced to eat food that is heavily processed and packaged. Packaging is not "modernization," rather it is a tactic used to displace cheaper and more efficient systems in which food is processed locally—in front of people's eyes—ensuring quality and freshness.

Hunger, Malnutrition, and the Politics of Food

Food riots make front-page news, but the daily hunger of nearly a billion people, the problem of malnutrition linked to obesity, and other food-related diseases are hidden. Malnutrition is a consequence both of the denial of access to food and of the disappearance of nutrition from our farms and processing systems. Malnutrition in childhood leads to malnutrition in adulthood. Malnutrition is a major cause of anemia in women and the most significant cause of maternal mortality. When underfed women become mothers, their babies have a low birth weight, leaving them vulnerable to disease and deprived of their right to a full, healthy, and wholesome personhood. These issues of health are not ordinarily acknowledged as being connected to farming and growing food, but just as nutrition begins on the farm, so does malnutrition.

We are what we eat, but what are we eating?

Food safety, food security, and agriculture are intimately interrelated. How we grow our food and what we grow determines what we eat and who eats. It determines the quality and safety of our food. Yet food safety, food security, and agriculture have been separated from each other. Food is being produced in ways that are robbing the majority of people of it, and compelling those who eat to consume bad food. One billion people on the planet are hungry; another 2 billion are suffering from food-related diseases such as obesity, diabetes, and hypertension. Those who are not able to access food are victims of the malnutrition of poverty; those who can buy food in the global supermarket are victims of a different kind of malnutrition. Third World countries carry the triple burden of food-related diseases, hunger, and obesity. The WHO/ FAO have predicted that by the year 2020 70 percent of ischemic-heart-disease deaths, 75 percent of stroke deaths, and 70 percent of diabetes deaths will occur in developing countries. These diseases are directly linked to diet.

The globalized, industrialized food system is creating hunger. Industrialized agriculture is based on the destruction of small farmers—uprooted and dispossessed, peasants join the ranks of the hungry. Industrialized agriculture is also capital-intensive. It is based on costly external inputs such as purchased and nonrenewable seeds, synthetic fertilizers, pesticides, and herbicides. Peasants incur huge debts to purchase these inputs; to pay them back they must sell their entire crop, thus depriving themselves of food. If they cannot repay their debts they lose their land—and they are increasingly losing their lives. More than 150,000 farmers in India have committed suicide as costs of inputs have increased and the price of their produce has fallen, trapping them in endless cycles of debt.

Malnutrition and hunger are also on the rise because farmers are being pushed into growing cash crops for export. The nature of agriculture and the nature of food are being transformed. Agriculture—the care of the land, the culture of growing good food—is being transformed into a corporate, industrial activity. Food is being transformed from a source of nutrition and sustenance into a commodity, and as a commodity, it flowed first to factory farms and now to automobiles. The poor will get the leftovers.

The Globalization and Industrialization of Agriculture and Food Systems

Across the world, a food tsunami is occurring, transforming small farms run largely by female peasants into "factories" producing "commodities."

Globalization has led to greater industrialization of agriculture, and industrial agriculture displaces women from productive work on the land.

Agricultural globalization has been driven by agribusinesses seeking global markets for their non-renewable inputs—seeds, fertilizers, and pesticides—as well as markets for their food commodities. The Agriculture Agreement of the WTO and the structural-adjustment programs of the World Bank have been the most important instruments for the globalization of agriculture. This globalization involves multiple shifts: it shifts control over food production from local and national levels to the global level, and from women farmers to global corporations, whether it be in the area of seed or systems of maintaining and renewing soil fertility.

Factory farms are a negative food system because they consume more food than they produce. Industrial beef requires 10 kilograms of feed to produce 1 kilogram of food. Industrial pork requires 4 to 5.5 kilograms of feed to produce 1 kilogram of food. Factory-farmed chicken requires two to three times more feed than it produces as food.

Industrial biofuels are placing new pressures on food. Prices of corn in Mexico, the staple for Mexican tortillas, have doubled as corn is increasingly being used to make ethanol for fuel. Corn, soy, and canola are all being diverted to feed cars while people starve.

The industrialization of agriculture marks a shift from internal inputs to purchased, external inputs, from ecological to chemical, from biodiversity to monocultures. And it is a shift from women as the primary source of knowledge and skills about farming—from seed saving to composting, cultivating polycultures in the right balance, harvesting, storing, processing—to an agriculture without women.

Humanity has eaten more than 80,000 edible plants through its evolution. More than 3,000 have been used consistently. However, we now rely on just eight crops to provide 75 percent of the world's food, and with genetic engineering, production has narrowed to three crops—corn, soy, canola. Now these, too, are being diverted to biofuel. Monocultures are destroying biodiversity, our health, and the quality and diversity of food, and they lead to malnutrition—for those who are underfed as well as those who are overfed. Monocultures have been promoted as necessary to produce more food. However, all they produce is more control and profits—for Monsanto, Cargill, and Archer Daniels Midland. They create pseudo surpluses and real scarcity.

Corporations are forcing us to eat untested food such as GMOs. Even soy is being consumed in ways never imagined and is now present in 60 percent of all processed food. It has high levels of isoflavones and phytoestrogens which produce hormone imbalances in humans; traditional fermentation found in the food cultures of China and Japan reduce levels of isoflavones. The promotion of soy in food is a huge experiment promoted with US$13 billion in subsidies from the U.S. government between 1998 and 2004, and US$80 million a year from the U.S. soy industry. Local food cultures have rich and diverse alternatives to soy; for protein there are thousands of varieties of beans and grain legumes—pigeon-pea, chickpea, mung bean, urad-bean, rice-bean, azuki bean, moth-bean, cow-pea, peas, lentils, horse gram, fava bean, winged bean. In edible oils we have sesame, mustard, linseed, niger, saffola, sunflower, groundnut.

By depending on monocultures, the food system is being made increasingly dependent on fossil fuels—for synthetic fertilizers, for running giant machinery, for long-distance transportation. With the spread of monocultures and the destruction of local farms, we are increasingly eating oil, not food. Moving beyond monocultures of the mind has become an imperative for repairing the food system. Biodiverse small farms have higher productivity and generate higher incomes for farmers, while biodiverse diets provide more nutrition and better taste. Bringing biodiversity back to our farms goes hand in hand with bringing small farmers back to the land. Corporate control thrives on monocultures; citizens' food freedom depends on biodiversity.

Biofuels, fuels from biomass, continue to be the most important energy source for the poor in the world. The ecological, biodiverse farm is not just a source of food, it is a source of energy. Energy for cooking comes from inedible biomass like cow-dung cakes, stalks of millets and pulses, farmed trees, and village woodlots. Managed sustainably, village commons have been a source of decentralized energy for centuries. Industrial biofuels are not the fuel of the poor; they are the food of the poor, transformed into heat, electricity, and transportation for the rich. Liquid biofuels, in particular ethanol and biodiesel, driven by the search for alternatives to fossil fuels to avoid the catastrophe of peak oil and to reduce carbon dioxide emissions, are one of the fastest-growing sectors of production. George Bush tried to legislate the mandatory use of 35 billion gallons of biofuels annually by 2017. Global production of biofuels is increasing at a rapid pace. Argentina, Australia, Canada, China, Colombia, Ecuador, India, Indonesia, Malawi, Malaysia, Mexico, Mozambique, the Philippines, Senegal, South Africa, Thailand, and Zambia have all enacted pro-biofuel policies in recent years.

There are two types of industrial biofuels—ethanol and biodiesel. Ethanol can be produced from products rich in sucrose—such as sugarcane and molasses—and substances rich in starch—such as maize, barley, and wheat, blended with gasoline. Biodiesel is produced from vegetables such as palm, soy, and rapeseed oil, and is blended with diesel. Representatives of organizations and social movements from Brazil, Bolivia, Costa Rica, Colombia, Guatemala, and the Dominican Republic in a declaration titled "Full Tanks at the Cost of Empty Stomachs" wrote, "The current model of production of bioenergy is sustained by the same elements that have always caused the oppression of our people." And in an article titled "Foodstuff as Imperial Weapon: Biofuels and Global Hunger," Fidel Castro declared, "More than three billion people are being condemned to a premature death from hunger and thirst." Worldwide, the biofuel sector has grown rapidly. The United States and Brazil have established ethanol industries, and the European Union is quickly catching up in its exploration of potential markets. Governments all over the world are encouraging biofuel production with favorable policies.

Inevitably this massive increase in the demand for grains will come at the cost of human needs, with poor people priced out of the food market. On February 28, 2008, the Brazilian Landless Workers' Movement (MST) wrote, "the expansion of the production of biofuels aggravates hunger in the world. We cannot maintain our tanks full while stomachs go empty." This diversion of food for fuel has already increased the price of corn and soy, and this is just the beginning. Imagine the land required to provide 25 percent of the world's oil from food.

One ton of corn produces 413 liters of ethanol; the 35 billion gallons of ethanol sought by President Bush would require 320 million tons of corn. This is more than the total U.S. output of corn (280.2 million tons in 2005). Such production would change the U.S. from an exporter of corn to an importer. And its impact on Mexico, which as a result of NAFTA became dependent on U.S. corn, would be devastating.

The change to industrial biofuels, which are being promoted as a source of renewable energy and as a means to reduce greenhouse gas emissions, risks not only a food crisis, but can actually aggravate climate chaos and the CO_2 burden. The deforestation caused by expanding soy and palm oil plantations is leading to increased CO_2 emissions. The FAO estimates that 1.6 billion tons (or 25 to 30 percent of all greenhouse gases released into the atmosphere each year) come from deforestation. By 2022, biofuel plantations could destroy 98 percent of Indonesia's rainforests.

According to Wetlands International, the destruction of Southeast Asian lands for palm-oil plantations is contributing 8 percent of global CO_2 emissions, and, according to Delft Hydraulics, every ton of palm oil results in 30 tons of carbon dioxide emissions or ten times as much as petroleum producers. However, this additional burden on the atmosphere is treated as a clean development mechanism in the Kyoto Protocol for reducing emissions. Biofuels are thus contributing to or even exacerbating the same global warming that they are supposed to reduce.

To make matters worse, the conversion of biomass to liquid fuel uses more fossil fuels than it replaces. One gallon of ethanol production requires 28,000 kilocalories of energy. This provides 19,400 kilocalories of energy. Thus the energy efficiency is 43 percent. If the U.S. uses 20 percent of its corn to produce 5 billion gallons of ethanol, it will substitute for just 1 percent of oil use. If 100 percent of the U.S. corn crop were used, only 7 percent of its oil would be substituted. This is clearly not a solution either to peak oil or to climate chaos. When you consider that corn (which produces ethanol) uses more nitrogen fertilizer, more insecticide, and more herbicide than any other crop, and that 1,700 gallons of water are used to produce one gallon of ethanol, the "solution" is even more damaging.

Agriculture Without Women Farmers, Society Without Girls

The prevailing view is that economic globalization will modernize society and improve women's status, but the opposite is happening. The patriarchal values of the market and religion are combining to lead not just to women's marginalization, but to their very dispensability. The growing phenomenon of female feticide in India illustrates how capitalist patriarchy and religious patriarchy converge to unleash new levels of violence against women.

This regression is no accident. The Green Revolution region of Punjab was the place where female feticide first began; it was also the first to turn amniocentesis into a tool for facilitating it. Between 1978 and 1983, 78,000 female fetuses were aborted after sex-determination tests. The child sex ratio has declined from 976 (women for every 1,000 men) in 1961 to 927 in 2001. The change has been most dramatic since 1981, when sex-determination technologies became increasingly available. To look at it another way, India's population grew 21 percent between 1991 and 2001 to 1.03 billion. While the population grew, girls were disappearing. Taking into account the change in sex ratio and the population growth, there are 36 million fewer females in the population than would be expected.

If female feticide were only a result of a traditional bias against women, it would be restricted to areas where the bias against girls has been extreme in the past, and would decline as socioeconomic changes eroded traditional structures. However, it is spreading like a plague across Indian society: regions with high economic growth and more rapid "modernization" and integration into the global economy exhibit higher rates of female feticide and lower child sex ratios. The greater the economic growth and prosperity, the larger the number of missing girls.

Worldwide, women are resisting the policies that destroy the basis of their livelihood and food sovereignty. They are also creating alternatives to guarantee food security for their communities based on different principles and methods than those governing the dominant, profit-oriented global economy. They are:

- *Localization and regionalization instead of globalization*

- *Nonviolence instead of aggressive domination*

- *Equity and reciprocity instead of competition*

- *Respect for the integrity of nature and her species*

- *Understanding humans as part of, instead of as masters over, nature*

- *Protection of biodiversity in production and consumption*

The future of food needs to be reclaimed by women, shaped by women, and democratically controlled by women. Only when food is in women's hands will both food and women be secure.

Delhi, 2010

INTRODUCTION

'Let them come and see men and women and children who know how to live, whose joy of life has not yet been killed by those who claimed to teach other nations how to live.'

—Chinua Achebe[1]

The Age of Enlightenment, and the theory of progress to which it gave rise, was centred on the sacredness of two categories: modern scientific knowledge and economic development. Somewhere along the way, the unbridled pursuit of progress, guided by science and development, began to destroy life without any assessment of how fast and how much of the diversity of life on this planet is disappearing. The act of living and of celebrating and conserving life in all its diversity—in people and in nature—seems to have been sacrificed to progress, and the sanctity of life been substituted by the sanctity of science and development.

Throughout the world, a new questioning is growing, rooted in the experience of those for whom the spread of what was called 'enlightenment' has been the spread of darkness, of the extinction of life and life-enhancing processes. A new awareness is growing that is questioning the sanctity of science and development and revealing that these are not universal categories of progress, but the special projects of modern western patriarchy. This book has grown out of my involvement with women's struggles for survival in India over the last decade. It is informed both by the suffering and insights of those who struggle to sustain and conserve life, and whose struggles question the meaning of a progress, a science, a development which destroys life and threatens survival.

The death of nature is central to this threat to survival. The earth is rapidly dying: her forests are dying, her soils are dying, her waters are

1 Chinua Achebe, *No Longer at Ease*, London: Heinemann, 1960, p. 45.

dying, her air is dying. Tropical forests, the creators of the world's climate, the cradle of the world's vegetational wealth, are being bulldozed, burnt, ruined or submerged. In 1950, just over 100 million hectares of forests had been cleared—by 1975, this figure had more than doubled. During 1950-75, at least 120 million hectares of tropical forests were destroyed in South and Southeast Asia alone; by the end of the century, another 270 million could be eliminated. In Central America and Amazonia, cattle ranching for beef production is claiming at least 2.5 million hectares of forests each year; in India 1.3 million hectares of forests are lost every year to commercial plantation crops, river valley projects, mining projects, and so on. Each year, 12 million hectares of forests are being eliminated from the face of the earth. At current rates of destruction, by the year 2050 all tropical forests will have disappeared, and with tropical forests, will disappear the diversity of life they support.

Up to 50 percent of all living things—at least five million species—are estimated to live in tropical forests. A typical four square-mile patch of rainforest contains up to 1,500 species of flowering plants, 750 species of trees, 125 of mammals, 400 of birds, 100 of reptiles, 60 of amphibians and 150 of butterflies. The unparalleled diversity of species within tropical forests means relatively few individuals of each; any forest clearance thus disrupts their life cycles and threatens them with rapid extinction. Current estimates suggest that we are losing one species of life a day from the 5-10 million species believed to exist. If present trends continue, we can expect an annual rate of loss as high as 50,000 species by the year 2000. In India alone, there exist 7,000 species of plant life not found anywhere else in the world; the destruction of her natural forests implies the disappearance of this rich diversity of animal and plant life.

Forests are the matrix of rivers and water sources, and their destruction in tropical regions amounts to the dessication and desertification of land. Every year 12 million hectares of land deteriorate into deserts and are unable to support vegetation or produce food. Sometimes land is laid waste through desertification, at other times through ill-conceived land use which destroys the fertility of fragile tropical soils. Desertification in the Sahel in Africa has already killed millions of people and animals. Globally, some 456 million people today are starving or malnourished because of the desertification of croplands. Most agricultural lands cropped intensively with green revolution techniques are either waterlogged or dessicated deserts. Nearly 7 million hectares of land in India brought under irrigation have already gone out of production due to severe salinity, and an additional 6 million hectares have been seriously affected by water-logging. Green revolution agriculture has decreased genetic diversity and increased the vulnerability of crops to failure through lowering resistance to drought and pests.

With the destruction of forests, water and land, we are losing our life-support systems. This destruction is taking place in the name of 'development' and progress, but there must be something seriously wrong with a concept of progress that threatens survival itself. The violence to nature, which seems intrinsic to the dominant development model, is also associated with violence to women who depend on nature for drawing sustenance for themselves, their families, their societies. This violence against nature and women is built into the very mode of perceiving both, and forms the basis of the current development paradigm. This book is an attempt to articulate how rural Indian women, who are still embedded in nature, experience and perceive ecological destruction and its causes, and how they have conceived and initiated processes to arrest the destruction of nature and begin its regeneration. From the diverse and specific grounds of the experience of ecological destruction arises a common identification of its causes in the developmental process and the view of nature with which it is legitimised. This book focuses on science and development as patriarchal projects not as a denial of other sources of patriarchy, such as religion, but because they are thought to be class, culture, and gender neutral.

Seen from the experiences of Third World women, the modes of thinking and action that pass for science and development, respectively, are not universal and humanly inclusive, as they are made out to be; modern science and development are projects of male, western origin, both historically and ideologically. They are the latest and most brutal expression of a patriarchal ideology which is threatening to annihilate nature and the entire human species. The rise of a patriarchal science of nature took place in Europe during the fifteenth and seventeenth centuries as the scientific revolution. During the same period, the closely related industrial revolution laid the foundations of a patriarchal mode of economic development in industrial capitalism. Contemporary science and development conserve the ideological roots and biases of the scientific and industrial revolutions even as they unfold into new areas of activity and new domains of subjugation.

The scientific revolution in Europe transformed nature from *terra mater* into a machine and a source of raw material; with this transformation it removed all ethical and cognitive constraints against its violation and exploitation. The industrial revolution converted economics from the prudent management of resources for sustenance and basic needs satisfaction into a process of commodity production for profit maximisation. Industrialism created a limitless appetite for resource exploitation, and modern science provided the ethical and cognitive license to make such exploitation possible, acceptable—and desirable. The new relationship of man's domination and mastery over nature was thus also associated with new patterns of domination and mastery over women, and their exclusion from participation *as partners* in both science and development.

Contemporary development activity in the Third World superimposes the scientific and economic paradigms created by western, gender-based ideology on communities in other cultures. Ecological destruction and the marginalisation of women, we know now, have been the inevitable results of most development programmes and projects based on such paradigms; they violate the integrity of one and destroy the productivity of the other. Women, as victims of the violence of patriarchal forms of development, have risen against it to protect nature and preserve their survival and sustenance. Indian women have been in the forefront of ecological struggles to conserve forests, land and water. They have challenged the western concept of nature as an object of exploitation and have protected her as Prakriti, the living force that supports life. They have challenged the western concept of economics as production of profits and capital accumulation with their own concept of economics as production of sustenance and needs satisfaction. A science that does not respect nature's needs and a development that does not respect people's needs inevitably threaten survival. In their fight to survive the onslaughts of both, women have begun a struggle that challenges the most fundamental categories of western patriarchy— its concepts of nature and women, and of science and development. Their ecological struggle in India is aimed simultaneously at liberating nature from ceaseless exploitation and themselves from limitless marginalisation. They are creating a feminist ideology that transcends gender, and a political practice that is humanly inclusive; they are challenging patriarchy's ideological claim to universalism not with another universalising tendency, but with diversity; and they are challenging the dominant concept of power as violence with the alternative concept of nonviolence as power.

The everyday struggles of women for the protection of nature take place in the cognitive and ethical context of the categories of the ancient Indian world-view in which nature is Prakriti, a living and creative process,

the feminine principle from which all life arises. Women's ecology movements, as the preservation and recovery of the feminine principle, arise
from a non-gender-based ideology of liberation, different both from the
gender-based ideology of patriarchy which underlies the process of ecological destruction and women's subjugation, and the gender-based
responses which have, until recently, been characteristic of the west

Inspired by women's struggles for the protection of nature as a condition for human survival, this book goes beyond a statement of women
as special victims of the environmental crisis. It attempts to capture
and reconstruct those insights and visions that Indian women provide
in their struggles for survival, which perceive development and science
from outside the categories of modern western patriarchy. These oppositional categories are simultaneously ecological and feminist: they allow
the possibility of survival by exposing the parochial basis of science and
development and by showing how ecological destruction and the marginalisation of women are not inevitable, economically or scientifically.

Chapter 1 traces the historical and conceptual roots of development
as a project of gender ideology, and analyses how the particular economic assumptions of western patriarchy, aimed exclusively at profits,
have subjugated the more humane assumptions of economics as the
provision of sustenance, to make for a crisis of poverty rooted in ecological devastation.

Chapter 2 addresses itself to the myth of the neutrality and universality of modern science. It traces its beginnings in the scientific revolution
which, on the one hand, subjugated nature, and on the other, excluded
women as knowers and experts. The structure and methodology of modern science are reductionist; this chapter shows how reductionism as a
patriarchal mode of knowing is necessarily violent to nature and women.

Chapter 3 goes on to describe the world that Indian women inhabit,
both philosophically as a world-view, and in their daily practice, in the
production and renewal of life. For the women who are leading ecological
struggles, the nature they protect is the living Prakriti. It is the awareness
of nature as a living force, and of themselves as partners with her in the
production of sustenance that guides their ecological struggles. These
movements, while dependent on women's insights, are not based on a
gender ideology, and make for an oppositional category, conceptually.

Chapter 4 traces the beginning of the destruction of forests and wom-
en's expertise in forestry with the colonisation of India's forests. It shows
how what is called 'scientific forestry' is actually a narrow, reductionist

view of forestry that has evolved from the western bias for maximisation of profits. Chipko, the famous movement of the peasant women of Garhwal is viewed here as a response to this paradigm. The destruction of forest ecosystems and the displacement of women who generate survival through the forest are structurally linked to this reductionist paradigm of forestry. Responses to the severe repercussions of deforestation that emerge from centres of capitalist patriarchy deepen both the ecological and survival crises. These attempts are contrasted with women's initiatives at forest protection and regeneration which are sustainable and just, recovering both the diversity of forests as well as sharing the wealth that they produce.

Chapter 5 is an analysis of the food crisis as rooted in masculinist agricultural science and development which have destroyed nature's capital and have excluded women as experts and producers of food. The violence inherent in the green revolution for food-crops and the white revolution for dairying, is located and linked to shifts in the perception of food as a commodity, produced and exchanged for profit.

Chapter 6 is about the water crisis which is threatening the survival of plant, animal, and human life on a cataclysmic scale. It is related to land and water use for profit, such that limited water resources are over-exploited or diverted from survival needs to the imperative of profit maximisation. The reductionist view of water and water management is contrasted with the holistic knowledge women have for conserving and using it for survival.

The concluding chapter recapitulates the rationale behind the dominant science and technology and development paradigm that is responsible for the current economic and ecological crises, and posits the reclaiming of the feminine principle as a nonviolent, non-gendered and humanly inclusive alternative.

Women of the Third World have conserved those categories of thought and action which make survival possible, and which therefore make justice and peace possible. Ecology movements, women's movements and peace movements across the world can draw inspiration from these categories as forces of opposition and challenge to the dominant categories of western patriarchy which rule the world today in the name of development and progress, even while they destroy nature and threaten the life of entire cultures and communities. It is to focus on and pay tribute to the leadership of millions of unknown women in India, struggling for a life that is simultaneously peaceful and just, that this book has been written.

CHAPTER ONE

Development, Ecology, and Women

Development as a new project of western patriarchy

'Development' was to have been a post-colonial project, a choice for accepting a model of progress in which the entire world remade itself on the model of the colonising modern west, without having to undergo the subjugation and exploitation that colonialism entailed. The assumption was that western style progress was possible for all. Development, as the improved well-being of all, was thus equated with the westernisation of economic categories—of needs, of productivity, of growth. Concepts and categories about economic development and natural resource utilisation that had emerged in the specific context of industrialisation and capitalist growth in a centre of colonial power, were raised to the level of universal assumptions and applicability in the entirely different context of basic needs satisfaction for the people of the newly independent Third World countries. Yet, as Rosa Luxemburg has pointed out, early industrial development in western Europe necessitated the permanent occupation of the colonies by the colonial powers and the destruction of the local 'natural economy'.[1] According to her, colonialism is a constant necessary condition for capitalist growth: without colonies, capital accumulation would grind to a halt. 'Development' as capital accumulation and the commercialisation of the economy for the

---

1 Rosa Luxemberg, *The Accumulation of Capital*, London: Routledge and Kegan Paul, 1951.

generation of 'surplus' and profits thus involved the reproduction not merely of a particular form of creation of wealth, but also of the associated creation of poverty and dispossession. A replication of economic development based on commercialisation of resource use for commodity production in the newly independent countries created the internal colonies.[2] Development was thus reduced to a continuation of the process of colonisation; it became an extension of the project of wealth creation in modern western patriarchy's economic vision, which was based on the exploitation or exclusion of women (of the west and non-west), on the exploitation and degradation of nature, and on the exploitation and erosion of other cultures. 'Development' could not but entail destruction for women, nature, and subjugated cultures, which is why, throughout the Third World, women, peasants and tribals are struggling for liberation from 'development' just as they earlier struggled for liberation from colonialism.

The UN Decade for Women was based on the assumption that the improvement of women's economic position would automatically flow from an expansion and diffusion of the development process. Yet, by the end of the Decade, it was becoming clear that development itself was the problem. Insufficient and inadequate 'participation' in 'development' was not the cause for women's increasing under-development; it was rather, their enforced but asymmetric participation in it, by which they bore the costs but were excluded from the benefits, that was responsible. Development exclusivity and dispossession aggravated and deepened the colonial processes of ecological degradation and the loss of political control over nature's sustenance base. Economic growth was a new colonialism, draining resources away from those who needed them most. The discontinuity lay in the fact that it was now new national elites, not colonial powers, that masterminded the exploitation on grounds of 'national interest' and growing GNPs, and it was accomplished with more powerful technologies of appropriation and destruction.

Ester Boserup[3] has documented how women's impoverishment increased during colonial rule; those rulers who had spent a few centuries

---

2 An elaboration of how 'development' transfers resources from the poor to the well-endowed is contained in J. Bandyopadhyay and V. Shiva, 'Political Economy of Technological Polarisations' in *Economic and Political Weekly*, Vol. XVIII, 1982, pp. 1827-32; and J. Bandyopadhyay and V. Shiva, 'Political Economy of Ecology Movements', in *Economic and Political Weekly*, forthcoming.

3 Ester Boserup, *Women's Role in Economic Development*, London: Allen and Unwin, 1970.

in subjugating and crippling their own women into de-skilled, de-intellectualised appendages, disfavoured the women of the colonies on matters of access to land, technology and employment. The economic and political processes of colonial under-development bore the clear mark of modern western patriarchy, and while large numbers of women and men were impoverished by these processes, women tended to lose more. The privatisation of land for revenue generation displaced women more critically, eroding their traditional land use rights. The expansion of cash crops undermined food production, and women were often left with meagre resources to feed and care for children, the aged and the infirm, when men migrated or were conscripted into forced labour by the colonisers. As a collective document by women activists, organisers and researchers stated at the end of the UN Decade for Women, 'The almost uniform conclusion of the Decade's research is that with a few exceptions, women's relative access to economic resources, incomes and employment has worsened, their burden of work has increased, and their relative and even absolute health, nutritional and educational status has declined.'[4]

The displacement of women from productive activity by the expansion of development was rooted largely in the manner in which development projects appropriated or destroyed the natural resource base for the production of sustenance and survival. It destroyed women's productivity both by removing land, water and forests from their management and control, as well as through the ecological destruction of soil, water and vegetation systems so that Nature's productivity and renewability were impaired. While gender subordination and patriarchy are the oldest of oppressions, they have taken on new and more violent forms through the project of development. Patriarchal categories which understand destruction as 'production' and regeneration of life as 'passivity' have generated a crisis of survival. Passivity, as an assumed category of the 'nature' of nature and of women, denies the activity of nature and life. Fragmentation and uniformity as assumed categories of progress and development destroy the living forces which arise from relationships within the 'web of life' and the diversity in the elements and patterns of these relationships.

The economic biases and values against nature, women and indigenous peoples are captured in this typical analysis of the 'unproductiveness' of traditional natural societies:

4 DAWN, *Development Crisis and Alternative· Visions: Third World Women's Perspectives*, Bergen: Christian Michelsen Institute, 1985, p. 21.

Production is achieved through human and animal, rather than mechanical, power. Most agriculture is unproductive; human or animal
manure may be used but chemical fertilisers and pesticides are unknown.... For the masses, these conditions mean poverty. [5]

The assumptions are evident: nature is unproductive; organic agriculture based on nature's cycles of renewability spells poverty; women
and tribal and peasant societies embedded in nature are similarly unproductive, not because it has been demonstrated that in cooperation they
produce *less* goods and services for needs, but because it is assumed that
'production' takes place only when mediated by technologies for commodity production, even when such technologies destroy life. A stable
and clean river is not a productive resource in this view: it needs to be
'developed' with dams in order to become so. Women, sharing the river as
a commons to satisfy the water needs of their families and society are not
involved in productive labour: when substituted by the engineering man,
water management and water use become productive activities. Natural forests remain unproductive till they are developed into monoculture
plantations of commercial species. Development thus, is equivalent to
maldevelopment, a development bereft of the feminine, the conservation, the ecological principle. The neglect of nature's work in renewing
herself, and women's work in producing sustenance in the form of basic, vital needs is an essential part of the paradigm of maldevelopment,
which sees all work that does not produce profits and capital as non or
unproductive work. As Maria Mies[6] has pointed out, this concept of surplus has a patriarchal bias because, from the point of view of nature and
women, it is not based on material surplus produced *over and above* the
requirements of the community: it is stolen and appropriated through
violent modes from nature (who needs a share of her produce to reproduce herself) and from women (who need a share of nature's produce to
produce sustenance and ensure survival).

From the perspective of Third World women, productivity is a measure of producing life and sustenance; that this kind of productivity has
been rendered invisible does not reduce its centrality to survival—it
merely reflects the domination of modern patriarchal economic categories which see only profits, not life.

5 M. George Foster, *Traditional Societies and Technological Change*, Delhi: Allied Publishers, 1973.
6 Maria Mies, *Patriarchy and Accumulation on a World Scale*, London: Zed Books, 1986.

Maldevelopment as the death of the feminine principle

In this analysis, maldevelopment becomes a new source of male-female inequality. 'Modernisation' has been associated with the introduction of new forms of dominance. Alice Schlegel[7] has shown that under conditions of subsistence, the interdependence and complementarity of the separate male and female domains of work is the characteristic mode, based on diversity, not inequality. Maldevelopment militates against this equality in diversity, and superimposes the ideologically constructed category of western technological man as a uniform measure of the worth of classes, cultures, and genders. Dominant modes of perception based on reductionism, duality and linearity are unable to cope with equality in diversity, with forms and activities that are significant and valid, even though different. The reductionist mind superimposes the roles and forms of power of western male-oriented concepts on women, all non-western peoples and even on nature, rendering all three 'deficient', and in need of 'development'. Diversity, and unity and harmony in diversity, become epistemologically unattainable in the context of maldevelopment, which then becomes synonymous with women's underdevelopment (increasing sexist domination), and nature's depletion (deepening ecological crises). Commodities have grown, but nature has shrunk. The poverty crisis of the South arises from the growing scarcity of water, food, fodder and fuel, associated with increasing maldevelopment and ecological destruction. This poverty crisis touches women most severely, first because they are the poorest among the poor, and then because, with nature, they are the primary sustainers of society.

Maldevelopment is the violation of the integrity of organic, interconnected and interdependent systems, that sets in motion a process of exploitation, inequality, injustice and violence. It is blind to the fact that a recognition of nature's harmony and action to maintain it are preconditions for distributive justice. This is why Mahatma Gandhi said, 'There is enough in the world for everyone's need, but not for some people's greed.'

Maldevelopment is maldevelopment in thought and action. In practice, this fragmented, reductionist, dualist perspective violates the integrity and harmony of man in nature, and the harmony between men and women. It ruptures the cooperative unity of masculine and feminine, and places man, shorn of the feminine principle, above nature and women,

---

7   Alice Schlegel (ed.), *Sexual Stratification: A Cross-Cultural View,* New York: Columbia University Press, 1977.

and separated from both. The violence to nature as symptomatised by the ecological crisis, and the violence to women, as symptomatised by their subjugation and exploitation arise from this subjugation of the feminine principle. I want to argue that what is currently called development is essentially maldevelopment, based on the introduction or accentuation of the domination of man over nature and women. In it, both are viewed as the 'other', the passive non-self. Activity, productivity, creativity which were associated with the feminine principle are expropriated as qualities of nature and women, and transformed into the exclusive qualities of man. Nature and women are turned into passive objects, to be used and exploited for the uncontrolled and uncontrollable desires of alienated man. From being the creators and sustainers of life, nature and women are reduced to being 'resources' in the fragmented, anti-life model of maldevelopment.

Two kinds of growth, two kinds of productivity

Maldevelopment is usually called 'economic growth', measured by the Gross National Product. Porritt, a leading ecologist has this to say of GNP:

> *Gross* National Product—for once a word is being used correctly. Even conventional economists admit that the heyday of GNP is over, for the simple reason that as a measure of progress, it's more or less useless. GNP measures the lot, all the goods and services produced in the money economy. Many of these goods and services are not beneficial to people, but rather a measure of just how much is going wrong; increased spending on crime, on pollution, on the many human casualties of our society, increased spending because of waste or planned obsolescence, increased spending because of growing bureaucracies: it's all counted.[8]

The problem with GNP is that it measures some costs as benefits (e.g. pollution control) and fails to measure other costs completely. Among these hidden costs are the new burdens created by ecological devastation, costs that are invariably heavier for women, both in the North and South. It is hardly surprising, therefore, that as GNP rises, it does not necessarily mean that either wealth or welfare increase proportionately. I would argue that GNP is becoming, increasingly, a measure of how real wealth—the wealth of nature and that produced by women for

8 Jonathan Porritt, *Seeing Green*, Oxford: Blackwell, 1984.

sustaining life—is rapidly decreasing. When commodity production as the prime economic activity is introduced as development, it destroys the potential of nature and women to produce life and goods and services for basic needs. More commodities and more cash mean less life—in nature (through ecological destruction) and in society (through denial of basic needs). Women are devalued first, because their work cooperates with nature's processes, and second, because work which satisfies needs and ensures sustenance is devalued in general. Precisely because more growth in maldevelopment has meant less sustenance of life and life-support systems, it is now imperative to recover the feminine principle as the basis for development which conserves and is ecological. Feminism as ecology, and ecology as the revival of Prakriti, the source of all life, become the decentred powers of political and economic transformation and restructuring.

This involves, first, a recognition that categories of 'productivity' and growth which have been taken to be positive, progressive and universal are, in reality, restricted patriarchal categories. When viewed from the point of view of nature's productivity and growth, and women's production of sustenance, they are found to be ecologically destructive and a source of gender inequality. It is no accident that the modern, efficient and productive technologies created within the context of growth in market economic terms are associated with heavy ecological costs, borne largely by women. The resource and energy intensive production processes they give rise to demand ever increasing resource withdrawals from the ecosystem. These withdrawals disrupt essential ecological processes and convert renewable resources into non-renewable ones. A forest for example, provides inexhaustible supplies of diverse biomass over time if its capital stock is maintained and it is harvested on a sustained yield basis. The heavy and uncontrolled demand for industrial and commercial wood, however, requires the continuous overfelling of trees which exceeds the regenerative capacity of the forest ecosystem, and eventually converts the forests into non-renewable resources. Women's work in the collection of water, fodder and fuel is thus rendered more energy and time-consuming. (In Garhwal, for example, I have seen women who originally collected fodder and fuel in a few hours, now travelling long distances by truck to collect grass and leaves in a task that might take up to two days.) Sometimes the damage to nature's intrinsic regenerative capacity is impaired not by over-exploitation of a particular resource but, indirectly, by damage caused to other related natural resources through ecological processes. Thus the excessive overfelling of trees in the catchment areas of streams and rivers destroys not only forest resources, but also renewable supplies of water, through hydrological destabilisation. Resource intensive industries disrupt essential ecological processes not only by their excessive demands for raw material, but by their pollution of air and water and soil. Often such destruction is caused by the resource demands of non-vital industrial products. In spite of of severe ecological crises, this paradigm continues to operate because for the North and for the elites of the South, resources continue to be available, even now. The lack of recognition of nature's processes for survival *as factors in the process of economic development* shrouds the political issues arising from resource transfer and resource destruction, and creates an ideological weapon for increased control over natural resources in the conventionally employed notion of productivity. All other costs of the economic process consequently become invisible. The forces which contribute to the increased 'productivity' of a modern farmer or factory worker for instance, come from the increased use of natural resources. Lovins has described this as the amount of 'slave' labour presently at work in the world.[9] According to him each person on earth, on an average, possesses the equivalent of about 50 slaves, each working a 40 hour week Man's global energy conversion from all sources (wood, fossil fuel, hydroelectric power, nuclear) is currently approximately 8×10^{12} watts. This is more than 20 times the energy content of the food necessary to feed the present world population at the FAO standard diet of 3,600 cal/day. The 'productivity' of the western male compared to women or Third World peasants is not intrinsically superior; it is based on inequalities in the distribution of this 'slave' labour. The average inhabitant of the USA for example has 250 times more 'slaves' than the average Nigerian. 'If Americans were short of 249 of those 250 'slaves', one wonders how efficient they would prove themselves to be?'

It is these resource and energy intensive processes of production which divert resources away from survival, and hence from women. What patriarchy sees as productive work, is, in ecological terms highly destructive production. The second law of thermodynamics predicts that resource intensive and resource wasteful economic development must become a threat to the survival of the human species in the long run. Political struggles based on ecology in industrially advanced countries are rooted in this conflict between *long term survival options* and *short*

9 A. Lovins, cited in S.R. Eyre, *The Real Wealth of Nations*, London: Edward Arnold, 1978.

term over-production and over-consumption. Political struggles of women, peasants and tribals based on ecology in countries like India are far more acute and urgent since they are rooted in the *immediate threat to the options for survival* for the vast majority of the people, *posed by resource intensive and resource wasteful economic growth* for the benefit of a minority.

In the market economy, the organising principle for natural resource use is the maximisation of profits and capital accumulation. Nature and human needs are managed through market mechanisms. Demands for natural resources are restricted to those demands registering on the market; the ideology of development is in large part based on a vision of bringing all natural resources into the market economy for commodity production. When these resources are already being used by nature to maintain her production of renewable resources and by women for sustenance and livelihood, their diversion to the market economy generates a scarcity condition for ecological stability and creates new forms of poverty for women.

Two kinds of poverty

In a book entitled *Poverty: The Wealth of the People*[10], an African writer draws a distinction between poverty as subsistence, and misery as deprivation. It is useful to separate a cultural conception of subsistence living as poverty from the material experience of poverty that is a result of dispossession and deprivation. Culturally perceived poverty need not be real material poverty: subsistence economies which satisfy basic needs through self-provisioning are not poor in the sense of being deprived. Yet the ideology of development declares them so because they do not participate overwhelmingly in the market economy, and do not consume commodities produced for and distributed through the market *even though they might be satisfying those needs through self-provisioning mechanisms.* People are perceived as poor if they eat millets (grown by women) rather than commercially produced and distributed processed foods sold by global agribusiness. They are seen as poor if they live in self-built housing made from natural material like bamboo and mud rather than in cement houses. They are seen as poor if they wear handmade garments of natural fibre rather than synthetics. Subsistence, as culturally perceived poverty,

10   R. Bahro, *From Red to Green*, London: Verso, 1984, p. 211.

does not necessarily imply a low physical quality of life. On the contrary, millets are nutritionally far superior to processed foods, houses built with local materials are far superior, being better adapted to the local climate and ecology, natural fibres are preferable to man-made fibres in most cases, and certainly more affordable. This cultural perception of prudent subsistence living as poverty has provided the legitimisation for the development process as a poverty removal project. As a culturally biased project it destroys wholesome and sustainable lifestyles and creates real material poverty, or misery, by the denial of survival needs themselves, through the diversion of resources to resource intensive commodity production. Cash crop production and food processing take land and water resources away from sustenance needs, and exclude increasingly large numbers of people from their entitlements to food. 'The inexorable processes of agriculture-industrialisation and internationalisation are probably responsible for more hungry people than either cruel or unusual whims of nature. There are several reasons why the high-technology-export-crop model increases hunger. Scarce land, credit, water and technology are pre-empted for the export market. Most hungry people are not affected by the market at all.... The profits flow to corporations that have no interest in feeding hungry people without money.'[11]

The Ethiopian famine is in part an example of the creation of real poverty by development aimed at removing culturally perceived poverty. The displacement of nomadic Afars from their traditional pastureland in Awash Valley by commercial agriculture (financed by foreign companies) led to their struggle for survival in the fragile uplands which degraded the ecosystem and led to the starvation of cattle and the nomads.[12] The market economy conflicted with the survival economy in the Valley, thus creating a conflict between the survival economy and nature's economy in the uplands. At no point has the global marketing of agricultural commodities been assessed against the background of the new conditions of scarcity and poverty that it has induced. This new poverty moreover, is no longer cultural and relative: it is absolute, threatening the very survival of millions on this planet.

The economic system based on the patriarchal concept of productivity was created for the very specific historical and political phenomenon

11 R.J. Barnet, *The Lean Years*. London: Abacus, 1981, p. 171.

12 U.P. Koehn, 'African Approaches to Environmental Stress: A Focus on Ethiopia and Nigeria in R.N. Barrett (ed.), *International Dimensions of the Environmental Crisis*, Colorado: Westview, 1982, pp. 253-89.

of colonialism. In it, the input for which efficiency of use had to be max-
imised in the production centres of Europe, was industrial labour. For
colonial interest therefore, it was rational to improve the labour resource
even at the cost of wasteful use of nature's wealth. This rationalisation has,
however, been illegitimately universalised to all contexts and interest
groups and, on the plea of increasing productivity, labour reducing technologies have been introduced in situations where labour is abundant
and cheap, and resource demanding technologies have been introduced
where resources are scarce and already fully utilised for the production
of sustenance. Traditional economies with a stable ecology have shared
with industrially advanced affluent economies the ability to use natural
resources to satisfy basic vital needs. The former differ from the latter in
two essential ways: first, the same needs are satisfied in industrial societies through longer technological chains requiring higher energy and
resource inputs and excluding large numbers without purchasing power;
and second, affluence generates new and artificial needs requiring the
increased production of industrial goods and services. Traditional economies are not advanced in the matter of non-vital needs satisfaction, but
as far as the satisfaction of basic and vital needs is concerned, they are
often what Marshall Sahlins has called 'the original affluent society'. The
needs of the Amazonian tribes are more than satisfied by the rich rainforest; their poverty begins with its destruction. The story is the same for the
Gonds of Bastar in India or the Penans of Sarawak in Malaysia.

Thus are economies based on indigenous technologies viewed as
'backward' and 'unproductive'. Poverty, as the denial of basic needs, is
not necessarily associated with the existence of traditional technologies,
and its removal is not necessarily an outcome of the growth of modem
ones. On the contrary, the destruction of ecologically sound traditional
technologies, often created and used by women, along with the destruction of their material base is generally believed to be responsible for the
'feminisation' of poverty in societies which have had to bear the costs of
resource destruction.

The contemporary poverty of the Afar nomad is not rooted in the in-
adequacies of traditional nomadic life, but in the *diversion of the productive pastureland of the Awash Valley.* The erosion of the resource base for
survival is increasingly being caused by the demand for resources by the
market economy, dominated by global forces. The creation of inequality
through economic activity which is ecologically disruptive arises in two
ways: first, inequalities in the distribution of privileges make for unequal

access to natural resources—these include privileges of both a political and economic nature. Second, resource intensive production processes have access to subsidised raw material on which a substantial number of people, especially from the less privileged economic groups, depend for their survival. The consumption of such industrial raw material is determined purely by market forces, and not by considerations of the social or ecological requirements placed on them. The costs of resource destruction are externalised and unequally divided among various economic groups in society, but are borne largely by women and those who satisfy their basic material needs directly from nature, simply because they have no purchasing power to register their demands on the goods and services provided by the modern production system. Gustavo Esteva has called development a permanent war waged by its promoters and suffered by its victims.[13]

The paradox and crisis of development arises from the mistaken identification of culturally perceived poverty with real material poverty, and the mistaken identification of the growth of commodity production as better satisfaction of basic needs. In actual fact, there is less water, less fertile soil, less genetic wealth as a result of the development process. Since these natural resources are the basis of nature's economy and women's survival economy, their scarcity is impoverishing women and marginalised peoples in an unprecedented manner. Their new impoverishment lies in the fact that resources which supported their survival were absorbed into the market economy while they themselves were excluded and displaced by it.

The old assumption that with the development process the availability of goods and services will automatically be increased and poverty will be removed, is now under serious challenge from women's ecology movements in the Third World, even while it continues to guide development thinking in centres of patriarchal power. Survival is based on the assumption of the sanctity of life; maldevelopment is based on the assumption of the sacredness of 'development'. Gustavo Esteva asserts that the sacredness of development has to be refuted because it threatens survival itself. 'My people are tired of development', he says, 'they just want to live.'[14]

13   Gustavo Esteva, 'Regenerating People's Space' in S.N. Mendlowitz and R.B. J. Walker, *Towards a Just World Peace: Perspectives From Social Movements*, London: Butterworths and Committee for a Just World Peace, 1987.

14   G. Esteva, Remarks made at a Conference of the Society for International Development, Rome, 1985.

The recovery of the feminine principle allows a transcendance and transformation of these patriarchal foundations of maldevelopment. It allows a redefinition of growth and productivity as categories linked to the production, not the destruction, of life. It is thus simultaneously an ecological and a feminist political project which legitimises the way of knowing and being that create wealth by enhancing life and diversity, and which deligitimises the knowledge and practise of a culture of death as the basis for capital accumulation.

Science, Nature, and Gender

The recovery of the feminine principle is an intellectual and political challenge to maldevelopment as a patriarchal project of domination and destruction, of violence and subjugation, of dispossession and the dispensability of both women and nature. The politics of life centred on the feminine principle challenges fundamental assumptions not just in political economy, but also in the science of life-threatening processes.

Maldevelopment is intellectually based on, and justified through, reductionist categories of scientific thought and action. Politically and economically each project which has fragmented nature and displaced women from productive work has been legitimised as 'scientific' by operationalising reductionist concepts to realise uniformity, centralisation, and control. Development is thus the introduction of 'scientific agriculture', 'scientific animal husbandry', 'scientific water management', and so on. The reductionist and universalising tendencies of such 'science' become inherently violent and destructive in a world which is inherently interrelated and diverse. The feminine principle becomes an oppositional category of nonviolent ways of conceiving the world, and of acting in it to sustain all life by maintaining the interconnectedness and diversity of nature. It allows an ecological transition from violence to nonviolence, from destruction to creativity, from anti-life to life-giving processes, from uniformity to diversity and from fragmentation and reductionism to holism and complexity.

It is thus not just 'development' which is a source of violence to women and nature. At a deeper level, scientific knowledge, on which the development process is based, is itself a source of violence. Modern reductionist science, like development, turns out to be a patriarchal project, which has excluded women as experts, and has simultaneously excluded ecological and holistic ways of knowing which understand and respect nature's processes and interconnectedness *as science*.

Modern science as patriarchy's project

Modern science is projected as a universal, value-free system of knowledge, which has displaced all other belief and knowledge systems by its universality and value neutrality, and by the logic of its method to arrive at objective claims about nature. Yet the dominant stream of modern science, the reductionist or mechanical paradigm, is a particular response of a particular group of people. It is a specific project of western man which came into being during the fifteenth and seventeenth centuries as the much-acclaimed Scientific Revolution. During the last few years feminist scholarship has begun to recognise that the dominant science system emerged as a liberating force not for humanity as a whole (though it legitimised itself in terms of universal betterment of the species), but as a masculine and patriarchal project which necessarily entailed the subjugation of both nature and women. Harding has called it a 'western, bourgeois, masculine project',[1] and according to Keller

> Science has been produced by a particular sub-set of the human race, that is, almost entirely by white, middle class males. For the founding fathers of modern science, the reliance on the language of gender was explicit; they sought a philosophy that deserved to be called 'masculine', that could be distinguished from its ineffective predecessors by its 'virile' powers, its capacity to bind Nature to man's service and make her his slave.[2]

Bacon (1561–1626) was the father of modern science, the originator of the concept of the modern research institute and industrial science, and the inspiration behind the Royal Society. His contribution to modern science and its organisation is critical. From the point of view of nature, women and marginal groups, however, Bacon's programme was not humanly inclusive. It was a special programme benefitting the middle class,

1 Susan Harding, *The Science Question in Feminism*, Ithaca: Cornell University Press, 1986, p. 8.
2 Evelyn F. Keller, *Reflections on Gender and Science*, New Haven: Yale University Press, 1985, p. 7.

European, male entrepreneur through the conjunction of human knowledge and power in science.

In Bacon's experimental method, which was central to this masculine project, there was a dichotomising between male and female, mind and matter, objective and subjective, rational and emotional, and a conjunction of masculine and scientific dominating over nature, women, and the non-west. His was not a neutral', 'objective', 'scientific' method—it was a masculine mode of aggression against nature and domination over women. The severe testing of hypotheses through controlled manipulations of nature, and the necessity of such manipulations if experiments are to be repeatable, are here formulated in clearly sexist metaphors. Both nature and inquiry appear conceptualized in ways modelled on rape and torture—on man's most violent and misogynous relationships with women—and this modelling is advanced as a reason to value science. According to Bacon 'the nature of things betrays itself more readily under the vexations of art than in its natural freedom'.[3] The discipline of scientific knowledge and the mechanical inventions it leads to, do not 'merely exert a gentle guidance over nature's course; they have the power to conquer and subdue her, to shake her to her foundations'.[4]

In *Tempores Partus Masculus* or *The Masculine Birth of Time*, translated by Farrington in 1951, Bacon promised to create 'a blessed race of heroes and supermen' who would dominate both nature and society.[5] The title is interpreted by Farrington as suggesting a shift from the older science, represented as female—passive and weak—to a new masculine science of the scientific revolution which Bacon saw himself as heralding. In *New Atlantis*, Bacon's Bensalem was administered from Solomon's House, a scientific research institute, from which male scientists ruled over and made decisions for society, and decided which secrets should be revealed and which remain the private property of the institute.

Science-dominated society has evolved very much in the pattern of Bacon's Bensalem, with nature being transformed and mutilated in modern Solomon's Houses—corporate labs and the university programmes they sponsor. With the new biotechnologies, Bacon's vision of controlling reproduction for the sake of production is being realised, while the green

3 F.H. Anderson, (ed.), *Francis Bacon: The New Organon and Related Writings*, Indianapolis: Bobbs-Merrill, 1960, p. 25.

4 J. Spedding, *et. al* (eds.) *The Works of Francis Bacon* (Reprinted), Stuttgart: F.F. Verlag, 1963, Vol. V, p. 506.

5 Quoted in Keller, *op. cit.*, pp. 38-39.

revolution and the bio-revolution have realised what in *New Atlantis* was only a utopia.

'We make by act trees and flowers to come earlier or later than their seasons, and to come up and bear more speedily than by their natural course they do. We make them by act greater, much more than their nature, and their fruit greater and sweeter and of differing taste, smell, colour and figure from their nature'.[6] For Bacon, nature was no longer Mother Nature, but a female nature, conquered by an aggressive masculine mind. As Carolyn Merchant points out, this transformation of nature from a living, nurturing mother to inert, dead and manipulable matter was eminently suited to the exploitation imperative of growing capitalism. The nurturing earth image acted as a cultural constraint on exploitation of nature. 'One does not readily slay a mother, dig her entrails or mutilate her body'. But the mastery and domination images created by the Baconian programme and the scientific revolution removed all restraint and functioned as cultural sanctions for the denudation of nature.

> The removal of animistic, organic assumptions about the cosmos constituted the death of nature—the most far-reaching effect of the scientific revolution. Because nature was not viewed as a system of dead, inert particles moved by external, rather than inherent forces, the mechanical framework itself could legitimate the manipulation of nature. Moreover, as a conceptual framework, the mechanical order had associated with it a framework of values based on power, fully compatible with the directions taken by commercial capitalism.[7]

Modern science was a consciously gendered, patriarchal activity. As nature carne to be seen more like a woman to be raped, gender too was recreated. Science as a male venture, based on the subjugation of female nature and female sex provided support for the polarisation of gender. Patriarchy as the new scientific and technological power was a political need of emerging industrial capitalism.

While on the one hand the ideology of science sanctioned the denudation of nature, on the other it legitimised the dependency of women and the authority of men. Science and masculinity were associated in domination over nature and feminity, and the ideologies of science and gender reinforced each other. The witch-hunting hysteria which was

6 Carolyn Merchant, *The Death of Nature : Women, Ecology and the Scientific Revolution*, New York: Harper & Row, 1980, p. 182.

7 Merchant, *op. cit.*, p. 193.

aimed at annihilating women in Europe as knowers and experts was co-
temporous with two centuries of scientific revolution. It reached its peak
with Galilee's *Dialogue* concerning the Two Chief World Systems and
died with the emergence of the Royal Society of London and the Paris
Academy of Sciences.[8]

> The interrogation of witches as a symbol for the interrogation of na-
> ture, the courtroom as model for its inquisition, and torture through
> mechanical devices as a tool for the subjugation of disorder were fun-
> damental to the scientific method as power. For Bacon, as for Harvey,
> sexual politics helped to structure the nature of the empirical method
> that would produce a new form of knowledge and a new ideology of
> objectivity seemingly devoid of cultural and political assumptions.[9]

The Royal Society, inspired by Bacon's philosophy, was clearly seen
by its organisers as a masculine project. In 1664, Henry Oldenberg, Sec-
retary of the Royal Society announced that the intention of the society
was to 'raise a *masculine philosophy* ... whereby the Mind of Man may be
ennobled with the knowledge of solid Truths'.[10] And for Glanvill, the masculine aim of science was to know 'the ways of captivating Nature, and
making her subserve our purposes, thereby achieving the Empire of Man
Over Nature'.[11] Glanvill advocated chemistry as one of the most useful
arts for 'by the *violence* of its artful fires it is made to confess those la-
tent parts, which upon less provocation it would not disclose'.[12] The 'de-
mothering' of nature through modern science and the marriage of
knowledge with power was simultaneously a source of subjugating
women as well as non-European peoples. Robert Boyle, the famous scientist who was also the Governor of the New England Company, saw the
rise of mechanical philosophy as an instrument of power not just over
nature but also over the original inhabitants of America. He explicitly declared his intention of ridding the New England Indians of their ridiculous
notions about the workings of nature. He attacked their perception of
nature, 'as a kind of goddess', and argued that 'the veneration, wherewith

8 Brian Easlea, *Science and Sexual Oppression: Patriarchy's Confrontation with Woman
and Nature*, London: Weidenfeld and Nicholson, 1981, p. 64.
9 Merchant, *op. cit.*, p. 172.
10 Easlea, *op. cit.*, p. 70.
11 Easlea, *op. cit.*, p. 70.
12 Merchant, *op. cit.*, p. 189.

men are imbued for what they call nature, has been a discouraging impediment to the empire of man over the inferior creatures of God'.[13]

Today, with new ecological awareness, ecologists the world over turn to the beliefs of native American and other indigenous peoples as a special source for learning how to live in harmony with nature. There are many today from the ecology and women's movements who see irrationality in Boyle's impulse for the empire of white man over nature and other peoples, and who see rationality in the words of Indian Chief Smohalla when he cried out: 'You ask me to plough the ground: shall I take a knife and tear my mother's bosom? You ask me to cut grass and make hay and sell it and be rich like white men; but how dare I cut off my mother's hair'?[14]

Chief Seattle's letter, which has become a major inspiration for the ecology movement states, 'This we know—the earth does not belong to man, man belongs to the earth. All things are connected like the blood which unites one family. Whatever befalls the earth befalls the sons of the earth. Man did not weave the web of life; he is merely a strand in it. Whatever he does to the web, he does to himself'.

The ecological and feminist alternatives to reductionist science are clearly not the first attempts to create a science of nature that is not gendered and disruptive. The period of the scientific revolution itself was full of alternatives to the masculine project of mechanistic, reductionist science, and it was also full of struggles between gendered and non-gendered science. Bacon and Paracelsus are the leading exponents of the two competing trends of modern science in seventeenth century Europe.[15] The Paracelsians belonged to the hermetic tradition which did not dichotomise between mind and matter, male and female. The mechanical school represented by Bacon created dichotomies between culture and nature, mind and matter, and male and female, and devised a conceptual strategy for the former to dominate over the latter. The two visions of science were also two visions of nature, power and gender relations. For Paracelsus the male did not dominate over the female, the two complemented each other, and knowledge and power did not arise from dominating over nature but from 'cohabiting with the elements',[16] which

13 Easlea, *op. cit.*, p. 73.

14 Easlea, *op. cit.*, p. 73.

15 J.P.S. Oberoi, *The Other Mind of Europe: Goethe as a Scientist*, Delhi: Oxford University Press, 1984.

16 Keller, *op. cit.*, p. 48.

were themselves interconnected to form a living organism. For the Paracelsian, 'The whole world is knit and bound within itself: for the world is a living creature, everywhere both female and male,' and knowledge of nature is derived through participating in these interconnections.[17]

With the formation of the Royal Society and in the context of emerging industrial capitalism, the contest between the mechanical and hermetic traditions was won by the masculine project which was the project of a particular class. Paracelsus and Bacon did not merely differ in their ideology of gender and science; they were also differently rooted in the politics of class, with Bacon committed to middle class values (finally becoming Lord Chancellor and Bacon Verulam in 1618 in the reign of James I) and identifying with capitalists, merchants and the State in his scientific project, and Paracelsus, on the side of the peasants in their uprising in the Tyrol.[18] Reductionist science became a major agent of economic and political change in the centuries to follow, dichotomising gender and class relations, and man's relationship with nature. 'Given the success of modern science, defined in opposition to everything female, fears of both Nature and Woman could subside. With the one reduced to its mechanical substrata, and the other to her sexual virtue, the essence of *Mater* could be both tamed and conquered'.[19]

For more than three centuries, reductionism has ruled as the only valid scientific method and system, distorting the history of the west as well as the non-west. It has hidden its ideology behind projected objectivism, neutrality, and progress. The ideology that hides ideology has transformed complex pluralistic traditions of knowledge into a monolith of gender-based, class-based thought and transformed this particular tradition into a superior and universal tradition to be superimposed on all classes, genders and cultures which it helps in controlling and subjugating. This ideological projection has kept modern reductionist science inaccessible to criticism. The parochial roots of science in patriarchy and in a particular class and culture have been concealed behind a claim to universality, and can be seen only through other traditions—of women and non-western peoples. It is these subjugated traditions that are revealing how modern science is gendered, how it is specific to the needs and impulses of the dominant western culture and how ecological destruction and nature's exploitation are inherent to its logic. It is

17 Merchant, *op. cit.*, p. 104.

18 Oberoi, *op. cit.*, p. 21.

19 Keller, *op. cit.*, p. 60.

becoming increasingly clear that scientific neutrality has been a reflection of ideology, not history, and science is similar to all other socially constructed categories. This view of science as a social and political project of modern western man is emerging from the responses of those who were defined into nature and made passive and powerless: Mother Earth, women, and colonised cultures. It is from these fringes that we are beginning to discern the economic, political and cultural mechanisms that have allowed a parochial science to dominate and how mechanisms of power and violence can be eliminated for a degendered, humanly inclusive knowledge.

The violence of reductionism

The myth that the 'scientific revolution' was a universal process of intellectual progress is being steadily undermined by feminist scholarship and the histories of science of non-western cultures. These are relating the rise of the reductionist paradigm with the subjugation and destruction of women's knowledge in the west, and the knowledge of non-western cultures. The witch-hunts of Europe were largely a process of delegitimising and destroying the expertise of European women. In 1511, England had an Act of Parliament directed against 'common artificers, as smythes, weavers and women who attempt great cures and things of great difficulties: in the witch they partly use sorcerye and witch-craft'.[20] By the sixteenth century women in Europe were totally excluded from the practice of medicine and healing because 'wise women ran the risk of being declared witches. A deeper, more violent form of exclusion of women's knowledge and expertise, and of the knowledge of tribal and peasant cultures is now under way with the spread of the masculinist paradigm of science through 'development'.

I characterise modern western patriarchy's special epistemological tradition of the 'scientific revolution' as 'reductionist' because it reduced the capacity of humans to know nature both by excluding other knowers and other ways of knowing, and it reduced the capacity of nature to creatively regenerate and renew itself by manipulating it as inert and fragmented matter. Reductionism has a set of distinctive characteristics which demarcates it from all other non-reductionist knowledge systems

---

20 Quoted in Muriel J. Hughes, *Women Healers in Medieval Life and Literature*, New York: Libraries Press, 1968, p. 86.

which it has subjugated and replaced. The basic ontological and epistemological assumptions of reductionism are based on homogeneity. It sees all systems as made up of the same basic constituents, discrete, unrelated, and atomistic, and it assumes that all basic processes are mechanical. The mechanistic metaphors of reductionism have socially reconstituted nature and society. In contrast to the organic metaphors, in which concepts of order and power were based on interconnectedness and reciprocity, the metaphor of nature as a machine was based on the assumption of separability and manipulability. As Carolyn Merchant has remarked: 'In investigating the roots of our current environmental dilemma and its connections to science, technology and the economy, we must re-examine the formation of a world-view and a science that, by reconceptualising reality as a machine, rather than a living organism, sanctioned the domination of both nature and women'.[21] This domination is inherently violent, understood here as the violation of integrity. Reductionist science is a source of violence against nature and women because it subjugates and dispossesses them of their full productivity, power, and potential. The epistemological assumptions of reductionism are related to its ontological assumptions: uniformity allows the knowledge of parts of a system to be taken as knowledge of the whole. Separability allows context-free abstraction of knowledge and creates criteria of validity based on alienation and non-participation, then projected as 'objectivity'. 'Experts' and 'specialists' are thus projected as the only legitimate knowledge seekers and justifiers.

Profits, reductionism, and violence

The close nexus between reductionist science, patriarchy, violence, and profits is explicit in 80 percent of scientific research that is devoted to the war industry, and is frankly aimed directly at lethal violence—violence, in modern times, not only against the enemy fighting force but also against the much larger civilian population. In this book I argue that modern science is related to violence and profits even in peaceful domains such as, for example, forestry and agriculture, where the professed objective of scientific research is human welfare. The relationship between reductionism, violence and profits is built into the genesis of masculinist science, for its reductionist nature is an epistemic response to

21 Merchant, *op. cit.*, p. xvii.

an economic organisation based on uncontrolled exploitation of nature for maximization of profits and capital accumulation.

Reductionism, far from being an epistemological accident, is a response to the needs of a particular form of economic and political organisation.[22] The reductionist world-view, the industrial revolution and the capitalist economy were the philosophical, technological, and economic components of the same process. Individual firms and the fragmented sector of the economy, whether privately owned or state owned, have only their own efficiency and profits in mind; and every firm and sector measures its efficiency by the extent to which it maximizes its gains, regardless of the maximization of social and ecological costs. The logic of this internal efficiency has been provided by reductionism. Only those properties of a resource system are taken into account which generate profits through exploitation and extraction; properties which stabilise ecological processes but are commercially non-exploitative are ignored and eventually destroyed.

Commercial capitalism is based on specialised commodity production. Uniformity in production, and the uni-functional use of natural resources is therefore required. Reductionism thus reduces complex ecosystems to a single component, and a single component to a single function. It further allows the manipulation of the ecosystem in a manner that maximizes the single-function, single-component exploitation. In the reductionist paradigm, a forest is reduced to commercial wood, and wood is reduced to cellulose fibre for the pulp and paper industry. Forests, land, and genetic resources are then manipulated to increase the production of pulpwood, and this distortion is legitimised scientifically as overall productivity increase, even though it might decrease the output of water from the forest, or reduce the diversity of life forms that constitute a forest community. The living and diverse ecosystem is thus violated and destroyed by 'scientific' forestry and forestry 'development'. In this way, reductionist science is at the root of the growing ecological crisis, because it entails a transformation of nature such that its organic processes and regularities and regenerative capacities are destroyed.

Women in sustenance economies, producing and reproducing wealth in partnership with nature, have been experts in their own right

---

22 J. Bandyopadhyay & V. Shiva, 'Ecological Sciences: A Response to Ecological Crises' in J. Bandyopadhyay, *et al., India's Environment*, Dehradun: Natraj, 1985, p. 196; and J. Bandyopadhyay & V. Shiva, 'Environmental Conflicts and Public Interest Science', in *Economic and Political Weekly*, Vol. XXI, No. 2, Jan. 11, 1986, pp. 84-90.

of a holistic and ecological knowledge of nature's processes. But these alternative modes of knowing, which are oriented to social benefits and sustenance needs, are not recognised by the reductionist paradigm, because it fails to perceive the interconnectedness of nature, or the connection of women's lives, work, and knowledge with the creation of wealth.

The rationality and efficacy of reductionist and non-reductionist knowledge systems are never *evaluated* cognitively. The rationality of reductionist science is, a priori, declared superior. If reductionist science has displaced non-reductionist modes of knowing, it has done so not through cognitive competition, but through political support from the state: development policies and programmes provide the financial and material subsidies *as well as* the ideological support for the appropriation of nature for profits. Since the twin myths of progress (material prosperity) and superior rationality lost their sheen in the working out of development patterns and paradigms, and were visibly exploded by widespread ecological crises, the state stepped in to transform the myths into an ideology. When an individual firm or sector directly confronts the larger society in its appropriation of nature on grounds of progress and rationality, people can assess social costs and private benefits for themselves; they can differentiate between progress and regression, rationality, and irrationality. But with the mediation of the state, subjects and citizens become objects of change rather than its determinants, and consequently lose both the capability and the right to assess progress. If they have to bear the costs instead of reaping the benefits of 'development', this is justified as a minor sacrifice for the 'national interest'.

The nexus between the state, the dominant elite, and the creation of surplus value provides the power with which reductionism establishes its supremacy. Institutions of learning in agriculture, medicine, and forestry, selectively train people in the reductionist paradigms, in the name of 'scientific' agriculture, medicine, and forestry to establish the superiority of reductionist science. Stripped of the power the state invests it with, reductionism can be seen to be cognitively weak and ineffective in responding to problems posed by nature. Reductionist forestry has destroyed tropical forests, and reductionist agriculture is destroying tropical farming. As a system of knowledge about nature or life reductionist science is weak and inadequate; as a system of knowledge for the market, it is powerful and profitable. Modern science, as we have noted earlier, has a world-view that both supports and is supported by the socio-political-economic system of western capitalist patriarchy which dominates and exploits nature, women, and the poor.

The ultimate reductionism is achieved when nature is linked with a view of economic activity in which money is the only gauge of value and wealth. Life disappears as an organising principle of economic affairs. But the problem with money is that it has an asymmetric relationship to life and living processes. Exploitation, manipulation, and destruction of the life in nature can be a source of money and profits but neither can ever become a source of nature's life and its life-supporting capacity. It is this asymmetry that accounts for a deepening of the ecological crises as a decrease in nature's life-producing potential, along with an increase of capital accumulation and the expansion of 'development' as a process of replacing the currency of life and sustenance with the currency of cash and profits. The 'development' of Africa by western experts is the primary cause for the destruction of Africa; the 'development' of Brazil by transnational banks and corporations is the primary cause for the destruction of the richness of Amazonian rainforests, the highest expression of life. Natives of Africa and Amazonia had survived over centuries with their ecologically evolved, indigenous knowledge systems. What local people had conserved through history, western experts and knowledge destroyed in a few decades, a few years even.

It is this destruction of ecologies and knowledge systems that I characterise as the violence of reductionism which results in: *a) Violence against women:* women, tribals, peasants as the knowing subject are violated socially through the expert/non-expert divide which converts them into non-knowers even in those areas of living in which through daily participation, they are the real experts—and in which responsibility of practice and action rests with them, such as in forestry, food, and water systems. *b) Violence against nature:* nature as the object of knowledge is violated when modern science destroys its integrity of nature, both in the process of perception as well as manipulation. *c) Violence against the beneficiaries of knowledge:* contrary to the claim of modern science that people in general are ultimately the beneficiaries of scientific knowledge, they—particularly the poor and women—are its worst victims, deprived of their productive potential, livelihoods, and life-support systems. Violence against nature recoils on man, the supposed beneficiary. *d) Violence against knowledge:* in order to assume the status of being the only legitimate mode of knowledge, rationally superior to alternative modes of knowing, reductionist science resorts *to the suppression and falsification of facts* and thus commits violence against science itself. It declares organic systems of knowledge irrational, and rejects the belief systems of others without full rational evaluation. At the same time it protects itself from the exposure and investigation of the myths it has created by assigning itself a new sacredness that forbids any questioning of the claims of science.

Two kinds of facts

The conventional model of science, technology, and society locates sources of violence in politics and ethics, in the *application* of science and technology, not in scientific knowledge itself. The assumed dichotomy between values and facts underlying this model implies a dichotomy between the world of values and the world of facts. In this view, sources of violence are located in the world of values while scientific knowledge inhabits the world of facts.

The fact-value dichotomy is a creation of modern reductionist science which, while being an epistemic response to a particular set of values, posits itself as independent of values. By splitting the world into facts vs. values, it conceals the real difference between two kinds of value-laden facts. Modern reductionist science is characterized in the received view as the discovery of the properties and laws of nature in accordance with a 'scientific' method which generates claims of being 'objective', 'neutral', and 'universal'. This view of reductionist science as being a description of reality *as it is,* unprejudiced by value, is being rejected increasingly on historical and philosophical grounds. It has been historically established that all knowledge, including modern scientific knowledge, is built on the use of a plurality of methodologies, and reductionism itself is only one of the scientific options available.

> There is no 'scientific method'; there is no single procedure, or set of rules that underlies every piece of research and guarantees that it is scientific and, therefore, trustworthy. The idea of a universal and stable method that is an unchanging measure of adequacy and even the idea of a universal and stable rationality is as unrealistic as the idea of a universal and stable measuring instrument that measures any magnitude, no matter what the circumstances. Scientists revise their standards, their procedures, their criteria of rationality as they move along and enter new domains of research just as they revise and perhaps entirely replace their theories and their instruments as they move along and enter new domains of research.[23]

23 Paul Feyerband, *Science in a Free Society*: New Left Books, 1978, p. 10.

The assumption that science deals purely with facts has no support from the practise of science itself. The 'facts' of reductionist science are socially constructed categories which have the cultural markings of the western bourgeois, patriarchal system which is their context of discovery and justification. Carolyn Merchant has shown how, until the sixteenth century in the west, organic metaphors were considered scientific and sane. 'An organically oriented mentality in which female principles played an important role was undermined and replaced by a mechanically oriented mentality that either eliminated or used female principles in an exploitative manner. As western culture became increasingly mechanized in the 1600s, the female earth and virgin earth spirit were subdued by the machine'.[24] The subjugation of other traditions of knowledge is similarly a displacement of one set of culturally constituted facts of nature by another, not the substitution of 'superstition' by 'fact'. The cultural categories of scientific knowledge are not merely cognitive, they are also ethical.

Whereas the nurturing earth image can be viewed as a cultural constraint restricting the types of socially and morally sanctioned human actions allowable with respect to the earth, the new images of mastery and domination functioned as cultural sanctions for the denudation of nature. Controlling images which construct facts also operate as ethical restraints or sanctions as subtle 'oughts' and 'ought-nots'.

In the Third World, the conflict between reductionist and ecological perceptions of the world are a contemporary and everyday reality, in which western trained male scientists and experts epitomise reductionist knowledge. The political struggle for the feminist and ecology movements involves an epistemological shift in the criteria of assessment of the rationality of knowledge. The worth and validity of reductionist claims and beliefs need to be measured against ecological criteria when the crisis of sustainability and survival is the primary intellectual challenge. The view of reductionist scientific knowledge as a purely factual description of nature, superior to competing alternatives, is found to be ecologically unfounded. Ecology perceives relationships between different elements of an ecosystem: what properties will be selected for a particular resource element will depend on what relationships are taken as the context defining the properties. The context is fixed by priorities and values guiding the perception of nature. Selection of the context is a value determined process and the selection in turn determines what

24 Merchant, *op. cit.*, p. 2.

properties are seen. There is nothing like a neutral fact about nature *independent of the value determined by human cognitive and economic activity.* Properties perceived in nature will depend on how one looks and how one looks depends on the economic interest one has in the resources of nature. The value of profit maximization is thus linked to reductionist systems, while the value of life and the maintenance of life is linked to holistic and ecological systems.

Two kinds of rationality

The ontological and epistemological components of the reductionist world-view provide the framework for a particular practice of science. According to Descartes, 'Method consists entirely in the order as a disposition of the objects towards which our mental vision must be directed if we would find out any truth. We shall comply with it exactly if we reduce involved and obscure propositions step by step to those that are simpler, and then starting with the intuitive apprehension of all those that are absolutely simple, attempt to ascend to the knowledge of all others by precisely similar steps'.[25] This method was, in Descartes' view, the method to 'render ourselves the masters and possessors of nature'. Yet it singularly fails to lead to a perception of reality (truth) in the case of living organisms such as nature (including man), in which the whole is not merely the sum of parts, because parts are so cohesively inter-related that isolating any one distorts the whole.

Kuhn, Feyerband, Polanyi, and others have convincingly argued that modern science is not practised according to a well defined and stable scientific method; all that can be granted it is that it is a single mode of thought, among many.

The controlled experiment and the laboratory are a central element of the methodology of reductionist science. The object of study is arbitrarily isolated from its natural surroundings, from its relationship with other objects and the observer(s). The context (the value framework) so provided determines what properties are perceived, and leads to a particular set of beliefs. The Baconian programme of domination over nature was centrally based on the controlled experiment which was formulated and conceived in the language and metaphor of rape, torture, and the inquisition. The 'controlled' experiment was therefore a political choice,

25 Descartes, *A Discourse on Method*, London: Everymans, 1981, p. xv.

aimed at control of nature and exclusion of other ways of knowing. It was assumed that the truth of nature was more accessible through violence, and it was recognised that this truth is a basis of power. In this way, 'human knowledge and human power meet as one'.[26] Sandra Harding has characterised this as the contemporary 'alliance of perverse knowledge claims with the perversity of dominating power'.

The knowledge and power nexus is inherent to the reductionist system because the mechanistic order, as a conceptual framework, was associated with a set of values based on power which were compatible with the needs of commercial capitalism. It generates inequalities and domination by the way knowledge is generated and structured, the way it is legitimised, and by the way in which such knowledge transforms nature and society. The domination of the South by the North, of women by men, of nature by westernised man are now being identified as being rooted in the domination inherent to the world-view created by western man over the last three centuries through which he could subjugate or exclude the rest of humanity on grounds of humanity. As Harding observes,

> We can now discern the effects of these cultural markings in the discrepancies between the methods of knowing and the interpretations of the world provided by the creators of modern western culture and those characteristic of the rest of us. Western culture's favoured beliefs mirror in sometimes clear and sometimes distorting ways not the world as it is or as we might want it to be, but the social projects of their historically identifiable creators.[27]

Exclusion of other traditions of knowledge by reductionist science is threefold: *(i)* ontological, in that other properties are just not taken note of; *(ii)* epistemological, in that other ways of perceiving and knowing are not recognized; and *(iii)* sociological, in that the non-specialist and non-expert is deprived of the right both to access to knowledge and to judging claims made on its behalf. All this is the stuff of politics, not science. Picking *one* group of people (the specialists), who adopt *one* way of knowing the physical world (the reductionist), to find *one* set of properties in nature (the mechanistic) is a political, not a scientific mode. Knowledge so obtained is presented as 'the laws of nature', wholly 'objective' and altogether universal. Feyerband is therefore right in saying: 'The *appearance* of objectivity that is attached to some value judgements

26 Quoted in Merchant, *op. cit.*, p. 171.
27 Harding, *op. cit.*, p. 15.

comes from the fact that a particular tradition is *used* but not recognised. Absence of the impression of subjectivity is not proof of objectivity, but an oversight'. The 'controlled' experiment which was assumed to be a mode for 'neutral' observation was, in effect, a political tool for exclusion such that people's experimentation in their daily lives was denied access to the status of the scientific.

It is argued in defence of modern science that it is not science itself but the political misuse and unethical technological application of it that lead to violence. The speciousness of this argument was always clear, but it is totally untenable today, when science and technology have become cognitively inseparable and the amalgam has been incorporated into the scientific-military-industrial complex of capitalist patriarchy. The fragmentation of science into a variety of specializations and sub-specializations is used as a smoke-screen to blur the perception of this linkage between science and a particular model of social organisation, that is, a particular ideology. Science claims that since scientific truths are verifiable and neutral, they are justified beliefs and therefore universal, regardless of the social context. Yet from the perspective of subjugated traditions, the 'truths' of reductionism are falsehoods for the subjugated. Why should we regard the emergence of modern science as a great advance for humanity when it was achieved only at the cost of a deterioration in social status for most of humanity including women and non-western cultures? Sandra Harding, locating the culture of destruction and domination in science-as-usual, not in bad science, asks,

> Could the uses of science to create ecological disaster, support militarism, turn human labour into physically and mentally mutilating work, develop ways of controlling 'others'—the colonised, the women, the poor—be just misuses of applied science? Or does this kind of conceptualisation of the character and purposes of experimental method ensure that what is called bad science or misused science will be a distinctively masculinist science as usual?[28]

Modern science and ecological crises

The supernatural-natural divide. It was not so long ago that most philosophers, sociologists and anthropologists, both western and non-western,

28 Harding, *op. cit.*, p. 102.

relegated all traditional thought to the realm of the supernatural, the mystical, and the irrational. Modern science, in contrast, was uniquely posed as natural, material, empirical, rational. Scientists, in accordance with an abstract scientific method, were viewed as putting forward statements corresponding to the realities of a directly observable world. The theoretical concepts in their discourse were in principle seen as reducible to directly verifiable observational claims. Of course, an elementary investigation into the nature of scientific theories showed that such a reduction was not possible and, instead, it was pervasive theoretical presuppositions which determined observation and facts. Further, the lack of existence of a theoretically neutral observational vocabulary excluded the possibility of definite and conclusive verification of theoretical claims. Scientific claims, like all others, were slowly recognised as arising not in accordance with a verificationist model but from the commitment of a specialist community of scientists to presupposed metaphors and paradigms which determined the meaning of constituent terms, concepts and the status of observation and facts. Meaning and validity were controlled by the social world of scientists and not by the natural world. These new accounts of modern science left no criteria to distinguish between the myths of traditional thought and the metaphors of modern science, between supernatural entities presupposed by traditional communities and theoretical entities presupposed by modern scientists.

Thus, awareness of and familiarity with the theorising and practise of both modern science and traditional thought forces a collapse in the distinction between the supernatural and natural, the irrational and rational, the social and scientific. It removes modern science from its presumed privileged epistemological status, and elevates traditional thought to the status of ethno-science, because it constitutes legitimate ways of knowing and because its claims are expressed in the everyday languages of the people and are influenced by the structures of their languages. To that extent they are particular to each society and its people. However, though theoretical explanation in traditional thought is now recognised as being about the natural and not the supernatural domain, and is of the same epistemological status as explanation in modern scientific thought, its cognitive power is seen as inferior to that of the latter. There are, however, a number of problems in holding on to such a perspective on the cognitive superiority of modern science while conceding epistemological status to traditional and modern belief systems.

Firstly, as Kuhn[29] has shown, scientists are not in practice typically and consistently aware of the existence of alternatives in any case. Science is not nearly as open as has been popularly thought. Scientific inquiry does not range freely amongst boundless alternatives as the popular image suggests, but at any given time is constrained by the currently dominant paradigm. On the other hand, one knows so little about traditional beliefs, especially in the diachronic perspective, that claims about their stagnation, lack of creativity etc., can only be speculation. Thus one cannot legitimately talk of the 'open' and 'closed' predicament but merely of rapidly versus slowly changing belief systems.

Why should more change in thinking per se amount to more rational and cognitively superior theorising? Popper's falsificationism seems to identify the willingness to give up beliefs with a critical spirit, and hence rapidly changing belief systems are viewed as evolving towards more rational and objective claims. However, this view of progress-through-revolution again faces problems. If, following Kuhn, scientific change is guided by social and political factors and not by purely logical and empirical criteria provided by an abstract scientific method, it becomes difficult to conceive how change in itself ensures progress. Even in Popper's unworldly third world of ideas and knowledge, it is therefore not possible to defend the claim that the higher the turnover of beliefs, the more rational one's beliefs will be. In the real world, however, where ideas and beliefs act as guides to action, and play a transformative as well as an interpretive role, too rapid a change in belief systems at times becomes a sign of irrationality and irresponsibility rather than rationality and a critical spirit. The most glaring example of such irrationality and irresponsibility is the situation of contemporary ecological crises. While traditional belief systems did, in rare cases, lead to material transformation of the environment that led to ecological disasters, in most cases ethnosciences have proved to be adequate in maintaining societies and nature. On the other hand, threatening the conditions of natural and human sustenance through human intervention seems to be the rule rather than the exception in modern scientific thought and the practise it gives rise to, especially in fields dealing with health, food production, and food consumption.

The new philosophies of science which have broken down the supernatural-natural divide and the society-science dualism, and have

29 T. Kuhn, *The Structure of Scientific Revolution*, Chicago: University of Chicago Press, 1972.

established epistemological equivalence between ethno-science and modern science, have however created models which do not allow one to discuss the status of beliefs about nature in the materialist perspective of the ecological crises. Kuhn's conclusion about nature fitting into the inelastic boxes of paradigms leaves no room to introduce those material situations when nature boomerangs. His view thus leads to material vacuity. Knowledge about nature can be materially assessed only when the dualism separating thought from action and belief from practice is broken.

This materialist criterion allows one to view belief systems as weak when the unanticipated and unpredicted change in the material environment is far more extensive and intensive than the predicted transformation. When antibiotics create super-infection and flood control measures accentuate floods and fertilizers rob soil of its fertility, the problem is not merely between use and misuse of technology. It is rooted in the very process of knowledge-creation in modern science, a process which is increasingly turning out to be more preoccupied with the material problems created by intervention through scientific beliefs, than material problems posed by nature itself.

The natural-unnatural divide

The belief-action and theory-practise unity which provides the unit of assessment in a materialist epistemology can be interpreted at two different levels in modern science. At the first level, the activity or practise which involves material transformation can be restricted to the scientist's practice in his specialised environment of a laboratory. This level however does not create conditions in which ecological instabilities arising from mistaken beliefs about natural processes can be seen. For an ecological evaluation of the materialist adequacy of theories it therefore becomes essential to consider a more general level of practise in which the material transformation is in the wider natural setting and not in the manipulated setting of a laboratory. Quite obviously, certain types of scientific theorising do not reach the second level of practise. Examples of this are theories in astrophysics or particle physics which, in their contemporary state, stop at the material transformation required to create an experimental situation and do not spill over into the larger environment. However, such theorising is uninteresting in the context of a comparison with ethno-science and an evaluation in an ecological perspective, though for a dualist philosophy of science restricted to the analysis of ideas alone it is just these fields which are most interesting since they are the most advanced in the reductionist-positivist scheme of thought. For our task, the scientific theory and practise that is of relevance is the type that does have ecological implications and involves scientific practise in a wider natural setting.

There is a third category of knowledge in modern science, which unlike particle physics, transcends the material context of the experimental laboratory and, unlike knowledge of fields related to health and food and agriculture, does not create ecological imbalances. Electronics and its background specializations are such an example. Such scientific domains are characterised by both the levels of practise taking place in materially artificial and man-made environments. The artifacts created as part of the transformative activity arising from such beliefs do not interfere with natural processes and relationships in nature. Though derived from nature, they continue to exist independent of it after creation. However, the creation of such artifacts does not replace the natural processes ensuring human survival; they merely supplement the natural material world and do not provide a substitute for it. What could be a better indication of man's continued dependence on nature than the fact that today's so-called post-industrial societies satisfy most of their food needs through imports from so-called underdeveloped countries? It is in the context of the continued central role of nature in human survival that the material inadequacy of scientific thought in the ecological perspective becomes essential.

For those who have internalised linearity in history and nature, taking guidance from ethno-science will seem like 'going backwards'. For others, who see plurality as the stable order for natural ecosystems and human societies, being enlightened by ethnoscience will amount to returning to the appropriate path after having gone astray for a while on the reductionist road. Nature is, after all, diverse, and authentic knowledge of nature should account for this diversity. Ethno-sciences are not less reliable because they are pluralistic, and reductionist science universalised does not provide a more reliable account of nature because it is singular. Objectivity cannot, after all, be equated with a singular inappropriate answer that destroys its very object.

Recent history has shown that in certain areas of human activity a return to ecological thought and action is possible and desirable. The primitive practise of breast-feeding had been discredited by the advertising and reductionist claims of the baby-food industry. The ecology of breast-feeding has, however, become appreciated once again, and the 'primitive' practise is enlightened practise today. Chemicalisation of health care seemed to be the only way to develop in the reductionist paradigm. Work in ethno-medicine is again bringing back wholesome drugs and treatment. Sustainable organic farming which created 'farmers of forty centuries' is on its way back, in all the diversity and plurality of its traditional base. Each of these steps towards ecological thought and action has been possible because contact was made with an ethno-scientific tradition. If the world is to be conserved for survival, the human potential for conservation must be conserved first. It is the only resource we have to foresee and forestall the destruction of our ecosystems.

Contemporary women's ecological struggles are new attempts to establish that steadiness and stability are not stagnation, and balance with nature's essential ecological processes is not technological backwardness but technological sophistication. At a time when a quarter of the world's population is threatened by starvation due to erosion of soil, water, and genetic diversity of living resources, chasing the mirage of unending growth, by spreading resource destructive technologies, becomes a major source of genocide. The killing of people by the murder of nature is an invisible form of violence which is today the biggest threat to justice and peace.

The emerging feminist and ecological critiques of reductionist science extend the domain of the testing of scientific beliefs into the wider physical world. Socially, the world of scientific experiments and beliefs has to be extended beyond the so-called experts and specialists into the world of all those who have systematically been excluded from it—women, peasants, tribals. The verification and validation of a scientific system would then be validation in practise, where practise and experimentation is real-life activity in society and nature. Harding says:

> Neither God nor tradition is privileged with the same credibility as scientific rationality in modern cultures. ...The project that science's sacredness makes taboo is the examination of science in just the ways any other institution or set of social practises can be examined. If we are not willing to try and see the favoured intellectual structures and practises of science as cultural artifacts rather than as sacred commandments handed down to humanity at the birth of modern science, then it will be hard to understand how gender symbolism, the gendered social structure of science, and the masculine identities and behaviours of individ-

ual scientists have left their marks on the problematics, concepts, theories, methods, interpretation, ethics, meanings and goals of science.[30]

The intellectual recovery of the feminine principle creates new conditions for women and non-western cultures to become principal actors in establishing a democracy of all life, as countervailing forces to the intellectual culture of death and dispensability that reductionism creates.

Ecology movements are political movements for a nonviolent world order in which nature is conserved for conserving the options for survival. These movements are small, but they are growing. They are local, but their success lies in non-local impact. They demand only the right to survival yet with that minimal demand is associated the right to live in a peaceful and just world. With the success of these grassroots movements is linked the global issue of survival. Unless the world is restructured ecologically at the level of world-views and life-styles, peace and justice will continue to be violated and ultimately the very survival of humanity will be threatened.

30 Harding, *op. cit.*, p. 30

CHAPTER THREE

Women in Nature

Nature as the feminine principle

Women in India are an intimate part of nature, both in imagination and in practise. At one level nature is symbolised as the embodiment of the feminine principle, and at another, she is nurtured by the feminine to produce life and provide sustenance.

From the point of view of Indian cosmology, in both the exoteric and esoteric traditions, the world is produced and renewed by the dialectical play of creation and destruction, cohesion and disintegration. The tension between the opposites from which motion and movement arises is depicted as the first appearance of dynamic energy (Shakti). All existence arises from this primordial energy which is the substance of everything, pervading everything. The manifestation of this power, this energy, is called nature (Prakriti).[1] Nature, both animate and inanimate, is thus an expression of Shakti, the feminine and creative principle of the cosmos; in conjunction with the masculine principle (Purusha), Prakriti creates the world.

Nature as Prakriti is inherently active, a powerful, productive force in the dialectic of the creation, renewal, and sustenance of *all* life. In *Kulacudamim Nigama,* Prakriti says:

---

1 'Prakriti' is a popular category, and one through which ordinary women in rural India relate to nature. It is also a highly evolved philosophical category in Indian cosmology. Even those philosophical streams of Indian thought which were patriarchal and did not give the supreme place to divinity as a woman, a mother, were permeated by the prehistoric cults and the living 'little' traditions of nature as the primordial mother goddess.

There is none but Myself
Who is the Mother to create.[2]

Without Shakti, Shiva, the symbol for the force of creation and destruction, is as powerless as a corpse. 'The quiescent aspect of Shiva is, by definition, inert ... Activity is the nature of Nature (Prakriti)'.[3]

Prakriti is worshipped as Aditi, the primordial vastness, the inexhaustible, the source of abundance. She is worshipped as Adi Shakti,
the primordial power. All the forms of nature and life in nature are the
forms, the children, of the Mother of Nature who is nature itself born of
the creative play of her thought.[4] Hence Prakriti is also called Lalitha,[5] the
Player because *lila* or play, as free spontaneous activity, is her nature. The
will-to-become many (Bahu-Syam-Prajayera) is her creative impulse and
through this impulse, she creates the diversity of living forms in nature.
The common yet multiple life of mountains, trees, rivers, animals is an
expression of the diversity that Prakriti gives rise to. The creative force
and the created world are not separate and distinct, nor is the created
world uniform, static, and fragmented. It is diverse, dynamic, and inter-
related.

The nature of Nature as Prakriti is activity *and* diversity. Nature symbols from every realm of nature are in a sense signed with the image of
Nature. Prakriti lives in stone or tree, pool, fruit or animal, and is identified with them. According to the *Kalika Purana*:

> Rivers and mountains have a dual nature. A river is but a form of wa-
> ter, yet is has a distinct body. Mountains appear a motionless mass, yet
> their true form is not such. We cannot know, when looking at a lifeless
> shell, that it contains a living being. Similarly, within the apparently
> inanimate rivers and mountains there dwells a hidden consciousness.
> Rivers and mountains take the forms they wish.[6]

2 For an elaboration of the concept of the feminine principle in Indian thought see Alain
Danielon, *The Gods of India*, New York: Inner Traditions International Ltd., 1985; Sir John
Woodroffe, *The Serpent Power*, Madras: Ganesh and Co., 1931; and Sir John Woodroffe,
Shakti and Shakta, London: Luzaz and Co., 1929

3 Woodroffe, *op. cit.*, (1931), p 27.

4 W.C. Beane, Myth, *Cult and Symbols in Sakta Hinduism: A Study of the Indian Mother
Goddess*, Leiden: EJ. Brill, 1977.

5 *Lalitha Sahasranama*, (Reprint), Delhi: Giani Publishing House, 1986.

6 *Kalika Purana*, 22.10-13, Bombay: Venkateshwara Press, 1927.

The living, nurturing relationship between man and nature here differs dramatically from the notion of man as separate from and dominating over nature. A good illustration of this difference is the daily worship of the sacred tulsi within Indian culture and outside it. Tulsi (*Ocimum sanctum*) is a little herb planted in every home, and worshipped daily. It has been used in Ayurveda for more than 3000 years, and is now also being legitimised as a source of diverse healing powers by western medicine. However, all this is incidental to its worship. The tulsi is sacred not merely as a plant with beneficial properties but as Brindavan, the symbol of the cosmos. In their daily watering and worship women renew the relationship of the home with the cosmos and with the world process. Nature as a creative expression of the feminine principle is both in ontological continuity with humans as well as above them. Ontologically, there is no divide between man and nature, or between man and woman, because life in all its forms arises from the feminine principle.

Contemporary western views of nature are fraught with the dichotomy or duality between man and woman, and person and nature. In Indian cosmology, by contrast, person and nature (Purusha-Prakriti) are a duality in unity. They are inseparable complements of one another in nature, in woman, in man. Every form of creation bears the sign of this dialectical unity, of diversity within a unifying principle, and this dialectical harmony between the male and female principles and between nature and man, becomes the basis of ecological thought and action in India. Since, ontologically, there is no dualism between man and nature and because nature as Prakriti sustains life, nature has been treated as integral and inviolable. Prakriti, far from being an esoteric abstraction, is an everyday concept which organises daily life. There is no separation here between the popular and elite imagery or between the sacred and secular traditions. As an embodiment and manifestation of the feminine principle it is characterised by *(a)* creativity, activity, productivity; (b) diversity in form and aspect; (c) connectedness and inter-relationship of all beings, including man; *(d)* continuity between the human and natural; and *(e)* sanctity of life in nature.

Conceptually, this differs radically from the Cartesian concept of nature as an 'environment' or a 'resource'. In it, the environment is seen as separate from man: it is his surrounding, not his substance. The dualism between man and nature has allowed the subjugation of the latter by man and given rise to a new world-view in which nature is *(a)* inert and passive; *(b)* uniform and mechanistic; (c) separable and fragmented within itself; *(d)* separate from man; and *(e)* inferior, to be dominated and exploited by man.

The rupture within nature and between man and nature, and its associated transformation from a life-force that sustains to an exploitable resource characterises the Cartesian view which has displaced more ecological world-views and created a development paradigm which cripples nature and woman simultaneously.

The ontological shift for an ecologically sustainable future has much to gain from the world-views of ancient civilisations and diverse cultures which survived sustainably over centuries. These were based on an ontology of the feminine as the living principle, and on an ontological continuity between society and nature—the humanisation of nature and the naturalisation of society. Not merely did this result in an ethical context which excluded possibilities of exploitation and domination, it allowed the creation of an earth family.

The dichotomised ontology of man dominating woman and nature generates maldevelopment because it makes the colonising male the agent and model of 'development'. Women, the Third World, and nature become underdeveloped, first by definition, and then, through the process of colonisation, in reality.

The ontology of dichotomisation generates an ontology of domination, over nature and people. Epistemologically, it leads to reductionism and fragmentation, thus violating women as subjects and nature as an object of knowledge. This violation becomes a source of epistemic and real violence—I would like to interpret ecological crises at both levels—as a disruption of ecological perceptions of nature.

Ecological ways of knowing nature are necessarily participatory. Nature herself is the experiment and women, as sylviculturalists, agriculturists and water resource managers, the traditional natural scientists. Their knowledge is ecological and plural, reflecting both the diversity of natural ecosystems and the diversity in cultures that nature-based living gives rise to. Throughout the world, the colonisation of diverse peoples was, at its root, a forced subjugation of ecological concepts of nature and of the Earth as the repository of all forms, latencies, and powers of creation, the ground and cause of the world. The symbolism of Terra Mater, the earth in the form of the Great Mother, creative and protective, has been a shared but diverse symbol across space and time, and ecology movements in the West today are inspired in large part by the recovery of the concept of Gaia, the earth goddess.[7]

The shift from Prakriti to 'natural resources', from Mater to 'matter' was considered (and in many quarters is still considered) a progressive shift from superstition to rationality. Yet, viewed from the perspective of nature, or women embedded in nature, in the production and preservation of sustenance, the shift is regressive and violent. It entails the disruption of nature's processes and cycles, and her interconnectedness. For women, whose productivity in the sustaining of life is based on nature's productivity, the death of Prakriti is simultaneously a beginning of their marginalisation, devaluation, displacement, and ultimate dispensability. The ecological crisis is, at its root, the death of the feminine principle, symbolically as well as in contexts such as rural India, not merely in form and symbol, but also in the everyday processes of survival and sustenance.

Nature and women as producers of life

With the violation of nature is linked the violation and marginalisation of women, especially in the Third World. Women produce and reproduce life not merely biologically, but also through their social role in providing sustenance. All ecological societies of forest-dwellers and peasants, whose life is organised on the principle of sustainability and the reproduction of life in all its richness, also embody the feminine principle. Historically, however, when such societies have been colonised and broken up the men have usually started to participate in life-destroying activities or have had to migrate; the women meanwhile, usually continue to be linked to life and nature through their role as providers of sustenance, food, and water. The privileged access of women to the sustaining principle thus has a historical and cultural, and not merely biological, basis. The principle of creating and conserving life is lost to the ecologically alienated, consumerist elite women of the Third World and the over-consuming west, just as much as it is conserved in the lifestyle of the male and female forest-dwellers and peasants in small pockets of the Third World.

Maria Mies has called women's work in producing sustenance the *production of life* and views it as a truly productive relationship to

7 Erich Neumann, *The Great Mother*, New York: Pantheon Books, 1955

nature, because 'women not only collected and consumed what grew in nature but they *made things grow*'.[8] This organic process of growth in which women and nature work in partnership with each other has created a special relationship of women with nature, which, following Mies, can be summarised as follows:

> *(a)* Their interaction with nature, with their own nature as well as the external environment, was a reciprocal process. They conceived of their own bodies as being productive in the same way as they conceived of external nature being so.
>
> *(b)* Although they appropriate nature, their appropriation does not constitute a relationship of dominance or a property relation. Women are not owners of their own bodies or of the earth, but they cooperate with their bodies and with the earth in order 'to let grow and to make grow'.
>
> *(c)* As producers of new life they also became the first subsistence producers and the inventors of the first productive economy, implying from the beginning social production and the creation of social relations, i.e. of society and history.

Productivity, viewed from the perspective of survival, differs sharply from the dominant view of the productivity of labour as defined for processes of capital accumulation. 'Productive' man, producing commodities, using some of nature's wealth and women's work as raw material and dispensing with the rest as waste, becomes the only legitimate category of work, wealth, and production. Nature and women working to produce and reproduce life are declared 'unproductive'.

With Adam Smith, the wealth created by nature and women's work was turned invisible. Labour, and especially male labour, became the fund which originally supplies it with all the necessities and conveniences of life. As this assumption spread to all human communities, it introduced dualities within society, and between nature and man. No more was nature a source of wealth and sustenance; no more was women's work in sustenance 'productive work' no more were peasant and tribal societies creative and productive. They were all marginal to the framework of the industrial society, except as resources and inputs. The transforming, productive power was associated only with male western labour and economic development became a design of remodelling

8 Maria Mies, *Patriarchy and Accumulation on a World Scale*, London: Zed Books, 1986, pp. 16-17, 55.

the world on that assumption. The devaluation and derecognition of nature's work and productivity has led to the ecological crises; the devaluation and derecognition of women's work has created sexism and inequality between men and women. The devaluation of subsistence, or rather sustenance economies, based on harmony between nature's work, women's work and man's work has created the various forms of ethnic and cultural crises that plague our world today.

The crisis of survival and the threat to sustenance arises from ecological disruption that is rooted in the arrogance of the west and those that ape it. This arrogance is grounded in a blindness towards the quiet work and the invisible wealth created by nature and women and those who produce sustenance. Such work and wealth are 'invisible' because they are decentred, local, and in harmony with local ecosystems and needs. The more effectively the cycles of life, as essential ecological processes, are maintained, the more invisible they become. Disruption is violent and visible; balance and harmony are experienced, not seen. The premium on visibility placed by patriarchal maldevelopment forces the destruction of invisible energies and the work of women and nature, and the creation of spectacular, centralised work and wealth. Such centralisation and the uniformity associated with it works further against the diversity and plurality of life. Work and wealth in accordance with the feminine principle are significant precisely because they are rooted in stability and sustainability. Decentred diversity is the source of nature's work and women's productivity; it is the work of 'insignificant' plants in creating significant changes which shift the ecological equilibrium in life's favour. It is the energy of all living things, in all their diversity, and together, the diversity of lives wields tremendous energy. Women's work is similarly invisible in providing sustenance and creating wealth for basic needs. Their work in the forest, the field and the river creates sustenance in quiet but essential ways. Every woman in every house in every village of rural India works invisibly to provide the stuff of life to nature and people. It is this invisible work that is linked to nature and needs, which conserves nature through maintaining ecological cycles, and conserves human life through satisfying the basic needs of food, nutrition, and water. It is this essential work that is destroyed and dispensed with by maldevelopment: the maintenance of ecological cycles has no place in a political economy of commodity and cash flows.

The existence of the feminine principle is linked with diversity and sharing. Its destruction through homogenisation and privatisation leads to the destruction of diversity and of the commons. The sustenance economy is based on a creative and organic nature, on local knowledge, on locally recycled inputs that maintain the integrity of nature, on local consumption for local needs, and on the marketing of surplus beyond the imperatives of equity and ecology. The commodity and cash economy destroys natural cycles and reduces nature to raw materials and commodities. It creates the need for purchase and sale to centralised inputs and commodity markets. When production is specialised and for export, surplus becomes a myth. There is only indebtedness, of peoples and nations. The debt trap is part of global commodity production and sale which destroys nurturing nature and nurturing economies in the name of development.

Sustenance, in the final analysis, is built on the continued capacity of nature to renew its forests, fields, and rivers. These resource systems are intrinsically linked in life-producing and life-conserving cultures, and it is in managing the integrity of ecological cycles in forestry and agriculture that women's productivity has been most developed and evolved. Women transfer fertility from the forests to the field and to animals. They transfer animal waste as fertilizer for crops and crop by-products to animals as fodder. They work with the forest to bring water to their fields and families. This partnership between women's and nature's work ensures the sustainability of sustenance, and it is this critical partnership that is torn asunder when the project of 'development' becomes a patriarchal project, threatening both nature and women. The forest is separated from the river, the field is separated from the forest, the animals are separated from the crops. Each is then separately developed, and the delicate balance which ensures sustainability and equity is destroyed. The visibility of dramatic breaks and ruptures is posited as 'progress'. Marginalised women are either dispensed with or colonised. Needs go unfulfilled, nature is crippled. The drama of violence and fragmentation cannot be sustained and the recovery of the feminine principle thus becomes essential for liberating not only women and nature, but also the patriarchal reductionist categories which give rise to maldevelopment.

The revolutionary and liberational potential of the recovery of the feminine principle consists in its challenging the concepts, categories and processes which have created the threat to life, and in providing oppositional categories that create and enlarge the spaces for maintaining and enriching all life in nature and society. The radical shift induced by a focus on the feminine principle is the recognition of maldevelopment as a culture of destruction. The feminine principle becomes a category of challenge which locates nature and women as the source of life and wealth, and as such, active subjects, maintaining and creating life-processes.

There are two implications that arise from the recognition of nature and women as producers of life. First, that what goes by the name of development is a maldevelopment process, a source of violence to women and nature throughout the world. This violence does not arise from the misapplication of an otherwise benign and gender-neutral model, but is rooted in the patriarchal assumptions of homogeneity, domination, and centralisation that underlie dominant models of thought and development strategies. Second, that the crises that the maldevelopment model has given rise to cannot be solved within the paradigm of the crisis mind. Their solution lies in the categories of thought, perception, and action that are life-giving and life-maintaining. In contemporary times, Third World women, whose minds have not yet been dispossessed or colonised, are in a privileged position to make visible the invisible oppositional categories that they are the custodians of. It is not only as victims, but also as leaders in creating new intellectual ecological paradigms, that women are central to arresting and overcoming ecological crises. Just as ecological recovery begins from centres of natural diversity which are gene pools, Third World women, and those tribals and peasants who have been left out of the processes of maldevelopment, are today acting as the intellectual gene pools of ecological categories of thought and action. Marginalisation has thus become a source for healing the diseased mainstream of patriarchal development. Those facing the biggest threat offer the best promise for survival because they have two kinds of knowledge that are not accessible to dominant and privileged groups. First, they have the knowledge of what it means to be the victims of progess, to be the ones who bear the costs and burdens. Second, they have the holistic and ecological knowledge of what the production and protection of life is about. They retain the ability to see nature's life as a *precondition* for human survival and the integrity of interconnectedness in nature as a precondition for life. Women of the Third World have been dispossessed of their base for sustenance, but not of their minds, and in their uncolonised minds are conserved the oppositional categories that make the sustenance of life possible for all. The producers of life alone can be its real protectors. Women embedded in nature, producing life with nature, are therefore taking the initiative in the recovery of nature.

To say that women and nature are intimately associated is not to say anything revolutionary. After all, it was precisely just such an assumption that allowed the domination of both women and nature. The new insight provided by rural women in the Third World is that women and nature are associated *not in passivity but in creativity and in the maintenance of life.*

This analysis differs from most conventional analyses of environmentalists and feminists. Most work on women and environment in the Third World has focussed on women as special victims of environmental degradation. Yet the women who participate in and lead ecology movements in countries like India are not speaking merely as victims. Their voices are the voices of liberation and transformation which provide new categories of thought and new exploratory directions. In this sense, this study is a post-victimology study. It is an articulation of the categories of challenge that women in ecology movements are creating in the Third World. The women and environment issue can be approached either from these categories of challenge that have been thrown up by women in the struggle for life, or it can be approached through an extension of conventional categories of patriarchy and reductionism. In the perspective of women engaged in survival struggles which are, simultaneously, struggles for the protection of nature, women and nature are intimately related, and their domination and liberation similarly linked. The women's and ecology movements are therefore one, and are primarily counter-trends to a patriarchal maldevelopment. Our experience shows that ecology and feminism can combine in the recovery of the feminine principle, and through this recovery, can intellectually and politically restructure and transform maldevelopment.

Maldevelopment is seen here as a process by which human society marginalises the play of the feminine principle in nature and in society. Ecological breakdown and social inequality are intrinsically related to the dominant development paradigm which puts man against and above nature and women. The underlying assumptions of dialectical unity and cyclical recovery shared by the common concern for the liberation of nature and of women, contrast deeply with the dominant western patriarchal assumptions of duality in existence and linearity in process. Within the western paradigm, the environmental movement is separate from the women's movement. As long as this paradigm with its assumptions of linear progress prevails, 'environmentalism' and 'feminism' independently ask only for concessions *within* maldevelopment, because in the absence of oppositional categories, that is the only 'development' that is conceivable. Environmentalism then becomes a new patriarchal project of technological fixes and political oppression. It generates a new subjugation of ecological movements and fails to make any progress towards sustainability and equity. While including a few women as tokens in 'women and environment', it excludes the feminine visions of survival that women have conserved. Fragmented feminism, in a similar way, finds itself trapped in a gender-based ideology of liberation—taking off from either the 'catching-up-with-men' syndrome (on the grounds that the masculine is superior and developed), or receding into a narrow biologism which accepts the feminine as gendered, and excludes the possibility of the recovery of the feminine principle in nature and women, *as well as* men.

Gender-ideology vs. the recovery of the feminine principle

We see the categories of 'masculine' and 'feminine' as socially and culturally constructed. A gender-based ideology projects these categories as biologically determined. The western concept of masculinity that has dominated development and gender relations has excluded all that has been defined by culture as feminine and has legitimised control over all that counts as such. The category of masculinity as a socially constructed product of gender ideology is associated with the creation of the concept of woman as the 'other'. In this asymmetrical relationship, femininity is ideologically constructed as everything that is not masculine and must be subjected to domination. There are two gender-based responses to the process of domination and asymmetry. The first, represented by Simone de Beauvoir, is based on the acceptance of feminine and masculine as biologically established, and the status of women as the second sex as similarly determined. Women's liberation is prescribed as the masculinisation of the female. The emancipation of the 'second sex' lies in its modelling itself on the first; women's freedom consists in freedom from biology, from 'bondage to life's mysterious processes.[9] It consists of women 'battling against the elements', and becoming masculine. The liberation that de Beauvoir conceives of is a world in which the masculine is accepted as superior and women are free to assume masculine values.

9 Simone de Beauvoir, *The Second Sex*, London: Penguin Books, 1972.

The process of liberation is thus a masculinisation of the world defined *within* the categories created by gender-based ideology.

De Beauvoir accepts the patriarchal categorisation of women as passive, weak, and unproductive. 'In no domain whatever did she create'; she simply 'submitted passively to her biologic fate', while men fought. The 'worst that was laid upon woman was that she should be excluded from these warlike forays. For it is not in giving life, but in risking life, that man is raised above the animal. That is why superiority has been accorded in humanity not to the sex that brings forth life but to that which kills'.[10] De Beauvoir subscribes to the myth of man-the-hunter as a superior being. She believes that instead of being the providers in hunting-gathering societies, women were a liability to the group because 'closely spaced births must have absorbed most of their strength and time so that they were incapable of providing for the children they brought into the world'.[11]

That traditional and tribal women, without access to modern contraception, could not regulate the number of their children and the number of births is turning out to be a commonly accepted patriarchal myth. Similarly, the myth of female passivity and masculine creativity has been critically analysed by recent feminist scholarship, which shows that the survival of mankind has been due much more to 'woman-the-gatherer' than to 'man-the-hunter'. Lee and de Vore have shown empirically how even among existing hunters and gatherers, women provide up to 80 percent of the daily food, whereas men contribute only a small portion by hunting. Elizabeth Fisher's studies indicate that gathering of vegetable food was more important for our early ancestors than hunting.[12] In spite of of this, the myth persists that man-the-hunter as the inventor of tools was the provider of basic needs and the protector of society. Evelyn Reed shows how sexism has been the underlying ideology of much work that passes as neutral, unbiased science, and has been the cause for much of the violence and destruction in history.[13] Finally, Maria Mies has argued that the relationship of man-the-hunter with nature was necessarily violent, destructive, and predatory, in sharp contrast to the relationship that woman-the-gatherer or cultivator had. Humanity, quite clearly, could not have survived if man-the-hunter's productivity had been the basis for the daily subsistence of early societies. Their

10 de Beauvoir, *op. cit.*, pp. 95-96.

11 *Ibid.*, p. 87.

12 Quoted in Elizabeth Fisher, *Woman's Creation*, New York: Anchor Press, 1979, p. 48.

13 E. Reed, *Sexism and Science*, New York: Pathfinder Press, 1978.

survival was based on the fact that this activity was only a small part of sustenance. Yet patriarchal ideology has made man-the-hunter the model of human evolution, and has thus adopted violence and domination as its structural component. Hunting, per se, need not be violent; most tribal societies apologise to the animals they have to kill, and their hunting is constrained by nature's cycles of production and reproduction. It is the elevation of the hunting to the level of ideology, that has laid the foundation of a violent relationship with nature. As Mies points out, the patriarchal myth of man-the-hunter implies the following levels of violence in man's relationship with nature:

(*a*) The hunters' main tools are not instruments with which to produce life but to destroy it. Their tools are not basically means of production but of destruction, and can also be used as means of coercion against fellow human beings.

(*b*) This gives hunters a power over living beings, both animal and human, which does not arise out of their own productive work. They can appropriate not only fruits and plants (like the gatherers) and animals, but also other (female) producers by virtue of arms.

(*c*) The objective relationship mediated through arms, therefore, is basically a predatory or exploitative one: hunters appropriate life, but they cannot produce life. It is an antagonistic and non-reciprocal relationship. All later exploitative relations between production and appropriation are, in the last analysis, upheld by arms as means of coercion.

(*d*) The objective relationship to nature mediated through arms constitutes a relationship of dominance and not of cooperation between hunter and nature. This relationship of dominance has become an integral element of all further production relations established by men. It has become, in fact, the main paradigm of their productivity. Without dominance and control over nature, men cannot conceive of themselves as being productive.

(*e*) 'Appropriation of natural substances' (Marx) now also becomes a process of one-sided appropriation, of establishing property relations, not in the sense of humanisation, but of exploitation of nature.[14]

Mies concludes that while the patriarchal paradigm has made man-the-hunter an exemplar of human productivity, he is 'basically a parasite—not a producer'. With the reversal of categories, made possible by focussing

14 Maria Mies, *op. cit.*, p. 62.

on the production of life, the masculinisation of the feminine is no longer a viable option for liberation.

Herbert Marcuse sees liberation as a feminisation of the world: 'Inasmuch as the male principle has been the ruling mental and physical force, a free society would be the "definite negation" of this principle—it would be a female society'.[15] While Marcuse opposes de Beauvoir's model, both share the assumptions of feminine and masculine as natural, biologically defined traits which have an independent existence, and both respond to patriarchy's gender ideology with categories that have been created by that ideology. Marcuse states: 'Beneath the social factors which determine male aggressiveness and female receptivity, a *natural* contrast exists; it is the woman who "embodies" in a literal sense, the promise of peace, of joy, of the end of violence. Tenderness, receptivity, sensuousness have become features (or mutilated features) of her body—features of her (repressed) humanity'.[16]

Gender ideology has created the dualism and disjunction between male and female. Simultaneously it has created a conjunction of activity and creativity with violence and the masculine, and a conjunction of passivity with nonviolence and the feminine. Gender-based responses to this dualism have retained these conjunctions and disjunctions, and within these dichotomised categories, have prescribed either the masculinisation or feminisation of the world.

There is, however, a third concept and process of liberation that is trans-gender. It is based on the recognition that masculine and feminine as gendered concepts based on exclusiveness are ideologically defined categories, as is the association of violence and activity with the former, and nonviolence and passivity with the latter. Rajni Kothari has observed, 'The feminist input serves not just women but also men. There is no limiting relationship between feminist values and being a woman'.[17] In this non-gender-based philosophy the feminine principle is not exclusively embodied in women, but is the principle of activity and creativity in nature, women, and men. One cannot really distinguish the masculine from the feminine, person from nature, Purusha from Prakriti. Though distinct, they remain inseparable in dialectical unity, as two aspects of one being. The recovery of the feminine principle is thus

15 Herbert Marcuse, *Counter-revolution and Revolt*, New York: Allen Lane, 1974, pp. 74-75.

16 Marcuse, *op. cit.*, p. 77.

17 Rajni Kothari, 'Lokayan's Efforts to Overcome the New Rift', FDA Dossier, Vol. 52, March-April 1986, p. 9.

associated with the non-patriarchal, non-gendered category of creative nonviolence, or 'creative power in peaceful form', as Tagore stated in his prayer to the tree.

It is this conceptual framework within which this book, and the experiences and struggles discussed in it are located. This perspective can recover humanity not in its distorted form of the victim and oppressor, but by creating a new wholeness in both that transcends gender because gender identity is, in any case, an ideological, social, and political construct.

The recovery of the feminine principle is a response to multiple dominations and deprivations not just of women, but also of nature and non-western cultures. It stands for ecological recovery and nature's liberation, for women's liberation and for the liberation of men who, in dominating nature and women, have sacrificed their own human-ness. Ashis Nandy says, one must choose the slave's standpoint not only because the slave is oppressed but also because he represents a higher-order cognition which perforce includes the master as a human, whereas the master's cognition has to exclude the slave except as a 'thing'.[18] Liberation must therefore begin from the colonised and end with the coloniser. As Gandhi was to so clearly formulate through his own life, freedom is indivisible, not only in the popular sense that the oppressed of the world are one, but also in the unpopular sense that the oppressor, too, is caught in the culture of oppression.

The recovery of the feminine principle is based on inclusiveness. It is a recovery in nature, woman and man of creative forms of being and perceiving. In nature it implies seeing nature as a live organism. In woman it implies seeing women as productive and active. Finally, in men the recovery of the feminine principle implies a relocation of action and activity to create life-enhancing, not life-reducing and life-threatening societies.

The death of the feminine principle in women and nature takes place through the association of the category of passivity with the feminine. The death of the feminine principle in men takes place by a shift in the concept of activity from creation to destruction, and the concept of power from empowerment to domination. Self-generated, nonviolent, creative activity as the feminine principle dies simultaneously in women, men and nature when violence and aggression become the masculine

18 Ashis Nandy, *The Intimate Enemy*, Delhi: Oxford University Press, 1986, p. xv.

model of activity, and women and nature are turned into passive objects of violence. The problem with a gender-based response to a gender-based ideology is that it treats ideologically constructed gender categorisation as given by nature. It treats passive nonviolence as biological givens in women, and violence as a biological given in men, when both non-violence and violence are socially constructed and need have no gender association. Gandhi, the modern world's leading practitioner and preacher of nonviolence was, after all, a man. The historical creation of a gender divide by a gender ideology cannot be the basis of gender liberation. And a gender-based ideology remains totally inadequate in either responding to the ecological crisis created by patriarchal and violent modes of relating to nature, or in understanding how Third World women are leading ecological struggles based on values of conservation which are immediately generalised as the concern for entire communities and regions, and even humanity as a whole.

CHAPTER FOUR

Women in the Forest

Aranyani: the forest as the feminine principle

Forests have always been central to Indian civilization. They have been worshipped as Aranyani, the Goddess of the Forest, the primary source of life and fertility, and the forest as a community has been viewed as a model for societal and civilizational evolution. The diversity, harmony and self-sustaining nature of the forest formed the organisational principles guiding Indian civilization; the *aranya saṁskriti* (roughly translatable as 'the culture of the forest' or 'forest culture') was not a condition of primitiveness, but one of conscious choice. According to Rabindranath Tagore the distinctiveness of Indian culture consists of its having defined life in the forest as the highest form of cultural evolution. In *Tapovan,* he writes:

> Contemporary western civilization is built of brick and wood. It is rooted in the city. But Indian civilization has been distinctive in locating its source of regeneration, material and intellectual, in the forest, not the city. India's best ideas have come where man was in communion with trees and rivers and lakes, away from the crowds. The peace of the forest has helped the intellectual evolution of man. The culture of the forest has fuelled the culture of Indian society. The culture that has arisen from the forest has been influenced by the diverse processes of renewal of life which are always at play in the forest, varying from species to species, from season to season, in sight and sound and smell. The unifying principle of life in diversity, of democratic pluralism, thus became the principle of Indian civilization.

Not being caged in brick, wood and iron, Indian thinkers were surrounded by and linked to the life of the forest. The living forest was for
them their shelter, their source of food. The intimate relationship between human life and living nature became the source of knowledge.
Nature was not dead and inert in this knowledge system. The experience of life in the forest made it adequately clear that living nature was
the source of light and air, of food and water. [1]

As a source of life nature was venerated as sacred and human evolution was measured in terms of man's capacity to merge with her rhythms
and patterns intellectually, emotionally, and spiritually. The forest thus
nurtured an ecological civilization in the most fundamental sense of harmony with nature. Such knowledge that came from participation in the
life of the forest was the substance not just of *Aranyakas* or forest texts,
but also of the everyday beliefs of tribal and peasant society. The forest as
the highest expression of the earth's fertility and productivity is symbolised
in yet another form as the Earth Mother,[2] as Vana Durga or the Tree Goddess. In Bengal she is associated with the *asvathha (Trophis aspera),* and
with the *sal (Shorea robusta)* and *asvathha (Ficus religiosa).* In Comilla she
is Bamani, in Assam she is Rupeswari. In folk and tribal cultures especially,
trees and forests are also worshipped as *Vana Devatas* or forest deities.

The sacred tree serves as an image of the cosmos, a symbol of the inexhaustible source of cosmic fertility. The Earth Mother as the primordial
Mother says:

> O ye gods, I shall support (i.e. nourish) the whole world with life-sus-
> taining vegetables which shall grow out of my body, during a period of
> heavy rain. I shall gain fame on earth then as Shakhambari (goddess
> who feeds the herbs), and in that very period, I shall slay the great asura
> named Durgama (a personification of drought).
>
> *Devimahatmya* 90:43-44.[3]

Sacred forests and sacred groves were created and maintained
throughout India as a cultural response for their protection. As Pant reports for the Himalaya:

1 Rabindranath Tagore, *Tapouan* (Hindi), Tikamgarh: Gandhi Bhavan, undated, p. 12.

2 W.C. Beane, *Myth, Cult and Symbols in Sakta Hinduism,* Leiden: E.J. Brill, 1977, p. 118,
states, 'We submit that the Dravidian goddess Kali was already a divinity as well as a per-
sonification of "forest phenomena", and quotes Tucci as saying that Durga is a mother
goddess originating in the Vindhyas as the 'vivifying force of the forest'.

3 Quoted in Beane, *op. cit.,* p. 57.

> A natural system of conservancy was in vogue; almost every hill-top is dedicated to some local deity and the trees on or about the spot are regarded with great respect so that nobody dare touch them. There is also a general impression among the people that everyone cutting a tree should plant another in its place.[4]

All religions and cultures of the South Asian region have been rooted in the forests, not through fear and ignorance but through ecological insight. Myers says: 'In contrast to the folklore of temperate zones, which often regards forests as dark places of danger, traditional perceptions of forests in the humid tropics convey a sense of intimate harmony, with people and forests equal occupants of a communal habitat, a primary source of congruity between man and nature'.[5]

For the tribes of Central India, the forest is the context and condition of survival. The *mohwa (Bassia latifolia)* is special for the tribals of Chattisgarh, of the Santhal Parganas, of Bastar and of the Satpuras. A large deciduous tree, usually with a short bole, spreading branches and a large rounded crown, it is one of the most important forest trees of India. Women collect the fleshy corollas of its flowers which are eaten raw or cooked, or dried, ground and mixed with flour for making cakes, or distilled into spirit. A thick white oil extracted from the seed is used by tribals for cooking and burning, and is sold for the manufacture of margarine, soap, and glycerine. The tree is never felled owing to the value of its flowers and fruits. Even when forest land is cleared for cultivation, the *mohwa* trees are carefully preserved and are found scattered over cultivated lands long after clearing has taken place. Trees bear crops of flowers and fruit when about ten years old and yield about 40 kgs. of flowers per year. In 1897 and 1900, serious famine years in Central India, the profuse blossoming of *mohwa* flowers was a famine insurance for the tribals. It is not surprising then, that to the forest dwellers of Central India, the *mohwa* is the tree of life.

India's people have traditionally recognised the dependence of human survival on the existence of forests. A systematic knowledge about plants and forest ecosystems was thus generated and informal principles of forest management formulated. It has often been stated that 'scientific' forestry and the scientific management of forest resources in India began with the British. The historical justification for such a statement

4 G.B. Pant, *The Forest Problem in Kumaon* (reprint), Nainital: Gyanodaya Prakashan. 1922, p. 75.

5 Norman Myers, *The Primary Source*, New York: W.W. Norton, 1984, p. 13.

becomes possible only if one accepts that modern western patriarchal science is the only valid science. In ancient Indian traditions, scientific knowledge of the plant kingdom is evident from such terms as *vriksayurveda,* which means the science of the treatment of plant diseases, and *vanaspati vidya* or plant sciences, while many ancient texts were called *Aranyakas* or forest texts. Being derived from the living forest, indigenous forestry science did not perceive trees as just wood; they were looked at from a multi-functional point of view, with a focus on diversity of form and function. For example, the noted lexicon, *Namalinganusasana,* popularly known as *Amarakosa,* lists a number of words to denote a tree, each describing it from a different point of view[6] (see Table 1). This is in distinct contrast to the western tradition of forest management, which views trees primarily in terms of their woody biomass.

TABLE 1

Sanskrit name	Functional description
Vraksha	that which is cut
Mahiruha	that which grows on the earth
Sakhi	that which has branches
Padapa	that which sucks water through the roots
Taru	that by which people get coolness
Agama	that which cannot move
Palasi	that which has leaves

Vegetation itself was divided into various categories. *Caraka*[7] for example, divided trees and plants into four classes.

(*i*) *Vanaspati:* those which are fruit bearing only
(*ii*) *Vanaspatya:* those that fruit and flower
(*iii*) *Osadhi:* those that die after the ripening of fruits
(*iv*) *Virudhi:* shrubs

A distinction has also been made between natural and cultivated forests, suggesting that afforestation and regeneration through the planting of trees has always been significant in the renewal of the forest wealth of the region. This tradition of seeing trees and plants as live has been continued into modern times by eminent Indian scientists like J.C. Bose, who did detailed experiments to show

6 S.C. Banerjee, *Flora and Fauna in Sanskrit Literature*, Calcutta: Naya Prakash, 1980.
7 Quoted in Banerjee, *op. cit.*, p. 16.

that the pretension of man and animals for undisputed superiority over their hitherto 'vegetative brethren' does not bear the test of close inspection. These experiments bring the plant much nearer than we ever thought. We find that it is not a mere mass of vegetative growth, but that its every fibre is instinct with sensibility. We are able to record the throbbings of its pulsating life, and find these wax and wane according to the life conditions of the plant, and cease in the death of the organism. In these and many other ways the life reactions in plant and man are alike.[8]

Ethnobotanical work among India's many diverse tribes is also uncovering the deep, systematic knowledge of forests among them. The diversity of forest foods used in India emerges from this knowledge. In south India, a study conducted among the Soliga in the Belirangan hills of Karnataka hows that they use 27 different varieties of leafy vegetables at different times of the year, and a variety of tubers, leaves, fruits, and roots are used for their medicinal properties by the tribals. A young illiterate Irula boy from a settlement near Kotagiri identified 37 different varieties of plants, gave their Irula names and their different uses.

In Madhya Pradesh, although rice (*Oryza sativa*) and lesser millets (*Panicum miliaceum, Eleusine coracana* and *Paspalum scrobiculatum*) form the staple diet of the tribals, almost all of them supplement it with seeds, grains, roots, rhizomes, leaves, and fruits of numerous wild plants which abound in the forests. Grigson noted that famine has never been a problem in Bastar as the tribes have always been able to draw half of their food from the innumerable edible forest products.[9] Tiwari prepared a detailed list of wild plant species eaten by the tribals in Madhya Pradesh.[10] He has listed 165 trees, shrubs, and climbers. Of these, the first category contains a list of 31 plants whose seeds are roasted and eaten. There are 19 plants whose roots and tubers are eaten after baking, boiling or processing; there are 17 whose juice is taken fresh or after fermenting; 25, whose leaves are eaten as vegetables, and 10 whose petals are cooked as vegetables. There are 63 plants whose fruits are eaten raw, ripe, or roasted or pickled; there are five species of Ficus which provide figs for the forest-dwellers. The fruits of the thorny shrub, *Pithcellobium dulce (Inga dulcis),* also called jungle jalebi, are favourites with the tribals. The sepals of *mohwa* are greedily eaten and also fermented for liquor. *Morus*

8 Quoted in M.S. Randhawa, *A History of Agriculture in India*, New Delhi: Indian Council for Agricultural Research. 1980, p. 97
9 Quoted in Randhawa, *op. cit.*, p. 99.
10 *Ibid.*, p. 99.

alba, the mulberry, provides fruit for both man and birds. Besides, the *her (Zizyphus mauritiana* and *Z Oenoplia)* provides delicious fruit, and has been eaten by jungle dwellers from the Mesolithic period onwards.

In non-tribal areas, too, forests provide food and livelihood through critical inputs to agriculture, through soil and water conservation, and through inputs of fodder and organic fertilizer. Indigenous sylvicultural practises are based on sustainable and renewable maximisation of all the diverse forms and functions of forests and trees. This common sylvicultural knowledge is passed on from generation to generation, through participation in the processes of forest renewal and of drawing sustenance from the forest ecosystem. In both forest and agriculture based economies, it is primarily women who use and manage the produce of forests and trees. In the Himalaya, where tree fodder is predominant in the agricultural economy even today, older women train the younger ones in the art of lopping (pollarding) and of collecting forest produce. In other regions also, lopping cycles and practices had evolved to maximise fodder production. Since food gathering and fodder collection has been women's work, primarily, women as foragers were critical in managing and renewing the diversity of the forest. Their work was complementary to that of men. The public and common domain of the forest was not closed to women—it was central to supporting life in the 'private' domain, the home, and community.

Indigenous forest management, as largely a women's domain for producing sustenance, was thus in an evolved state when the British arrived. Since the British interest in forests was exclusively for commercial timber, indigenous expertise became redundant for their interest and was replaced by a one-dimensional, masculinist science of forestry.

Colonialism and the evolution of masculinist forestry

When the British colonised India, they first colonised her forests. Ignorant of their wealth and of the wealth of knowledge of local people to sustainably manage the forests, they displaced local rights, local needs, and local knowledge and reduced this primary source of life into a timber mine. Women's subsistence economy based on the forest was replaced by the commercial economy of British colonialism. Teak from Malabar was extracted for the King's Navy, and the *sal* of Central India and the conifers of the Himalaya were exploited for the railway system. Although it is always local people who are held responsible for deforestation, it is commercial demands that have more frequently resulted in large-scale forest destruction. In the Himalayan region there is evidence that it was the needs of the Empire and not of the local people that led to rapid forest denudation. According to Atkinson's *Gazetteer,*

> the forests were denuded of good trees in all places. The destruction of trees of all species appears to have continued steadily and reached its climax between 1855 and 1861, when the demands of the Railway authorities induced numerous speculators to enter into contracts for sleepers, and these men were allowed, unchecked, to cut down old trees very far in excess of what they could possibly export, so that for some years after the regular forest operations commenced, the department was chiefly busy cutting up and bringing to the depot the timber left behind by the contractors.[11]

When the British started exploiting Indian timber for military purposes, they did it rapaciously and in ignorance, because the 'great continent appeared to hold inexhaustible tracts covered with dense jungles, but there was no apparent necessity for their detailed exploration, even had this been a possibility. In the early years of our occupation the botany of the forests, the species of trees they contained and their respective values was an unopened book'.[12]

To the colonial government and its officials the critical role that forests play in nature and the great influence they exercise on the physical well-being of a country went unrecognised. In view of the large forest wealth that existed, the government for some years obtained its full requirement without difficulty, while local needs were also met. The early administrators appear to have been convinced that this state of affairs could go on for an unlimited period. In many localities forests were viewed as an obstruction to agriculture, which was taxed, and were seen therefore as a limiting factor to the prosperity of the coloniser. The policy was to extend agriculture and the watchword was to clear the forests with this end in view. Virgin forests of the Doon Valley were thus clearfelled for land grants made exclusively to British settlers.[13]

The military requirement for Indian teak led to an immediate proclamation declaring that the royalty right in teak trees claimed by the former government in the south of the continent, was vested in the East

11 E.T. Atkinson. *Himalayan Gazetteer,* Vol. Ill, Allahabad: Government Press, 1882, p. 852.

12 E.P. Stebbing, *The Forests of India* (reprint), New Delhi: AJ. Reprints Agency, 1982, p. 61.

13 J. Bandyopadhyay, *et. al.,* *The Doon Valley Ecosystem,* mimeo, 1983.

India Company. In the year 1799 alone, 10,000 teak trees were brought down the Beypur River in Malabar. Under further pressure from the Home Government to ensure the maintenance of the future strength of the King's Navy, a decision was taken to appoint a special officer to superintend forest work—his duties were to preserve and improve the production of teak and other timber suitable for shipbuilding. Captain Watson of the police was appointed the first Conservator of Forests in India on November 10, 1806. Under the proclamation of April 1807, he wielded great powers. He soon established a timber monopoly throughout Malabar and Travancore and furnished the government, as did his immediate successors, with a plentiful supply of cheap timber. But the methods by which this was done were intolerable and gradually gave rise to seething discontent amongst both local peasants as well as proprietors. The feeling rose to such a pitch that the Conservatorship was abolished in 1823.[14]

The introduction of colonial forestry was thus established not because of superior forestry knowledge or scientific management, but through dominant military need and power. It was only after more than half a century of uncontrolled forest destruction by British commercial interests that an attempt was made to control exploitation. In 1865 the first Indian Forest Act (VII of 1865) was passed by the Supreme Legislative Council, which authorised the government to declare forests and wastelands *(benap* or unmeasured lands) as reserved forests.

The introduction of this legislation marks the beginning of what is called the 'scientific management' of forests; it amounted basically to the formalisation of the erosion both of forests and of the rights of local people to forest produce. Commercial forestry, which is equated with 'scientific forestry' by those narrow interests exemplified by western patriarchy is reductionist in intellectual content and ecological impact, and generates poverty at the socioeconomic level for those whose livelihoods and productivity depend on the forest. Reductionism has been characteristic of this forestry because it sunders forestry from water management, from agriculture, and from animal husbandry. Within the forest ecosystem it has reduced the diversity of life to the dead product, wood, and wood in turn to commercially valuable wood only. A commercial interest has the primary objective of maximising exchange value on the market through the extraction of commercially valuable species—forest ecosystems are therefore reduced to the timber of such species. By ignoring the complex

14 Stehbing, *op. cit*, p. 65.

relationship within the forest community and between plant life and other resources like soil and water, this pattern of resource use generates instabilities in the ecosystem and leads to counterproductive use of nature as a living and self-reproducing resource. The destruction of the forest ecosystem and the multiple functions of forest resources in turn hurts the economic interest of those groups of society, mainly women and tribals, who depend on the diverse resource functions of the forests for their survival. These include soil and water stabilisation and the provision of food, fodder, fuel, fertilizer, etc. In the alternative feminine forestry science which has been subjugated by the masculinist science, forests are not viewed as merely a stock of wood, isolated from the rest of the ecosystem, nor is their economic value reduced to the commercial value of timber. 'Productivity', 'yield', and 'economic value' are defined for nature and for women's work as *satisfying basic needs through an integrated ecosystem managed for multipurpose utilisation.* Their meaning and measure is therefore entirely different from the meaning and measure employed in reductionist masculinist forestry. In a shift from ecological forestry to reductionist forestry all scientific terms are changed from ecosystem-dependent to ecosystem-independent ones. Thus while for women, tribals, and other forest communities a complex ecosystem is productive in terms of water, herbs, tubers, fodder, fertilizer, fuel, fibre, and as a genepool, for the forester, these components are useless, unproductive waste, and dispensable. Two economic perspectives lead to two notions of 'productivity' and value'. As far as women's productivity in survival and overall productivity are concerned, the natural tropical forest is a highly productive ecosystem. Examining the forests of the humid tropics from an ecological perspective Galley has noted, 'A large biomass is generally characteristic of tropical forests. The quantities of wood especially are large in tropical forests and average about 300 tons per ha. compared with about 150 tons per ha. for temperate forests'.[15] However, in reductionist commercial forestry, overall productivity is subordinated to industrial use, and large biomass to species that can be profitably marketed—industrial and commercial biomass prevail; all the rest is waste. As Bethel, an international forestry consultant says, referring to the large biomass typical of forests in the humid tropics:

> It must be said that from a standpoint of industrial material supply, this is relatively unimportant. The important question is how much of

15 F.B. Golley, *Productivity and Mineral Cycling in Tropical Forests' Productivity of World Ecosystems*, Washington: National Academy of Sciences, 1975, pp. 106-15.

this biomass represents trees and parts of trees of *preferred species that
can be profitably marketed* ... By today's utilisation standards, *most of
the trees in these humid tropical forests are, from an industrial materials
standpoint, clearly weeds.*[16]

The 'industrial materials standpoint' is the standpoint of a capitalist and patriarchal reductionist forestry which splits the living diversity
and democracy of the forest into commercially useful dead wood which
it valorises, and ecologically valuable weeds which it characterises as
waste. This waste, however, is the wealth of biomass that maintains nature's water and nutrient cycles and satisfies the needs of food, fuel, fodder, fertilizer, fibre, and medicine of agricultural communities.

Since it is women's work that protects and conserves nature's life in
forestry and in agriculture, and through such conservation work, sustains human life through ensuring the provision of food and water, the
destruction of the integrity of forest ecosystems is most vividly and con-
cretely experienced by peasant women. For them forestry is married to
food production; it is essential for providing stable, perennial supplies
of water for drinking and for irrigation, and for providing the fertility
directly as green manure or as organic matter cycled through farm animals. Women's agricultural work in regions like the Himalaya is largely
work in and with the forest, yet it is discounted both in forestry and in
agriculture. The only forestry-related work that goes into census data is
lumbering and tree-felling; cutting trees then becomes a source of *roti* or
food for the men engaged in lumbering operations; for the women however, forests are food, not in death, but in life. The living forest provides
the means for sustainable food production systems in the form of nutrients and water, and women's work in the forest facilitates this process.
When, for example, women lop trees they enhance the productivity of
the oak forest under stable conditions and under common ownership
and control. While an unlopped tree has leaves that are too hard for cattle, lopping makes them soft and palatable, especially in early spring.
Maintaining the diversity of living resources is critical to the feminine
use of the forest: thus oak-leaf along with a mixture of dried grasses and
agricultural by-products is fed to cattle through the late autumn, win-
ter, and into spring. In the monsoon, the green grass becomes the dominant fodder, and in October and November, agricultural waste such as

16 James A. Bethel, 'Sometimes the Word is "Weed", in *Forest Management*, June, 1984,
pp. 17-22.

rice straw, *mandua* straw and *angora* straw become the primary supply of fodder. Lopping has never been viewed as a forest management strategy for using tree produce while conserving the tree. Yet, as Bandyopadhyay and Moench[17] have shown, lopping under appropriate conditions can actually *increase* the forest density and fodder productivity of the forest. Groups of women, young and old, go together to lop for fodder, and expertise develops by participation and through learning-by-doing. These informal forestry colleges of the women are small and decentred, creating and transferring knowledge about how to maintain the life of living resources. The visible forestry colleges by contrast are centralised and alienated: they specialise in a forestry of destruction, on how to transform a living resource into a commodity and subsequently, cash.

The dispossession of the local people of their rights, their resources and their knowledge has not gone unchallenged. Forest struggles have been taking place throughout the country for over two centuries to resist the colonisation of the people's forests in India. The access and rights of the people to forests were first severely encroached upon with the introduction of the Forest Acts of 1878 and 1927. The following years witnessed the spread of forest satyagrahas throughout India, as a protest against the reservation of forests for exclusive exploitation by British commercial interest, and their concommitant transformation from a common resource into a commodity. Villagers ceremonially removed forest products from the reserved forests to assert their right to satisfy their basic needs. The forest satyagrahas were[18] especially successful in regions where survival of the local population was intimately linked with access to the forests, as in the Himalaya, the Western Ghats, and the Central Indian hills. These nonviolent protests were systematically crushed by the British; in Central India, Gond tribals were gunned down for participating in the protests; in 1930 dozens of unarmed villagers were killed and hundreds injured in Tilari village in Tehri Garhwal, when they gathered to protest against the Forest Laws of the local rulers. After enormous loss of life, the satyagrahis were successful in reviving some of the traditional rights of the village communities to various forest products. The Forest Policy of post-colonial India continued on the colonial path of commercialisation and reductionism, and with it continued people's

17 J. Bandyopadhyay & M. Moench, 'Local Needs and Forest Resource Management in the Himalaya', in Bandyopadhyay *et al.*, *India's Environment: Crisis and Responses*. Dehradun: Natraj Publishers, 1985, p. 56.

18 J. Bandyopadhyay & V. Shiva, 'Chipko: Politics of Ecology' in *Seminar*, No. 330, 1987.

resistance to a denial of their basic needs, both through alienation of rights and through ecological degradation.

In the mountain regions of the Himalaya, the women of Garhwal started to protect their forests from commercial exploitation even at the cost of their lives, by starting the famous Chipko movement, embracing the living trees as their protectors. Beginning in the early 1970s in the Garhwal region of Uttar Pradesh, the methodology and philosophy of Chipko has now spread to Himachal Pradesh in the north, to Karnataka in the south, to Rajasthan in the west, to Orissa in the east, and to Central Indian highlands.

The women of Chipko

Women's environmental action in India preceded the UN Women's Decade as well as the 1972 Stockholm Environment Conference. Three hundred years ago more than 300 members of the Bishnoi community in Rajasthan, led by a woman called Amrita Devi, sacrificed their lives to save their sacred *khejri* trees by clinging to them. With that event begins the recorded history of Chipko.[19]

The recent Chipko movement has popularly been referred to as a women's movement, but it is only some male Chipko activists who have been projected into visibility. The women's contribution has been neglected and remains invisible, in spite of of the fact that the history of Chipko is a history of the visions and actions of exceptionally courageous women. Environmental movements like Chipko have become historical landmarks because they have been fuelled by the ecological insights and political and moral strengths of women. I will dwell at some length on some of these exceptional women because I have personally been inspired by my interaction with them, and because I feel that it is unjust that the real pillars of the movement are still largely unknown. The experience of these powerful women also needs to be shared to remind us that we are not alone, and that we do not take the first steps: others have walked before us.

In the history of social and political movements, the evolution is generally neglected, and only the end result focussed on. This creates two problems: first, future organisational work does not benefit from the lessons of perseverence and patience born of years of movement building;

19 R.S. Bishnoi, *Conservation as Creed*, Dehradun: Jugal Kishore, 1987, letter from Gandhi to Mirabehn, Jan. 16, 1948.

people start looking for instant solutions because it is the instant successes that have been sold through pseudo-history. Second, while the historical evolution of movements involves significant contributions from thousands of participants over extended periods, their climaxes are localised in space and time. This facilitates the appropriation of the movement by an individual or group who then erases the contributions of others. Movements are major social and political processes, however, and they transcend individual actors. They are significant precisely because they involve a multiplicity of people and events which contribute to a reinforcement of social change.

The Chipko process as a resurgence of woman power and ecological concern in the Garhwal Himalaya is a similar mosaic of many events and multiple actors. The significant catalysers of the transformations which made Chipko resistance possible have been women like Mira Behn, Sarala Behn, Bimala Behn, Hima Devi, Gauri Devi, Gunga Devi, Bachni Devi, Itwari Devi, Chamun Devi, and many others. The men of the movement like Sunderlal Bahuguna, Chandi Prasad Bhatt, Ghanshyam Shailani and Dhoom Singh Negi have been their students and followers. Mira Behn was one of Gandhi's closest disciples who moved to the Himalayan region in the late '40s. Between Rishikesh and Hardwar she started a cattle centre called Pashulok, because cattle are central to sustainable agriculture. Writing to Mira Behn fifteen days before his death, Gandhi said:

> I see that you are destined for serving the cow and nothing else. But I seem to see a vital defect in you. You are unable to cling to anything finally. You are a gypsy, never happy unless you are wandering. You will not become an expert in anything and your mother is also likely to perish in your lap. The only person, and that a woman, who really loves the cow, will fail her. Shall I pity you, the cow or me, for I, the originator of the real idea of serving and saving the cow for humanity, have never cared or perhaps never had the time to become even a moderate expert.[20]

As Gandhi had expected, Mira Behn moved on, from the ecology of the cow to the ecology of forests and water, to the links between deforestation and water crises. As she recollected later,

> Pashulok being situated as it is at the foot of the mountains, just where the Ganga emerges from the Himalayan valleys, I became very realistically aware of the terrible floods which pour down from the Ganga

20 *The Collected Works of Mahatma Gandhi*, Vol. 90, New Delhi: Government of India Publications, 1984.

catchment area, and I had taken care to have all the buildings constructed above the flood high-mark. Within a year or two I witnessed
a shocking flood: as the swirling waters increased, (there) came first
bushes and boughs and great logs of wood, then in the turmoil of more
and more water came whole trees, cattle of all sizes and from time to
time a human being clinging to the remnants of his hut. Nothing could
be done to save man or beast from this turmoil; the only hope was for
them to get caught up somewhere on the edge of an island or riverbank
prominence. The sight of these disastrous floods led me each summer
to investigate the area north of Pashulok whence they came. Merciless
deforestation as well as cultivation of profitable pines in place of broad-
leaf trees was clearly the cause. This in turn led me to hand over charge
of Pashulok to the government staff and to undertake a community
project in the valley of the Bhilangana. Here I built a little centre, Gopal
Ashram, and concentrated on the forest problem.[21]

During her stay in Garhwal Mira studied the environment intimately
and derived knowledge about it from the local people. From the older
ones she learnt that, earlier, Tehri Garhwal forests consisted largely of
oak, and Garhwali folksongs, which encapsulate collective experience
and wisdom, tell repeatedly of species such as *banj* and *kharik*.* They
create images of abundant forests of *banj*, grasslands, and fertile fields,
large herds of animals and vessels full of milk. In Mira's view the primary
reason for degeneration in this region was the disappearance of the *banj*
trees. According to her, if the catchment of the Ganga was not once again
clothed with *banj*, floods and drought would continue to get aggravated.

The issue was not merely one of planting trees, but of planting *ecologically appropriate* trees. As Mira Behn pointed out, the replacement of
banj and mixed forests by the commercially valuable pine was a major
reason for the increasing ecological instability of the Himalaya and the
growing economic deprivation of Garhwali women, since pine failed to
perform any of the ecological and economic functions of *banj*.

Mira Behn's ecological insights were inherited by Sunderlal Bahuguna
who had worked with her in the Bhilangana valley. Bahuguna had joined
the independence struggle at the tender age of 13, and was Congress Sec-
retary of Uttar Pradesh at the time of Independence. In 1954 he married
Bimla Behn, who had spent eight years with Sarala Behn, another close
disciple of Gandhi's. Sarala Behn had started an ashram for the education of hill women in Kausani and her full-time commitment was to make

21 Mira Behn, 'Something Wrong in the Himalaya', mimeo, undated.
* *Quercus incana* and *Celtis australis*.

them recognise that they were not beasts of burden but goddesses of wealth since they rear cattle and produce food, performing 98 percent of all labour in farming and animal husbandry. Influenced by Sarala Behn's ideas of women's freedom, Bimla agreed to marry Sunderlal Bahuguna only if he left the Congress Party and settled down in a remote village so that they could awaken the hill people by living with and through them. Writing twelve years after the establishment of the Silyara Ashram, Sunderlal, and Bimla Bahuguna wrote: 'One of us, Sunderlal, was inspired to settle in a village by Mira Behn and the other, Bimla, was inspired by living continuously with Sarala Behn'.[22] Sunderlal Bahuguna, in turn, drew in other activists like Ghanshyam Raturi, Chandi Prasad Bhatt, and Dhoom Singh Negi to lend support to a movement generated by women's power. As he often says 'We are the runners and messengers—the real leaders are the women'.

In the early stages of the Chipko movement, when the exploitation of forest resources was carried out by non-local forest contractors, the women's special concern with forestry for survival, which provided the base for Chipko, was temporarily merged with a largely male concern for raw material supply for sawmills and resin factories set up by local cooperatives.[23] These male cooperatives, set up by Gandhian organisations, saw the Chipko demand primarily as one of the supply of resin and timber for their industrial units. Among the many small scale forest industries that mushroomed in the hill regions in the 1960s were those run by Dasholi Gram Swaraj Sangh, Purola Gram Swaraj Sangh, Gangotri Gram Swaraj Sangh, Berinag Gram Swaraj Sangh, Kathyur Gram Swaraj Sangh, Takula Gram Swaraj Sangh, etc. Soon, however, a new separation took place between local male interests for commercial activity based on forest products, and local women's interests for sustenance activity based on forest protection. Bahuguna has been an effective messenger of the women's concern. He has developed these insights into the philosophy of natural forests as life-support systems and the Chipko struggle as a struggle to conserve them. It is largely through listening to the quiet voices of the women during his padyatras that Bahuguna has retained an ability to articulate the feminine-ecological principles of Chipko. When asked in 1977 why he did not set up resin units and sawmills like other voluntary agencies in Garhwal, he replied:

22 Bimla and Sunderlal Bahuguna, 'Twelve Years of Working in Villages' in *Uttarkband Smarika*, Chamba: Uttrakhand Sarvodaya Mandai, 1969.

23 *Uttar ke Shikharo Mein Chetna ke Ankur*, New Delhi: Himalaya Seva Sangh, 1975, p. 129.

If you had proposed the setting up of sawmills as hill development six years ago, I would have considered it. But today I see clearly that establishing sawmills in the hills is to join the project to destroy Mother Earth. Sawmills have an endless appetite for trees and wipe out forests to satisfy their appetite.[24]

While the philosophical and conceptual articulation of the ecological view of the Himalayan forests has been done by Mira Behn and Bahuguna, the organisational foundation for it being a women's movement was laid by Sarala Behn with Bimla Behn in Garhwal and Radha Bhatt in Kumaon.

In a commemorative column dedicated to Sarala Behn on her 75th birthday (which coincided with International Women's Year in 1975) the activists of Uttarakhand called her the daughter of the Himalaya and the mother of social activism in the region. Sarala Behn had come to India in search of nonviolence. As a close follower of Gandhi, she worked mainly in the hill areas during the independence movement. Reflecting on the Gandhian legacy in her 75th year, she wrote:

> From my childhood experience I have known that law is not just; that the principles that govern humanity are higher than those that govern the state; that a centralised government, indifferent to its peoples, is a cruel joke in governance; that the split between the private and public ethic is the source of misery, injustice and exploitation in society. Each child in India understands that bread (*roti*) is not just a right to the one who has money in his pocket. It is a more fundamental right of the one whose stomach is hungry. This concept of rights works within the family, but is shed at the societal level. Then the ethics of the market reigns, and men get trapped in it.[25]

Sarala Behn knew that the ethics of sharing, of producing and maintaining life, that women conserved in their activity, was the countervailing force to the masculinist morality of the market which came as 'development' and created a cash economy, but also created destitution and drunkenness. The early women's movement in Uttarakhand was therefore an anti-alcohol movement aimed at controlling alcohol addiction among men who earned cash incomes from felling trees with one hand and lost the cash to liquor with the other. For the women, drunkenness

---

24 S.L Bahuguna, 'Water is the Primary Product of the Hill Forests', interview in *Hummlika*, Yuvak Sangh, Jajal, Tehri Garhwal, 1980-81.

25 Sarala Behn, 'From Revolt to Construction' in *Uttar ke Shikharo Mein Chetna ke Ankur*.

meant violence and hunger for their children and themselves, and it was the organisational base created among them through the anti-alcohol movement that was inherited by Chipko. In 1965 the women of Garhwal raised their voice for prohibition in Ghansyali. In November that year, when thousands of women in Tehri demonstrated and picketted at shops, prohibition came into effect in five districts—Tehri, Uttarkashi, Chamoli, Garhwal, and Pithoragarh. In 1978 Sarala Behn wrote her *Blueprint for Survival* in which she reiterated the women's Chipko demand:

> We must remember that the main role of the hill forests should be not to yield revenue, but to maintain a balance in the climatic conditions of the whole of northern India and the fertility of the Gangetic Plain. If we ignore their ecological importance in favour of their short term economic utility, it will be prejudicial to the climate of northern India and will dangerously enhance the cycle of recurring and alternating floods and droughts.[26]

Sarala Behn established the Laxmi Ashram in Kausani primarily to empower the hill women. Bimla Behn who spent seven years with her, widened her project and established the Navjivan Ashram in Silyara, which then became the energizing source for Chipko.

The organisational base of women was thus ready by the 1970s, and this decade saw the beginning of more frequent popular protest concerning the rights of the people to utilise local forest produce. Nineteen seventy-two saw widespread, organised protests against the commercial exploitation of forests by outside contractors: in Purola on December 11, in Uttarkashi on December 12, and in Gopeshwar on December 15. It was then that Raturi composed his famous poem:

> *Embrace our trees*
> *Save them from being felled*
> *The property of our hills*
> *Save it from being looted.*

While the concept of saving trees by embracing them is old, as recalled by the case of the Bishnois, in the context of the current phase of the movement for forest rights, this popular poem is the earliest documentary source of the now famous name, 'Chipko'.

The movement spread throughout Garhwal and into Kumaon, through the totally decentred leadership of local women, connected to

---

26 Sarala Behn, 'A Blueprint for Survival of the Hills', supplement to *Himalaya: Man and Nature*, New Delhi: Himalaya Seva Sangh, 1980.

each other not vertically, but horizontally—through the songs of Ghan-shyam Raturi, through 'runners' like Bahuguna, Bhatt, and Negi who carried the message of Chipko happenings from one village to the next, from one region to another. For hill women, food production begins with the forest. Disappearing forests and water are quite clearly an issue of survival for hill women, which is why thousands of Garhwal women have protested against commercial forestry which has destroyed their forests and water resources.

In March 1973, when 300 ash trees which had been auctioned to a manufacturer of sports goods, were to be felled in Mandai the villagers went to the forest, beating drums. They declared that they would embrace the trees and not allow them to be cut. The labourers withdrew, but the manufacturer obtained an alternative contract in the Rampur Fata forest in Kedar Ghati. On receiving this information, people started walking towards Kedar Ghati. Seventy-two year-old Shyama Devi, who in 1975 had picketted a wine shop in Chandrapuri, brought her leadership experience to Kedar Ghati and mobilised the local women; the forest of Rampur Fata resounded with Chipko slogans from June to December, when the contractor finally withdrew.

Chipko now shifted to the Alakananda Valley, to the village Reni, that lies on the road from Joshimath to Niti Ghati. Devastation in the Alakananda Valley had been the first major signal that the Himalaya was dying when, in 1970, a major flood inundated several villages and fields for miles together. The women of Reni had not forgotten the Alakananda disaster; they linked the landslide that blocked the river and aggravated the floods with the felling of trees in the catchment area. In 1973, a woman grazing her cows spotted a few persons with axes in their hands; she whistled and collected all her companions who surrounded the contractor's men and said: 'This forest is our mother. When there is a crisis of food, we come here to collect grass and dry fruits to feed our children. We dig out herbs and collect mushrooms from this forest. You cannot touch these trees'.[27] The leadership to protect the Reni forest was provided by 50-year old Gauri Devi and 52-year old Gunga Devi, with co-workers Rupsa, Bhakti, Masi, Harki, Malti, Phagli, and Bala Devi. Together, in small groups, they formed vigilance parties to keep an eye on the axemen till the government was forced to set up a committee, which recommended a 10-year ban on commercial green-felling in the Alakananda catchment.

27 Quoted in Bimla Bahuguna, 'Contribution of Women to the Chipko Movement', in *Indian Farming*, November 1975

The Chipko movement then started mobilising for a ban on commercial exploitation throughout the hill districts of Uttar Pradesh because the overfelling of trees was leading to mountain instability everywhere. In 1975, more than 300 villages in these districts faced the threat of landslides and severe erosion. Genvala, Matli, and Dharali in Uttar Kashi, Pilkhi and Nand Gaon in Tehri, Chimtoli and Kinjhani in Chamoli, Baghar and Jageshwar in Almora, Rayer Agar and ajardeval in Pithoragarh are evident examples. The movement for a total ban was spurred by women like 50-year old Hima Devi who had earlier mobilised public opinion against alcoholism in 1965, and was now moving from village to village to spread the message to save the trees. She spoke for the women at demonstrations and protests against auctions throughout the hill districts: 'My sisters are busy in harvesting the kharif crop. They are busy in winnowing. I have come to you with their message. Stop cutting trees. There are no trees even for birds to perch on. Birds flock to our crops and eat them. What will we eat? The firewood is disappearing: how will we cook?'[28]

In January, 1975 women of the hill regions started a 75-day trek from Uttarkashi to Kausani and another 50-day trek from Devprayag to Naugaon to mobilise public opinion on women's increasing workload due to deforestation. Bimla Behn and Radha Bhatt were part of these padyatras. In June 1977 a meeting of all the activists in the hills held in Sarala Behn's ashram further strengthened the movement and consolidated the resistance to commercial felling as well as to excessive tapping of resin from the pine trees. In the Gotar forests in the Tehri range the forest ranger was transferred because of his inability to prevent the illegal overtapping of pine resin. It was in this period that the methodology of hugging trees to save them from being felled was actually used for the first time by Dhoom Singh Negi in Salet forest near the village of Pipleth in Henwal.

Among the numerous instances of Chipko successes throughout the Garhwal Himalaya in the years to follow, are those of Adwani, Amarsar, Chanchnidhar, Dungari, Paintoli, and Badiyagarh. The auction of the Adwani forests took place in October 1977 in Narendernagar, the district headquarters. Sunderlal Bahuguna undertook a fast against the auction and appealed to the forest contractors and the district authorities to refrain from their mission. The auction took place despite expressions of popular discontent, and the forests were scheduled to be felled in the first week of December 1977. Large groups of women, led by Bachhni Devi (the wife of the local village headman, himself a contractor)

28 Quoted in Bimla Bahuguna *op. cit.*, 1975.

gathered together. Chipko activist Dhoom Singh Negi supported the women's struggle by beginning a fast in the forest itself. The women tied sacred threads to the trees as a token of their vow of protection. Between December 13 and 20, a large number of women from 15 villages guarded the forests while discourses from ancient texts on their role in Indian life went on uninterruptedly.

The axe-man withdrew, only to return on February 1, 1978, with two truckloads of armed police. The plan was to encircle the forests with their help in order to keep the people away during the actual felling. Even before they reached the area, the volunteers of the movement entered the forest and told their story to the forest labourers who had been brought in from distant places. By the time the contractors arrived with the policemen, each tree was being guarded by three volunteers. The police, having been defeated in their own plan and seeing the determination and awareness of the people, hastily withdrew.

There are in India, today, two paradigms of forestry—one life-enhancing, the other life-destroying. The life-enhancing paradigm emerges from the forest and the feminine principle; the life-destroying one from the factory and the market. The former creates a sustainable, renewable forest system, supporting and renewing food and water sources. *The maintenance of conditions for renewability is its primary management objective,* while the maximising of profits through commercial extraction is the primary management objective of the latter. Since the maximising of profits is consequent upon the destruction of conditions of renewability, the two paradigms are cognitively and ecologically incommensurate. The first paradigm has emerged from India's ancient forest culture, in all its diversity, and has been renewed in contemporary times by the women of Garhwal through Chipko.

It is these two distinct knowledge and economic systems which clashed in 1977 in Adwani when the Chipko movement became explicitly an ecological *and* feminist movement. The women, of course, had always been the backbone of Chipko and for them the struggle was ever the struggle for the living, natural forest. But in the early days when it was directed against removing the non-local forest contractors, local commercial interest had also been part of the resistance. Once non-local private contractors were removed and a government agency (the Forest Development Corporation) started working through local labour contractors and forest cooperatives, *the women continued to struggle against the exploitation of the forests.* It did not matter to them whether the forest was destroyed by outsiders or their own men. The most dramatic turn in this new confrontation took place when Bachni Devi of Adwani led a resistance against her own husband who had obtained a local contract to fell the forest. The forest officials arrived to browbeat and intimidate the women and Chipko activists, but found the women holding up lighted lanterns in broad daylight. Puzzled, the forester asked them their intention. The women replied, 'We have come to teach you forestry'. He retorted, 'You foolish women, how can you who prevent felling know the value of the forest? Do you know what forests bear? They produce profit and resin and timber'. And the women immediately sang back in chorus:

What do the forests bear?
Soil, water and pure air.
Soil, water and pure air
Sustain the earth and all she bears.

The Adwani satyagraha created new directions for Chipko. The movement's philosophy and politics now evolved to reflect the needs and knowledge of the women. Peasant women came out, openly challenging the reductionist commercial forestry system on the one hand and the local men who had been colonised by that system, cognitively, economically, and politically, on the other.

Afforestation projects and reductionism

The main thrust of conservation struggles like Chipko is that forests and trees are life-support systems, and should be protected and regenerated for their biospheric functions. The crisis mind on the other hand sees the forest and trees as weed, valued commercially, and converts even afforestation into deforestation and desertification. From life-support systems, trees are converted into green gold—all planting is motivated by the slogan, 'Money grows on trees'. Whether it is schemes like social forestry wasteland development, afforestation programmes are conceived at the international level by 'experts' whose philosophy of tree-planting falls within the reductionist paradigm of producing wood for the market, not biomass for maintaining ecological cycles or satisfying local needs of food, fodder, and fertilizer. All official programmes of afforestation, based on heavy funding and centralised decision making, act in two ways against the feminine principle in forestry—they destroy the forest as a diverse and self-reproducing system, *and* destroy it as commons, shared by a diversity of social groups with the smallest having rights, access, and entitlements.

'Social' forestry and the 'miracle' tree

Social forestry projects are a good example of single-species, single commodity production plantations, based on reductionist models which divorce forestry from agriculture and water management, and needs from markets.

A case study of World Bank sponsored social forestry in Kolar district of Karnataka[29] is an illustration of reductionism and maldevelopment in forestry being extended to farmland. Decentred agroforestry, based on multiple species and private and common treestands, has been India's age-old strategy for maintaining farm productivity in arid and semi-arid zones. The *honge,* tamarind, jackfruit, and mango, the *jola, gobli, kaglz** and bamboo traditionally provided food and fodder, fertilizer and pesticide, fuel and small timber. The backyard of each rural home was a nursery, and each peasant woman the sylviculturalist. The invisible, decentred agroforestry model was significant because the humblest of species and the smallest of people could participate in it, and with space for the small, *everyone* was involved in protecting and planting.

The reductionist mind took over tree-planting with 'social forestry'. Plans were made in national and international capitals by people who could not know the purpose of the *honge* and the *neem,* and saw them as weeds. The experts decided that indigenous knowledge was worthless and 'unscientific', and proceeded to destroy the diversity of indigenous species by replacing them with row after row of eucalyptus seedlings in polythene bags, in government nurseries. Nature's locally available seeds were laid waste; people's locally available knowledge and energies were laid waste. With imported seeds and expertise came the import

---

29 V. Shiva, H.C. Sharatchandra & J. Bandyopadhyay. *The Social, Ecological and Economic Impact of Social Forestry in Kolar,* (mimeo), Indian Institute of Management, Bangalore, 1981; V. Shiva, H.C. Sharatchandra & J. Bandyopadhyay, 'The Challenge of Social Forestry' in W. Fernandes & S. Kulkarni (eds.) *Towards a New Forest Policy,* New Delhi: Indian Social Institute, 1983; and V. Shiva, H. C. Sharatchandra & J. Bandyopadhyay, 'No Solution Within the Market', in *Ecologist,* October 1982.

* *Pongamia globra, Azadirachta indica, Tamarindus indica, Autocarpus integrijolia, Mangzfera indica, Acacia jernesiana* and *Acacia catechu*

of loans and debt and the export of wood, soils—and people. Trees, as a living resource, maintaining the life of the soil and water and of local people, were replaced by trees whose dead wood went straight to a pulp factory hundreds of miles away. The smallest farm became a supplier of raw material to industry and ceased to be a supplier of food to local people. Women's work, linking the trees to the crops, disappeared and was replaced by the work of brokers and middlemen who brought the eucalyptus trees on behalf of industry. Industrialists, foresters, and bureaucrats loved the eucalyptus because it grows straight and is excellent pulp·wood, unlike the *bonge* which shelters the soil with its profuse branches and dense canopy and whose real worth is as a living tree on a farm. The *bonge* could be nature's idea of the perfect tree for arid Kamataka. It has rapid growth of precisely those parts of the tree, the leaves and small branches, which go back to the earth, enriching and protecting it, conserving its moisture and fertility. The eucalyptus, on the other hand, when perceived ecologically, is unproductive, even negative, because this perception assesses the 'growth' and 'productivity' of trees in relation to the water cycle and its conservation, in relation to soil fertility and in relation to human needs for food and food production. The eucalyptus has destroyed the water cycle in arid regions due to its high water demand and its failure to produce humus, which is nature's mechanism for conserving water. Most indigenous species have a much higher biological productivity than the eucalyptus, when one considers water yields and water conservation. The non-woody biomass of trees has never been assessed by forest measurements and quantification within the reductionist paradigm, yet it is this very biomass that functions in conserving water and building soils. It is little wonder that Garhwal women call a tree *dati* or branch, because they see the productivity of the tree in terms of its non-woody biomass which functions critically in hydrological and nutrient cycles within the forest, and through green fertilizer and fodder in cropland.

In the context of ecological cycles and of the food needs of people and livestock, the eucalyptus actually makes negative contributions. It is destructive to nature's work and women's work in agriculture, for by destroying the water and land and organic matter base for food production, women's productivity in sustenance is killed. Kolar, which is the most successful social forestry district in Karnataka, has already lost more than 13 percent of its agricultural land to eucalyptus cultivation; most of this has been at the cost of its staple food, the millet, *ragi,* and associated food crops. Table 2 gives the decline in the area under *ragi* cultivation since the beginning of the social forestry programme. Today Kolar is the most severely hit by drought and food scarcity, for eucalyptus undermines not just food production but the long-term productivity of the soil.

TABLE 2
Area and production of ragi in Kolar district

Year	Area (ha)	Production (tons)
1977-78	1,41,772	1,75,195
1978-79	1,46,361	1,65,174
1979-80	1,40,862	99,236
1980-81	48,406	13,340

Malur, a region in Kolar district which has 30 percent of its land under eucalyptus was compared to Korategere in neighbouring Tumkur where indigenous farm forestry continues to provide a diversity of organic inputs to agriculture. Table 3 shows how eucalyptus has induced food and nutrition deficiencies in Malur.

TABLE 3
Food availability per day per individual

Land holdings (ha)	Korategere		Malur	
	Cereals (gms)	Pulses (gms)	Cereals (gms)	Pulses (gms)
1 ha	.55	.06	.21	.03
1-2 ha	.58	.07	.29	.01
2-4 ha	1.23	.07	.47	.03
4 ha	3.65	3.65	1.60	.06

'Greening' with eucalyptus is a violence against nature and its cycles, and it is a violence against women who depend on the stability of nature's cycles to provide sustenance in the form of food and water. Eucalyptus guzzles nutrients and water and, in the specific conditions of low rainfall zones, gives nothing back but terpenes to the soil. These inhibit the growth of other plants and are toxic to soil organisms which are responsible for building soil fertility and improving soil structure.[30] The eucalyptus certainly increased cash and commodity flows, but it resulted in a disastrous interruption of organic matter and water flows within the local ecosystem. Its proponents failed to calculate the costs in terms of

30 V. Shiva & J. Bandyopadhyay, *Ecological Audit of Eucalyptus Cultivation*, Dehradun: EBD Publishers, 1985.

the destruction of life in the soil, the depletion of water resources and the scarcity of food and fodder that eucalyptus cultivation creates. Nor did they, while trying to shorten rotations for harvesting, see that tamarind, jackfruit, and *honge* have very short rotations of one year in which the biomass harvested is far higher than that of eucalyptus, which they nevertheless declared a 'miracle' tree. The crux of the matter is that fruit production was never the concern of forestry in the reductionist paradigm—it focussed on wood, and wood for the market, alone. Eucalyptus as an exotic, introduced in total disregard of its ecological appropriateness, has thus become an exemplar of anti-life afforestation.

Women throughout India have resisted the expansion of eucalyptus because of its destruction of water, soil, and food systems. On August 10, 1983, the women and small peasants of Barha and Holahalli villages in Tumkur district (Karnataka) marched en masse to the forest nursery and pulled out millions of eucalyptus seedlings, planting tamarind and mango seeds in their place. This gesture of protest, for which they were arrested, spoke out against the virtual planned destruction of soil and water systems by eucalyptus cultivation. It also silently challenged the domination of a forestry science that had reduced all species to one (the eucalyptus), all needs to one, (that of the pulp industry), and all knowledge to one (that of the World Bank and forest officials). It challenged the myth of the miracle tree: tamarind and mango are symbols of the energies of nature and of local people, of the links between these seeds and the soil, and of the needs that these trees—and others like them—satisfy in keeping the earth and the people alive. Forestry for food— food for the soil, for farm animals, for people—all women's and peasants' struggles revolve around this theme, whether in Garhwal or Karnataka, in the Santhal Parganas or Chattisgarh, in reserved forests, farmlands, or commons. Destruction of diversity and life, and colonisation of the commons is built into reductionist forestry and its new avatar, 'wasteland development'.

The approaching tragedy of the commons

Recovering five million hectares of the commons in India each year could signal the end of rural poverty and a reversal of the ecological collapse of critical life-support systems like soil, water, and vegetation. Yet the wasteland development programme, far from being a recovery of the commons project, will in fact, privatise the commons, accentuate rural poverty, and increase ecological instability. In one stroke it will rob the poor of their remaining common resources, the only survival base to which they have access. The usurpation of the commons which began with the British will reach its final limit with the wasteland development programme as is. Chattrapati Singh of the Indian Law Institute argues:

> It is evident that till the end of the last century and in all historical periods before that, at least 80 percent of India's natural resources were common property, with only 20 percent being privately utilised.... This extensive common property has provided the resource base for a non-cash, non-market economy. A whole range of necessary resources has been freely available to the people. Thus commonly available wood, shrubs and cowdung have been utilised for cooking and heating; mud, bamboo and palm leaves for housing, wild grass and shrubs as animal fodder, and a variety of fruits and vegetables as food.[31]

These free commons have historically been the survival base for rural India and the domain of productivity of women. With the reservation of forests a century ago the first step towards the privatisation of commons took place. Today, 'wasteland development' constitutes the last step in their disappearance. N.S. Jodha, who has worked extensively on common property resources, has shown how women's work and the livelihoods of poorer sections of rural society are intimately linked to trees and grasslands in the commons, which support the farm animals and thus take pressure off cropland, while increasing organic inputs to crop through animal waste.[32] Small peasants and landless labourers can own livestock largely because of the existence of the commons. Further, in arid zones, traditional farming systems partly derive their stability and viability from the commons which allow for an integrated and diversified production strategy using crops, livestock, and trees, which cushion the dry-land economy by supplying food, fodder, and fuel in years of crop failure. Nearly 10 percent of the nutrition of poorer families has been found to come directly from the commons. Women's work in the sustenance economy of the poorest groups is thus closely tied to the existence of the commons.

The privatisation of the commons through wasteland development is not an aberration but an outcome of the dominance of development

31 Chattrapati Singh, *Common Property and Common Poverty*, Delhi: Oxford Publishing House, 1985, p. 2.

32 N. S. Jodha. 'Common Property Resources', mimeo, 1986.

agencies like the World Bank, and their indifference to the needs of nature, and vulnerable social groups. For such organisations and agencies, self-provisioning is not economic activity. In 1984, the World Bank wrote up a National Forestry Project for India, a significant component of which was the privatisation of wastelands. In 1985, it floated a Tropical Forestry Action Plan of eight billion dollars based on the same logic of the corporate takeover of commons. In 1985 the Wasteland Development Board was set up with the laudable objective of bringing five million hectares of wasteland under tree cover annually. The regeneration of ecologically appropriate tree cover with socially appropriate community control could help rebuild people's resource base, and re-establish their control over the commons. Yet the Wasteland Board schemes will primarily privatise the commons by transferring rights and control from the community as a whole, to the World Bank, private business, and a few local people. The Wasteland Board had recommended the entry of the corporate sector in wasteland development, and proposals have been cleared for a variety of industries from strawboard and paper to plastics and polythene. This attempt at appropriating the commons is being facilitated by a number of confusions: *(a)* the confusion between wastelands as commons and wastelands as ecologically degraded land, private or common; and *(b)* tree planting as forestry. In afforestation of wastelands risks arise both from what is understood as wasteland and as afforestation. Ecologically, wastelands are lands which have lost their biological productivity, a process also known as desertification. It is this meaning that is invoked to undertake a massive afforestation programme. However, a second meaning is invoked to administer the programme, and this meaning has nothing to do with whether or not the land is currently unproductive in the ecological sense.

The colonial heritage: commons as 'wasteland'

'Wastelands' as a land use category is, like much else, a part of our colonial heritage, loaded with the biases of colonial rule, where meaning was defined by the interest of the rulers. The colonial concept of wastelands was not an assessment of the biological productivity of land, but of its revenue generating capacity: 'wasteland' was land that did not pay any revenue because it was uncultivated. Under such wasteland came the forested districts of Chittagong, Darjeeling, Jalpaiguri, Chota Nagpur and

Assam—and the vast trail of forest land towards the mouth and delta of the Hooghly and other rivers, known as the Sundarbans. These lands were taken over by the British and leased to cultivators to transform into revenue generating lands. While in the Gangetic plains 'wastelands' were allotted to villages, in the heavily forested region of Dehradun, Mirzapur, etc., forest tracts were retained as 'government waste'. In Punjab, 20 per-cent of the cultivated area of a village was given away as village waste. These lands were kept partly as forest and grazing lands, and partly in-tended for the extension of cultivation. In 1861, under the viceroyalty of Lord Canning, the wasteland rules were formulated to administer these non-revenue generating, but often biologically productive, lands. As Baden-Powell records, 'The value of state forests—to be made out of the best and most usefully situated wooded and grasslands—was not even recognised, and the occupation of the 'waste' by capitalists and settlers was alone discussed'.[33] Rich forests were also considered waste in the early colonial period: the large scale destruction of the primeval forests of the Doon Valley for land grants to Britishers is one example of how an admin-istrative category of waste actually created an ecological one. What was not economically of value to the British was declared value-less, in spite of high ecological and local use value.

The extensive clearfelling of forests for agricultural land use was a typically colonial view of turning waste into wealth, created by the notion of agricultural surplus as an important source of revenue. *As* the *Eighth Settlement Report* of the Doon Valley admitted:

> Perhaps no mistake was more common in the early days of British rule than to suppose that the extension of the cultivation, wherever cultur-able land could be found, and the clearing of forest and jungle to extend cultivation, must necessarily benefit the country and the government, and should be pushed as much as possible.[34]

It was not until later in the nineteenth century that the value of forests was realised. Ecological considerations were not, however, the central objective of the reservation of forests through the notification of the Forest Act of 1878. It was the revenue generating capacity of for-ests which led to their reservation, and protection was defined as the exclusion of villagers' access to forests as a common resource. Forests in

33 B.H.. Baden-Powell, *Land Revenue in British India*, London: Oxford, 1907.

34 J. Baker, *Eighth Settlement Report*, Dehradun, 1888.

themselves now constituted a property of great value and might be made to yield an annual revenue equal to cultivation. The shift in the colonial perspective of seeing forests as wealth and not waste also led to their conversion from a common resource for local use, under local community control, to a commodity for commercial use under bureaucratic control. This robbery of the commons was seriously resisted through 'forest satyagrahas' throughout the country.

A second robbery of the commons is now under way through 'wastelands development', which is a euphemism for the privatisation of the commons. The last resource of the poor for fodder and fuel will now disappear through privatisation. As usual, in every scheme that worsens the position of the poor, it is the poor who are invoked as beneficiaries. Leases to some token landless people are aimed at covering up the large-scale appropriation of the common resources of the majority of the poor.

Manno Rakshana Koota: saving the soil, protecting the commons

An example of how such a scheme goes awry can be taken from the Karnataka experience. Village commons in Shimoga and Chikmagalur are being taken away from people for wasteland development. These village commons are C and D class lands in revenue records. Categorised as wasteland, they are meant for fulfilling the basic needs of villagers, for whom 'wastelands' are their common wealth, supporting their agricultural ecology. Attempts to change the vegetational and land use characteristics of these village commons are, in their perception, attempts at robbing their land of its biological wealth. There is a proposal for transferring all these village commons, within a radius of 100 kms of Harihar Polyfibres, and utilising about 45,000 acres of commons for growing eucalyptus and selling it to Harihar Polyfibres. The commons are to be leased individually to a few landless beneficiaries.

The people of the affected villages have protested by uprooting newly planted eucalyptus seedlings from these 'wastelands' in large numbers. (Some of the wastelands are in fact, under natural evergreen or semi-green forests, and the average tree population has been found to be 50-200 per acre of diverse tree species.) The cultivation of eucalyptus in the village commons consisting of these C and D class lands is seen by the people as a programme for the *creation* of wastelands, not a programme for their development. The conversion of ecologically productive village commons to feedstock for the wood and fibre industry is in direct conflict with the basic biomass needs of the local villages, and their diversion to industrial plantations through a project for wasteland development has generated a major popular resistance movement for the protection of the commons, called 'Mann u Rakshana Koota' or 'Movement for Saving the Soil'. The government seems determined to take over the commons and manage them commercially throughout the country. Poor people's needs and the need for ecological stahility are to be sacrificed in this ultimate privatisation of the commons.

The national programme for privatising the commons is the tree *patta* scheme of breaking up the commons and leasing them out to individuals or groups of individuals for tree planting. The scheme will have a far-reaching social and ecological impact—largely detrimental to the poorest who have traditionally sustained themselves on the commons, a shared resource to which *all* in the local community have access. Privatisation amounts to closing off the access of large numbers, granting exclusively to some. On paper, preference will be given to the landless; in practise, we know how beneficiaries are identified in the absence of community check and control. The World Bank National Social Forestry Plan admits that such schemes could at most benefit 10 percent of landless and marginal farmers and remains silent about the 90 percent who no longer have a commons to survive on. The planting will be financed through government loans. Since such loans must be paid back, the lessee will be forced to plant commercially and to harvest at short rotations. This has already been the trend of the tree *patta* scheme in West Bengal's World Bank funded project. The economics of the market will, as always, exclude those who have no purchasing power, and whose zero cost biomass sources in the commons have been usurped to create a commodity. The economy of the commons does not need purchasing power, the economy of the market does. Local needs will therefore be less satisfied through tree *pattas* than through commons. Further, since the banks which give the loans will also design the afforestation package, permanent and sustainable forestry can hardly be expected to be the outcome. Short-term commercial wood production, which mines soil nutrients and moisture, will result. The market, and not the needs of local people or local ecosystems will determine the planting pattern. As the report of the group constituted to evolve guidelines for tree *pattas* states, 'NABARD Banks and the implementing agencies could consider preparing some model schemes for adoption in different areas so that technical feasibility and economic viability are given due consideration'. The expertise for forestry has now shifted further away from the life of the forest and the lives of those who depend on forestry for survival. There is no reference in the new projects to *ecological* viability or issues of entitlements and rights for those for whom the panchayat and community lands were a free common resource. We have enough evidence to show that whenever this happens poor people are further deprived and ecosystems further degraded. The 'eucalyptisation' phenomenon has shown how the people (especially women) and nature can be wounded simultaneously with inappropriate tree planting. The wasteland development programme as it stands today is merely a plan that will destroy the commons for the rule of the market. And with the commons will be destroyed the survival base of those who depend on them for their' subsistence, and the production base for womanly work in sustenance.

There is, of course, the popular *triage* thesis that the poor have no right to survival and should be dispensed with. Hardin's tragedy of the commons scenario emerges from male reductionist assumptions about nature and the logic of *triage* that such reductionism and its principles of exclusion and dispensability entail.[35] Hardin is just a symbol of the new trend in reductionist science which uses the language of ecology and conservation to unleash another attack of violence against nature. More centralisation, more uniformity, more manipulation become new and false prescriptions for overcoming the ecological crisis. Yet neither nature nor people can be saved when the destruction of the former and the dispensability of the latter are the presupposition for creating the new reductionist science of nature.

Breeding 'super-trees': the ultimate reductionism

The forest crisis was an outcome of a reductionist forestry which viewed the forest as a timber mine, not as a central mechanism in soil and water conservation. The separation of the life-giving and life-maintaining functions of the forest from its commercial value has thus led to the destruction of the essential ecological processes to which forests and trees contribute.

35 G. Hardin, 'The Tragedy of the Commons', in *Science*, Vol. 162, December 1968, pp. 1243-48.

The struggles of women, tribals, and peasants, guided by a perception of the forest as a life-support system, are coinciding with failed projects of maldevelopment—of non-sustainable agricultural and energy policies. It is easy to invoke the environmental crisis and the poor people's energy crisis to open up new avenues for reductionist science and commodity production. The entry of biotechnologies in forestry for instance is guided by

> the incentive provided by the knowledge that fossil fuels must run out
> and that a need exists for new commodities to improve the profitability
> of agriculture, encourages the development of new biomass crops as
> energy sources for the failure. Most projections for increased crop pro-
> duction rely on the new biotechnologies that promise to introduce the
> grand period of the 'science power' phase of agriculture. Hence, land
> and other resources should not constrain the development of biomass
> as a renewable energy source for the future.[36]

> The new technologies and the new aid programmes in forestry are mo-
> tivated by the future existence of markets for biomass-based industrial
> and commercial energy of the era beyond fossil fuels. As Flavin predicts
> in the 1986 *State of the World* report, 'Oil will have been largely eliminat-
> ed as a fuel for power plants and many industries'.[37]

The fuel-gathering Third World woman will once again be bypassed by the new sources of energy which will be produced on the land which gave her food and fodder and fuel. Industrial energy from weeds will be derived at the cost of sustenance needs that land in the Third World now satisfies.

The reductionist mind further entrenches colonisation. The dysjunction process, which underlies the existing ecological and economic chaos, is then applied at newer and deeper levels to resolve the chaos; all it achieves, instead, is further irreversible chaos. The breakdown of ecological cycles for example, is reduced to the problem of planting trees. The cycles recede, trees become a universal solution, and as a universal solution can only be engineered for a market which must go against nature, hastening the breakdown and making recovery less possible. Ecological

36 W.H. Smith, 'Energy from Biomass: A New Commodity', in J.W. Rosenblum (ed.) *Agriculture in the 21st Century*, New York: John Wiley and Sons, 1983.

37 C. Flavin, 'Moving Beyond Oil', in *State of the World*, Washington: World Watch, 1986, pp. 78-97

crises signal the breakdown of scientific arrogance—the crisis mind turns this into yet another domain for its colonisation, promising new miracles and inducing the closure of options even while they exist. Tissue culture—as opposed to forest culture—is now proposed as the afforestation strategy of the future in India. But this solution works only through the logic of uniformity or indifference to the diversity of life in nature. Tissue culture will be the ultimate *triage* of the earth in its diversity, and of her people in their diversity.

The organic recovery of nature cannot be a recovery of reductionism. The machine cannot be a metaphor for nature without sundering it apart, because nature is not mechanistic and Cartesian. The ecological crisis suggests the indispensability of nature and the impossibility of substituting its life-support processes. The reductionist response to eco-crises assures an extension of the logic of dispensability: it presupposes that life-support can be manufactured in the laboratory and factory. In fact, in the reductionist response to the ecological crisis, the lab, and factory merge, the distinction between science and business blurs. With engineering entering the life-sciences, the renewability of life as a self-reproducing system comes to an end. Life must be engineered now, not reproduced. A new commodity set is created as inputs, and a new commodity is created as output. Life itself is the new commodity. Linkages that lay within nature to create conditions for self-renewal are destroyed, and in their place come linkages of the market and multinationals. The ultimate masculinist perception of trees as money is captured in Greenwood's statement, 'Knocking even one year off this interval has a net present value well into millions of dollars for organisations that own and plant large acreages'. [38]

The breeding strategy is to search for trees with 'superior' characteristics. From nature providing its own seed, the laboratories of multinationals will become the new monopolies for the supply of seed and seedlings. This centralised, global control leads to a new colonisation of nature and its commons, and will lead to new degrees of homogeneity and uniformity. In clonal propagation, all members of a clone are genetically identical. This uniformity in trees as resources allows the Taylorism logic to enter forest management at an even deeper level than the monoculture plantation of the same species. The uniformity assumes a greater dispensability of species that the market and industry consider 'inferior'.

38 M.S. Greenwood, 'Shortening Generations', in *Journal of Forestry*, January, 1986, p. 38.

And linked with the imperative of genetic engineering to dispense with species other than its favourites, is the political economy of dispensing with the small person and her needs for survival. As Hollowell and Porterfield point out, for the genetic 'improvement' of tree stands, a land base of 150,000 to 200,000 acres or more is required to assure an acceptable rate of return'.[39] According to them,

> ... gains in desired traits are most meaningful when converted to economic gains. Growth gains may be expressed as obtaining more volume per acre for a given rotation or reaching rotation volume and/or desired piece size at an earlier age. Economics will favour the shorter rotation.
>
> Straightness improvement is reflected in increased yield of lumber or veneer per unit volume of raw material. Increases in wood specific gravity can result in improved fibre yields or higher grade lumber.
>
> Once quantified, incremental gains can be converted into higher expected values using a forecast of future produce prices. Timing of expected gains is necessary to construct a cash flow stream for economic analysis.

Resource flows to maintain nature's cycles and local needs of water and diverse vegetation have been replaced by cash-flows as a measure of 'yield' and 'growth'. Nature's ecology, its yields and growth are further pushed aside. The market and factory define the 'improvement' sought through the new biotechnologies. This reductionism induced by global markets for wood resources is the ultimate violence, when super-firms decide which super-trees are useful. Nature's integrity and diversity and people's needs are thus simultaneously violated.

Susan Griffin, in *Woman and Nature,* parodied the reductionist mind when she wrote:

> The trees in the forest should be tall and free from knot-causing limbs for most of their height. They should be straight. Trees growing in the forest should be useful trees. For each tree ask if it is worth the space it grows in. Aspen, scrub pine, chokeberry, black gum, scrub oak, dogwood, hemlock, beech are weed trees which should be eliminated.
>
> For harvesting trees, it is desirable that a stand be all of the same variety and age. Nothing should grow on the forest floor, not seedling trees, not grass, not shrubbery.[40]

---

39 R.R. Hollowell & R.L. Porterfield, 'Is Tree Improvement a Good Investment? Yes, if You've got the Time and Money', in *Journal of Forestry,* February 1986, p. 46.

40 Susan Griffin, *Woman and Nature,* London: The Women's Press, 1984.

She contrasts this uniformity with the logic of diversity in the forest as feminine. The voices of women join the voices of nature.

> The way we stand, you can see we have grown up this way together, out of the same soil, with the same rains, leaning in the same way toward the sun.... And we are various and amazing in our variety, and our differences multiply, so that edge after edge of the endlessness of possibility is exposed. You know we have grown this way for years. And to no purpose you can understand. Yet what you fail to know we know, and the knowing is in us, how we have grown this way, why these years were not one of them heedless, why we are shaped the way we are, not all straight to your purpose, but to ours. And how we are each purpose, how each cell, how light and soil are in us, how we are in the soil, how we are in the air, how we are both infinitesimal and great and how we are infinitely without any purpose you can see, in the way we stand, each moment heeded in this cycle, no detail unlovely.

It is such a recovery of life in diversity, of a diversity shared and protected that the invisible Chipko struggles for. Giving value and significance to Prakriti, to nature as the source, to the smallest element of nature in its renewal, giving value to collective needs, not private action, women in Kangad, Sevalgaon, Rawatgaon work in partnership with nature to recreate and regenerate. Without signboards, without World Bank loans, without wire-fencing, they are working to allow nature's play in reproducing the life of the forest—grasses and shrubs, small trees and big, each useful to nature if not to man, are all coming alive again.

Recovering diversity, recovering the commons

At an altitude of 6,000 ft., deep in the Balganga Valley in Garhwal lies Kangad, a hamlet of 200 families. In 1977, the already degraded forest of Kangad was marked for felling by the forest department. The women, who had to walk long distances for fuel, fodder, and water, were determined to save the last patch of trees. The men of Kangad were employed by the forest department for felling operations. With the gender fragmentation of the interests of the village community—the women representing the conservation interests, and the men representing the exploitation demand—launching Chipko was not easy. The women contacted Bimla Bahuguna in Silyara, just 15 kms from Kangad. Bimla Behn, with Chipko activists Dhoom Singh Negi and Pratap Shihar, came to support the women's struggle. After four months of resistance, the women succeeded in saving their forest.

The women's organisation, the Mahila Mandai Dal, then decided to regenerate the degraded forests. On the basis of cattle owned by each family, contributions were raised to support a village forest guard who was paid Rs. 300 per month. For three years the arrangement worked and then failed because the watchman became inefficient and corrupt: he would allow some people to extract fodder and fuelwood. Once the women learnt of this, they unanimously decided to abolish the post of the forest guard and guard the forest themselves.

Now the Mahila Mandai has allocated duties to a group of village women. About ten or twelve women are on duty every day, allocated in such a manner that the work is distributed among all the families. Thus the duty for one family or group of women comes in a cycle of 15 to 20 days. As one woman said, 'On these days we leave our own work and protect the forest because our oak trees are like our children'. Oak trees are now generating naturally in Kangad.

Once, when a Gujjar grazier allowed his goats to graze in the regenerated area, the women confiscated the goats and fined the Gujjar Rs. 200. Villagers are fined up to Rs. 50 per person for lopping the regenerating oak and Rs. 100 for cutting trees for firewood. On another occasion, when a fire threatened to destroy the forest, all the women joined hands to put out the forest fire. As one woman reported, 'The men were at home, but they decided to stay back rather than join with us to put out the fire. The men are least bothered about saving trees'. In 1986, the Mahila Mandai decided to assist the forest department in tree planting. They dug 15,000 pits but found that the forest department wanted to plant only poplars. The women refused to plant this exotic, and forced the forest department to bring diverse indigenous fodder species instead.

The strength of nature and the strength of women is the basis of the recovery of the forest as commons in Kangad. The capital is not debt and aid. The market is not the guiding force. Nature's and women's energy are the capital, and local needs of water, food, fodder, and fuel provide the organising principle of managing a shared, living resource. This is merely a renewal of the conservation ethic and conservation work of hill women, that they think of the needs of their families. This is symbolised by their putting aside some leaves for Patna Devl (the goddess of the leaves) each time they go to collect fodder. These are small, perhaps invisible, but significant steps towards the recovery of the feminine principle in the forest.

This recovery re-establishes the integration of forestry with food production and water management and it allows the possibility of a re-emergence of the diversity and integrity of life in the forest, of fauna and flora, of plants big and small, each crucial to the life of the forest, each valuable in itself, each having a right to participate in the democracy of the forest's life, and each contributing in invisible, unknown ways to all life. Diversity of living resources in the forest, natural or in an agro-ecosystem, is critical to soil and water conservation, it is critical for satisfying the diversity of needs of people who depend on the forest, and the diversity of nature's needs in reproducing herself.

The annihilation of this diversity has destroyed women's control over conditions of producing sustenance. The many colonisations—through 'reserved' forests, through 'social forestry', through 'wasteland' development—have implied not forest development but the maldevelopment of both forestry and agriculture. A maldeveloped forestry has meant new resources and raw material supplies for industry and commerce; for nature and women it has meant a new impoverishment, a destruction of the diverse means of production through which both provide sustenance in food and water, and reproduce society. The Chipko struggle is a struggle to recover the hidden and invisible productivity of vital resources, and the invisible productivity of women, to recover their entitlements and rights to have and provide nourishment for sustained survival, and to create ecological insights and political spaces that do not destroy fundamental rights to survival. Chipko women provide a nonviolent alternative in forestry to the violence of reductionist forestry with its inherent logic of dispensability. They have taken the first steps towards recovering their status as the *other* silviculturists and forest managers, who participate in nature's processes instead of working against them, and share nature's wealth for basic needs instead of privatising it for profit.

CHAPTER FIVE

Women in the Food Chain

Green revolution: a western paradigm

Nature and women have historically been the primary food providers in natural farming, based on sustainable flows of fertility from forests and farm animals to croplands. The food system has always included the forest and animal systems in its processes. The women of Chipko fight for their forests primarily as peasants whose productivity in agriculture depends centrally on inputs from the forest, either directly as fertilizer to the soil, or indirectly as fodder for their cattle, which in turn produce fertilizer for fields. The feminine principle of food production is based on the intimate links between trees, animals, and crops, and on the work of women in maintaining these links. Women's work in agriculture has traditionally been work in integrating forestry and animal husbandry with farming. Agriculture modelled on nature and based on women's participation with nature has been self-reproducing and sustainable because the internally recycled resources provide the necessary inputs for seeds, soil moisture, soil nutrients, and pest control.

The masculinist paradigm of food production which has come to us under the many labels of 'green revolution', 'scientific agriculture', etc. involves the disruption of the essential links between forestry, animal husbandry, and agriculture, which have been the basis of the sustainable model. The renewable base of agriculture provided by women through carrying green manure and fodder to farms and carrying compost and organic matter to fields has been destroyed by reductionist agriculture which replaces renewable inputs from the farm by non-renewable inputs from factories, and displaces women's work in providing sustainable inputs with the work of men and machines to produce hazardous agri-chemicals as inputs to green revolution agriculture.

This paradigm, which results in the disruption of nature's ecological cycles and displaces women from maintaining those cycles, sees this process of fragmentation as one of increasing efficiency. Market efficiency and profits do increase through fragmentation, but at the cost of nature's capital in fertile and living soils and the destruction of women's work in keeping the inherent fertility of soils alive. From seeing farming as a process of nurturing the earth to maintain her capacity to provide food, a masculinist shift takes place which sees farming as a process of generating profits. Ecological destruction is one inevitable result of this commercial outlook. Economic deprivation is the other, because production for profits instead of needs excludes larger numbers of women and peasants from food production and even larger numbers of women, children, and the poor from entitlements to food. The fact that larger numbers of the poor in the Third World are victims of hunger and famine today is intimately related to a patriarchal model of progress which sees sales and profits as indicators of well-being and thus destroys the real well-being of people.

It is from the ecological perspective, that focusses on nature and needs, that it is possible to see that what has been called scientific agriculture and the green revolution is in reality a western patriarchal anti-nature model of agriculture, which shifts the control of food systems from women and peasants to food and agribusiness multinationals and disrupts natural processes. In the ecological perspective, it is impossible to see food production as distinct from forests, water, and animal systems. Movements by rural women to protect forests or rivers have always been rooted in protecting their agricultural base: for the Chipko women, forests provide food, and the movement to protect them is a movement to provide food to their families, their cattle (which they perceive as an extension of the human family) and their soils. In 1974, when the women of Reni protected their forest they told the contractors' men: 'This forest is our mother's home. When we have food scarcity, we come here to collect fruits for our children. We collect herbs and ferns and mushrooms. Do not cut this forest, otherwise we will embrace the trees and protect them with our lives.' In 1986, Chipko women of Nahi Kala were protecting their forests for food production. As Chamundeyi said, 'We need our forests for growing *mandua*, jhanjora, rajma, adrak, and mirch to feed our families and ourselves'. And throughout the hill areas, women sing: 'Give me an oak forest and I will give you pots full of milk and baskets full of grain'.

The link between forests and food is clear to the women who produce food in partnership with trees and animals. The patriarchal model, in contrast, sees forestry as independent of agriculture, and reduces the multiple outputs of the forest including fertilizer and fodder, into a single product—commercial wood. Animals are no longer seen as providing fertilizer and energy for agriculture, and through the 'white revolution', animal husbandry is reduced to the production of milk for the centralised dairy industry. Organic inputs from forests and animals are no longer seen as mechanisms for conserving soil moisture; large dams become the patriarchal option for providing water for food production. Organic manure is no longer a fertilizer; it is fertilizer factories that are seen to be the only source of soil fertility. Rich soils and appropriate cropping patterns are no longer mechanisms for pest control; poisons for killing pests become an inevitable component of patriarchal agriculture. The destruction of forests as a hand-maiden of agriculture has already been discussed in Chapter 4; the destruction of water systems as a result of demands of green revolution farming will be discussed in Chapter 6; in this chapter we will look at how seeds, soil fertility and pest control have ceased to be provided largely by women as internal resources of the farm, and are now produced by a handful of agribusiness companies. It will also analyse how the rupture of agriculture from animal husbandry and the reductionist evolution of each through the green and white revolutions has violated nature's balance and women's productivity, as well as people's right to food.

The displacement of women from food production

For more than forty centuries, Third World peasants, often predominantly women, have innovated in agriculture. Crops have crossed continents, crop varieties have been improved, patterns of rotational and mixed cropping have been evolved to match the needs of the crop community and the ecosystem. These decentred innovations have been lasting and sustainable. They stayed because they struck an ecological balance. Peasants as experts, as plant breeders, as soil scientists, as water managers, have kept the world fed all these centuries.

Twenty years ago, forty centuries of knowledge of agriculture began to be eroded and erased as the green revolution, designed by multinational corporations and western male experts, homogenised nature's diversity and the diversity of human knowledge on a reductionist pattern of agriculture, evolved by global research centres like the International Rice Research Institute, (IRRI) in the Philippines and the CIMMYT (the International Maize and Wheat Improvement Centre) in Mexico. Thirteen such institutes exist today run by CGIAR (the Consultative Group for International Agricultural Research).[1] Table 1 lists some important agricultural research institutions.

TABLE 1

International agricultural research institutions

Institution	Location	Research	Coverage
IRRI (1960) International Rice Research Institute	Los Banos, Philippines	Rice under irrigation; multiple cropping systems; upland rice	Worldwide, special emphasis in Asia
CIMMYT (1964) International Centre for the Improvement of Maize and Wheat	El Batan, Mexico	Wheat (also triticale, barley); maize	Worldwide
IITA (1965) International Institute of Tropical Agriculture	Ibadan, Nigeria	Farming systems; cereals (rice and maize as regional relay stations for IRRI and CIMMYT); grain legume (cow-pea, soyabean, lima bean, pigeon-pea), root and tuber crops, cassava, sweet potatoes, yams	Worldwide in lowland tropics, special emphasis in Africa
CIAT (1968) International Center for Tropical Agriculture	Palmira, Colombia	Beef; cassava, field beans; farming systems; swine (minor); maize and rice (regional relay stations to CIMMYT and IRRI)	Worldwide in lowland tropics, special emphasis in Latin America

1 'The Corporate Seed,' in *Balai Asian Journal*, No.7, 1983, Manila; and Anderson et at, *Science, Politics and the Agricultural Revolution in Asia*, Boulder: Westview, 1982.

WARDA (1971) West African Rice Development Association	Monrovia, Liberia	Regional cooperative effort in adaptive rice research among 13 nations with IITA and IRRI support	West Africa
CIP (1972) (International Potato Center)	Lima, Peru	Potatoes (for both tropics and temperate regions)	Worldwide, includ- ing linkages with developed countries
ICRISAT (1972) International Crop Research Institute for the Semi-Arid Tropics	Hyderabad, India	Sorghum; pearl millet, pigeon-pea; chick-pea; farming systems; groundnut	Worldwide, special emphasis on dry, semi-arid tropics, non-irrigated farming.
IBPGR (1973) International Board for Plant Genetic Resources	FAO, Rome, Italy	Conservation of plant genetic material with special reference to cereals	Worldwide

TABLE 2
IRRI finances according to source (1961-1980)
(U.S. dollars)

Contributor	Amount	% of total	Year(s) of grant
Ford Foundation	23,950,469	18.84	1961-80
Rockefeller Foundation	20,460,431	16.1	1961-80
US AID	28,982,114	22.80	1967-80
International Organizations	20,334,788	16	
Asian Development Bank	800,000		1975,1977
European Economic Community	3,011,219		1978-80
Fertilizer Development Center	70,939		1979-80
Foundation for International Potash Research	7,375		1963-65
International Board for Plant Genetic Resources	208,100		1977, 1979-80
International Center of Insect Physiology and Ecology	125,432		1978-80

International Development Research Center	3,710,736		1972-73, 1975-76, 1978-80
International Development Association	7,775,000		1973-80
International Fund for Agricultural Research	500,000		1980
International Potash Institute/ Potash Institute of North America	68,064		1963, 1965-66 1968-69, 1971-79
Fertilizer Development Center	70,939		1979-80
OPEC Special Fund	200,000		1980
UN Economic and Social Commission	6,000		1970, 1979
UN Food and Agriculture Organization (FAO)	2,650		1969
UN Environment Program	280,000		1974-78
UN Development Program	3,559,273		1974-78, 1978.
World Phosphate Rock Institute	10,000		1975
National governments	31,920,619	25.11	
Australia	4,185,459		1975-80
Belgium	148,677		1977
Canada	6,507,862		1974-80
Denmark	443,048		1978-80
Federal Republic of Germany	3,459,159		1974-80
Indonesia	1,619,119		1973-80
Iran	250,000		1977
Japan	8,882,145		1971-77, 1979-80
Korea	82,259		1980
The Netherlands	1,168,673		1971-79
New Zealand	137,450		1973, 1976-78
Philippines	100,000		1980
Saudi Arabia	274,300		1976-77, 1980
Sweden	302,944		1977-80
Switzerland	285,700		1979-80
United Kingdom	4,073,824		1973-76, 1979-80

Corporations	345,726	0.27
Bayer	9,333	1971, 1973
Boots Company	1,000	1977
Chevron Chemicals	2,993	1972, 1977
Ciba-Geigy	20,500	1968, 1970, 1972, 1975 1978-80
Cyanamid	19,000	1975-76, 1978, 1980
Dow Chemical	10,153	1967-70
Eli Lilly & Co (ELANCO)	6,000	1968-70
Esso Engineering and Research Company	4,306	1964-68
FMC	9,000	1975-77, 1980.
Gulf Research and Development Company	3,500	1969, 1972
Hoechst	11,891	1972, 1975-76, 1978
Imperial Chemical Industries	55,000	1967-69, 1971-76 1979-80
International Business Machines Corp. (IBM)	7,000	1967
International Minerals and Chemical Corp.	60,000	1966-67, 1975
Kemanobel	500	1980
Minnesota Mining and Manufacturing Company	1,000	1974
Monsanto	12,500	1967, 1969, 1971-72, 1976, 1978-80
Montedison	8,982	1977-78, 1980
Occidental Chemical	500	1971
Pittsburg Plate Glass Co.	2,000	1967
Plant Protection Ltd	5,000	1966
Shell Chemical Company	42,872	1969-70, 1972-73 1975, 1977-78, 1980
Stauffer Chemical Company	40,000	1967-69, 1971-76, 1978-80
Union Carbide	11,000	1968, 1970

Uniroyal Chemical	496		1980
Upjohn	1,200		1972
Government agencies	1,030,872	0.81	
National Institute of Health (US)	383,708		1978-80
National Food and Agriculture Council (Philippines)	276,859		1973, 1976-80
National Science Development Board (Philippines)	104,172		1963, 1965, 1967-68, 1973, 1975-76 1964-68, 1976.
Philippine Council for Agricultural Resources and Research	198,911		1976-80
Universities	13,634	0.01	
East-West Center (Hawaii)	1,500		1976, 1978
University Hohenheim (Stuttgart)	4,370		1980
United Nations University	7,764		1980
Others	61,557	0.05	1966, 1969, 1977
Total	127,100,210		

Source: International Rice Research Institute, *Annual Report* from 1962–1980.

In 1941, the Rockefeller Foundation established a research centre near Mexico City primarily devoted to plant breeding, that in 1961 took the name CIMMYT (International Maize and Wheat Improvement Centre). By the late 1950s the Centre created HYV wheat which later provided the basis of the green revolution in India. Private capital and global aid provided the inputs for the capital intensive, resource intensive, profit oriented farming of the green revolution.

The very meaning of agriculture was transformed with the introduction of the western green revolution paradigm. It was no longer an activity that worked towards a careful maintenance of nature's capital in fertile soils and provided society with food and nutrition. It became an activity aimed primarily at the production of agricultural commodities for profit. With the shift in the nature of the activity came a shift in the nature of the actors; nature, women, and peasants were no longer seen as primary producers of food. The shift from thinking in the context of nature's economy and the survival economy, to thinking exclusively in the context of the market economy, created the specificity of the hybrid seeds, chemical fertilizers and pesticides, mechanisation and large scale irrigation. These technologies were responses to the need for maximising profits from agriculture. They were aimed neither at protecting the soil and maintaining its fertility, nor at making food available to all as a basic human right or providing livelihoods in food production. The emergence of a new breed of agricultural 'experts' with fragmented knowledge of individual components of the farm system, and with a total integration of this fragmented knowledge with the market system, led to the displacement of the traditional agricultural experts-women and peasants.

Women were the world's original food producers, and continue to be central to food production systems in the Third World in terms of the work they do in the food chain. In agriculture—as in other sciences and areas of economic activity, women's scientific and economic contribution has been obscured by the male writing of history and anthropology, and by the use of the market and profits as a patriarchal base for the evaluation of the significance of technologies. Feminist scholarship has now begun to focus on the hidden contribution of women to plant and animal domestication when human societies made a transition from gathering/hunting to agricultural and nomadic ways of life. The paradigm of man-the-hunter based on assumptions of male dominance, competition, exploitation and aggression is slowly giving way to alternative perceptions which allow a recognition of the contribution of woman-the-gatherer, and the interdependence of the sexes in making survival possible through cooperation and nurturing. As Lee and De Vore[2] have pointed out, the contribution of women to food provisioning in gathering/hunting societies was 80 percent while hunting yielded only 20 percent. Because food collection required a thorough knowledge of plant and animal growth, maturation and fruition or reproduction, women have been credited with the discovery of domestication and cultivation of plants and animals. Food-gathering inventions attributable to women are the digging stick (precursor of the plough), the carrying sling, the sickle, and other knives. The mortar, the pounder, the drying, roasting, grinding, fermenting technologies, the storage of food in baskets, or day-lined storage pits are all inventions connected with food processing and preservation that are still alive in self-provisioning societies. According to Murdock's ethnographic atlas[3], in one half of the 142 advanced horticultural societies, farming was the exclusive domain of women, and it was shared on an equal footing with men in another 27 percent. Only in slightly more than one-fifth of these societies was agriculture the sole responsibility of men. Women

2 R.B.Lee & I. de Vore (eds.) *Man, the Hunter*, Chicago: Aldini, 1968.
3 G.P. Murdock& D.C. White, 'Standard Cross-Cultural Sample', *Ethnology*, Vol. 5 No. 4, pp. 329-369, 1969.

domesticated plants and animals and invented selective breeding. They
discovered propagation by shoots and cuttings, seed selection and the
construction of seedling beds. Stanley[4] lists the following inventions credited to women in cultivation: the use of ash as fertilizer; the creation of
work tools such as the hoe, spade, shovel, and simple plough; fallowing
and crop rotation; mulching, terracing, contour planting, irrigation, and
land recuperation through tree planting. She says that the eight most important cereals (wheat, rice, maize, barley, oats, sorghum, millet, and rye)
were all domesticated by women.

The worldwide destruction of the feminine knowledge of agriculture,
evolved over four to five thousand years, by a handful of white male scientists in less than two decades has not merely violated women as experts; since their expertise in agriculture has been related to modelling
agriculture on nature's methods of renewability, its destruction has gone
hand in hand with the ecological destruction of nature's processes and
the economic destruction of the poorer people in rural areas.

Half a century ago, Sir Alfred Howard, the father of modern sustainable farming wrote in his classic, An Agricultural Testament, that, 'In
the agriculture of Asia we find ourselves confronted with a system of
peasant farming which, in essentials, soon became stabilized. What is
happening today in the small fields of India and China took place many
centuries ago. The agricultural practises of the Orient have passed the
supreme test—they are almost as permanent as those of the primeval
forest, of the prairie, or of the ocean'.[5] Howard identified the principles
of sustainable agriculture as those of renewability as seen in the primeval forest. An Agricultural Testament is a record of practises that had
maintained the soil fertility of India over centuries. Historical records
indicate that the alluvial soils of the Gangetic plains have produced fair
crops year after year, without falling in fertility. According to Howard,
this has been possible because a perfect balance had been reached between the manurial requirements of crops harvested and natural processes which recuperate fertility. The conservation of soil fertility has
been achieved through a combination of mixed and rotational cropping
with leguminous crops, a balance between livestock and crops, shallow
and light ploughing, and organic manuring. John A. Voelker, too, had
challenged the colonial belief that traditional agriculture was primitive

4 A. Stanley, 'Daughters of Isis, Daughters of Demeter: When Women Sowed and Reaped'
in J. Rothschild (ed.), *Women, Technology and Innovation*, New York: Pergamon, 1982.

5 A. Howard, *An Agricultural Testament*, London: Oxford University Press, 1940.

and backward. Describing the perfection and permanence of Indian peasant farming he wrote: 'Nowhere would one find better instances of keeping land scrupulously clean from weeds, of ingenuity in device of water-raising appliances, of knowledge of soils and their capabilities, as well as of the exact time to sow and reap, as one would find in Indian agriculture. It is wonderful, too, how much is known of rotation, the system of "mixed crops" and of fallowing.... I, at least, have never seen a more perfect picture of cultivation'.[6]

People, cattle, and living things derive nutrition from the soil through plants, trees, and vegetation. Returning nutrition to the earth is therefore central to maintaining the food cycle and sustaining the productivity of the soil. The central role of farm animals in Indian agriculture came from the recognition that we cannot have an exploitative relationship with the earth; it must be one of reciprocity. That is why men, cattle, and trees have been treated as an integral unit in maintaining the food cycle; Kamadhenu, the sacred cow, and Kalpataru, the sacred tree have been the inviolable links of the inviolable food chain in Indian agriculture.[7]

Howard saw in India's peasants a knowledge of farming far more advanced than that of the west. He recognised the secret of India's sustainable land use as lying in the return of organic matter and humus to the soil. A balance between livestock and crops was always kept in order to maintain the food cycle and return organic matter to the soil. The method of mixed cropping is part of the adaptation of nature's ways in which cereal crops like millet, wheat, barley, and maize are mixed with pulses, providing nutrition to each other, and thus a balanced diet to people. Mixtures of crops give better results than monocultures; Howard notes that, 'Here we have another instance where the peasants of the East have anticipated and acted upon the solution of one of the problems which western science is only now beginning to recognise'.[8]

Rotational cropping is another strategy for maintaining the nutritional balance in the soil, especially with leguminous plants like pulses, although it was not till 1888, after a protracted controversy lasting thirty years, that western science finally accepted the important part played by pulse crops in enriching the soil.

6 J.A. Voelker, *Report on the Improvement of Indian Agriculture*, London: Eyre and Spottiswode, 1893, p. 11.

7 K.M. Munshi in *Towards Land Transformation*, Government of India, Ministry of Food and Agriculture, 1951.

8 Howard, *op. cit.*

Shallow and superficial ploughing was the fourth aspect of sustainable land use. It was recognized that too much cultivation and deep ploughing would oxidise the reserves of organic matter in the soil and the balance of soil fertility would soon be destroyed. The concept of the sacred earth as inviolable was also a constraint in overuse and destruction of the soil. Women's productive work on the farm has therefore been crucial to sustainable food production. It has been based on contributions to the land, not just exploitation of and benefit from it. In a paradigm that sees 'productivity' only in terms of output for markets and profits, contributing to the soil's organic fertility for sustainable land use is rendered invisible and unproductive. It is precisely because these essential links in the food chain have been ignored and destroyed by 'developed' and 'scientific' agriculture that the croplands of the world are rapidly being turned into deserts.

Women's work in organic agriculture also supports the work of decomposers and soil-builders which inhabit the soil. Organic manure is food for the community of living beings which depend on the soil. Soils treated with farmyard manure have from two to two-and-a-half times as many earthworms as untreated soils. Farmyard manure encourages the build-up of earthworms through increasing their food supply, whether they feed directly on it or on the micro-organisms it supports. Earthworms contribute to soil fertility by maintaining soil structure, aeration and drainage and by breaking down organic matter and incorporating it into the soil. The work of earthworms in soil formation was Darwin's major concern in later years. When finishing his book on earthworms he wrote: 'It may be doubted whether there are many other animals which have played so important a part in the history of creatures'.[9]

The little earthworm working invisibly in the soil is actually the tractor and fertilizer factory and dam combined. Worm-worked soils are more water stable than unworked soils, and worm-inhabited soils have considerably more organic carbon and nitrogen than parent soils. By their continuous movement through soils, earthworms make for the formation of channels which help in soil aeration. It is estimated that they increase soil-air volume by up to 30 percent. Soils with earthworms drain four to ten times faster than soil without earthworms and their water-holding capacity is higher by 20 percent. Earthworm casts, which can be 4-36 tons dry weight/acre/year contain more nutritive materials containing

9 Charles Darwin, *The Formation of Vegetable Mould through the Action of Worms with Observations on their Habits*, London: Faber and Faber, 1927.

carbon, nitrogen, calcium, magnesium, potassium, sodium, and phosphorous than the parent soil. Their work on the soil promotes microbial activity which is essential to the fertility of most soils. Yet the earthworm was never seen as a worker in 'scientific' agriculture.[10] The woman peasant who works invisibly with the earthworm in building soil fertility has also not been seen as doing 'productive' work or providing an 'input' to the food economy. We need to look beyond the mentality that tells us that fertility is 'bought' from fertilizer companies; we need to look beyond the fertilizer factory for maintaining soil fertility; and we need to recover the work of women and peasants who work with nature, not against her. In regions of India which have not yet been colonised by the green revolution, women peasants continue to work as soil builders rather than soil predators, and it is from these remaining pockets of natural farming that the ecological struggles to protect nature are emerging.

In sustainable agriculture based on maintaining the integrity and the fertility of the soil, women have played a major productive role, particularly in work linked to maintaining the food cycle. In feeding animals from trees or crop by-products, in nurturing cows and animals, in composting and fertilizing fields with organic manure, in managing mixed and rotation cropping, this critical work of maintaining ecological cycles was done by women, in partnership with the land, with trees, with animals and with men. Singh[11] has made estimates of the different kinds of work a woman in the hill areas of the Garhwal Himalaya currently puts into agricultural operations which are dependent on organic inputs. A woman's work is more than that of men and farm animals. For a one hectare farm, women put in 640 hours for interculture operations like weeding; 384 hours for irrigation; 650 hours for transporting organic manure and transferring it to the field; 557 hours for seed sowing (with men) and 984 hours for harvesting and threshing. Surveys have shown that in this hill region, a pair of bullocks works for 1,064 hours, men for 1,212 hours and women for 3,485 hours on a one hectare farm. Bhati and Singh, in a study in neighbouring Himachal Pradesh[12] show that women do 37 percent of the work in sowing, 59 percent in interculture (including weeding, hoeing, irrigation, etc.), 66 percent in harvesting, 59 percent in threshing and 69 percent in tending farm animals. In terms of overall farm work they

10 J.E. Satchel, *Earthworm Ecology*, London: Chapman and Hall, 1983.

11 Vir Singh, 'Hills of Hardship', *The Hindustan Times Weekly*, January 18, 1987.

12 J.B. Bhati & D.V. Singh, 'Women's Contribution to Agricultural Economy in Hill Regions of North-West India,' *Economic and Political Weekly*, Vol. 22. No. 17, April 25, 1987.

put in 61 percent of the total. K. Saradamoni's study[13] of women agricultural labourers and cultivators in three rice growing states—Kerala,
Tamil Nadu and West Bengal—challenges the view that the male agricultural labourer is the real worker, breadwinner, and supporter of women
and children. Through their work, knowledge, and skills, both categories
of women make crucial contributions to the production and processing
of rice, and their contributions have a nurturant quality. As Saradamoni
observes, the women involved in the study revealed their 'knowledge
about cultivation and their concern and participation. They have shown
a tenderness to paddy crop and fields almost similar to what they would
show to their own children'. She concludes that without these women,
their households would not have survived, yet their work is unrecognised
and, too often, uncounted and unrecorded.

Women's and nature's work and productivity are rendered invisible
when agricultural development becomes a project of western capitalist
patriarchy. Each increase in 'productivity' in this system is a decrease in
the productivity of women as food producers and processors. With the
green revolution food from fish in rice fields is destroyed by poisonous
pesticides, and reeds for fibre and ropemaking are destroyed by weedicides. The little spaces which ensure sustenance are slowly closed as the
world shrinks in its bounty. The shrinkage is always rooted in a reductionist attempt at 'growth'. Thus when wheat and rice are taken from the
home to the mill, not only do women lose work, but society loses nutrition. Rice and white bran which are eaten in home-processed grain are
destroyed by mechanised milling. The most nutritious part of the food is
turned into waste because the efficiency of the machine for profit generation is the determining factor, not the efficiency of women for the generation of nutrition. A woman anthropologist at the International Rice
Research Institute in the Philippines had the sensitivity to observe how
male categories of 'efficiency' created the mechanisation imperative.
Barog, a process of shaving off the already beaten stalks of rice to glean
the grain that remains, used to be undertaken by women who did this in
between childcare and cooking. They kept all the grain they got (none
going to the owner of the field) which at times, was as high as 10 percent
of the total yield. Mechanising the barog process was inspired because
the male IRRI scientists saw women's gain as a 'loss'. The woman anthropologist asks, 'How can IRRI defend counting barog gram as a "loss"? It is

13 K. Saradamoni, 'Labour, Land and Rice Production: Women's Involvement in Three
States,' *Economic and Political Weekly*, Vol. 22, No. 17, April 25, 1987.

TABLE 3

Gender division of agricultural work in Himachal Pradesh, 1983-84

(percentages)

Farm activity	Marginal farms		Small farms		Other farms		All farms	
	Male	Female	Male	Female	Male	Female	Male	Female
Crop production								
Field preparation	82	18	80	20	84	16	82	18
Manuring	62	38	63	37	66	34	63	37
Sowing	59	41	55	47	52	48	56	44
Interculture*	49	51	34	66	27	73	41	59
Harvesting	38	62	32	68	25	75	34	66
Threshing, etc	40	60	41	59	43	57	41	59
Total	64	36	60	40	59	41	61	39
Tending of animlas	29	71	33	67	34	66	31	69
Other farm work	87	13	87	13	83	17	86	14
Total farm work	36	64	40	60	42	58	39	61

*Includes weeding, hoeing, irrigation, etc.

Source : CSS, Agro-Economic Research Centre, Shimla (India).

true that the field owner does not get his hands on it. But the fact that the grain passes out of his hands does not reflect the technical inefficiency of the traditional method. The barog gram is by no means "lost" either to the national economy or to the production system itself. Village families eat it—and, what makes our report more embarrassing, it is usually the poorest villagers that eat. At best our failure to credit the traditional system with this gain reflects an evaluation of rice in terms of money rather than consumable food'.[14]

Mechanised processing and milling generate profits by first destroying the nutritional value of food and the productivity of women, and then by putting nutrition back into it through the processing industry. An advertisement for rice bran oil states: 'Did you know that your plate of rice has only half its nutrition? Yes! The other half is lost when rice is milled. That's the nutrition Harvest pure refined rice oil puts back into your meal. Making your meal complete.'

Women's expertise and role in food production and processing is displaced with 'Japanese knowhow' which packs into a plastic bottle the nutrition that Third World rural women conserve through their traditional food processing technologies. As the image of women is transformed from being conservers and producers to being consumers, their productive roles in agriculture recede further into invisibility.

In other parts of the Third World also, women are found to work more than men in the food system. White's study of rural Java noted that women of 15 years and over worked an average of 11.1 hours per day, compared to 8.7 hours for men. In annual terms, women worked for 4,056 hours and men for 3,173. Quizon and Evenson and King have reported that in the Philippines too, women put in more total work-time than men.[15]

In Africa, basic food production continues to be in the hands of women, even as their control over agriculture is increasingly being eroded through green revolution and cash-crop farming. Women there do 70–80 percent of all agricultural work and produce 40 to 50 percent of all staple food crops. Shimwaayi Muntemba has argued that women's ability to produce and supply food has been deteriorating over time. The

14 Anonymous, 'From a Woman Anthropologist's Note-pad: IRRI Memos', *Balai*, No 7, 1983.

15 Bina Agarwal, 'Women and Technological Change in Agriculture: The Asian and African Experience', in I. Ahmed, (ed.). *Technology and Rural Women: Conceptual and Empirical Issues*, London: George Allen and Unwin, 1985.

Male and female share of agricultural work (Africa)

	Male	%	Female
Ploughing	70		30
Planting	50		50
Hoeing/weeding	30		70
Transporting	20		80
Storing	20		80
Processing	10		90
Marketing	40		60
Husbandry	50		50

Source : Economic Commission for Africa, 1975.

penetration of capitalism and the money economy has led to a marked and devastating erosion of the productive power of land and the power of women.[16] The commercialisation of agriculture puts constraints on the amount of land available for the production of food crops. Women's productivity, particularly of food crops, has stagnated and in some cases actually diminished, while cash crop production under male control has led to reduced food availability for the household.

Agricultural 'development' or modernisation has split the activity into two sectors—the highly visible, globally planned and controlled and state subsidised production for profits and markets, and the less visible, sometimes invisible, decentred self-provisioning of food through what is commonly called subsistence farming. The 'masculinisation' of modem, chemical intensive and mechanised, capital intensive agriculture, and the 'feminisation' of traditional subsistence food production which feeds the bulk of the rural poor, is now being recognised worldwide.[17] This dichotomy has been accentuated with modern production and distribution systems which are integrated into global markets and are introduced through male-oriented international aid and financing which has become a major factor in excluding women's access to conditions for producing food. Their control over food systems has diminished while their responsibility as the main providers for their dependants has increased. As more land is diverted to cash crops and is impoverished

16 S. Muntemba, 'Women, the Farmers of Africa', speech delivered on 'The Position of Women in Rural Development', Amhem, Netherlands, 1985, and 'Dispossession and Counter-strategies in Zambia 1930-1970,' *Development*, Vol 4, 1984, p. 15.

17 E.A. Cebotarev, 'Women in Agricultural Science and Technology: Implications for Today's Food System,' mimeo, University of Guelph; 1986.

through the ecological impact of green revolution technologies, women have decreased space but increased burdens in food production. With the market as the measure of all productivity, the 'value' of women's work and status falls, while their work in producing food for survival increases. By splitting the agricultural economy into a cash-mediated masculinised sector, and a subsistence, food-producing 'feminised' sector, capitalist patriarchy simultaneously increases the work burden and the marginalisation of women. The cash economy first draws men away from basic food production, thus increasing women's workload for producing subsistence; then, ecological disruption caused by cash crop and green revolution farming forces them to walk longer distances for water, fodder, and fuel.

A study by Bandyopadhyay and Moench[18] of biomass utilisation in Garhwal has shown clearly what a shift away from staple food crops to vegetables for export implies for women's work and nature's stability. In the Garhwal Himalaya at least, two-thirds of the fodder needs of farm animals are derived from the straw of cereal crops; this is stored and provides animal feed in periods of low biological productivity. The shift to vegetables earns cash, but it destroys the food and fodder source on the farm. The pressure for fodder on forests thus immediately increases three-fold, as if the population had tripled. The invisible costs of deforestation and forest degradation generated by commercial agriculture, with the associated cost of water and soil instability, are never calculated by the market transactions of commercial farming. For the women, the destruction of fodder sources on the farm means more energy expenditure in fodder collection from forests, which means more deforestation and higher rates of soil and water erosion. Finally, the disruption of ecological cycles turns both farms and forests into unproductive and desertified wastelands.

The point, however, is not so much that in farming systems women labour more than men in agriculture but that, traditionally, they are productive in precisely those links in farm operations which involve a partnership with nature and are crucial for maintaining the food cycle— in the soil, and in the local food economy. And it is these cycles that are broken when cash crop, green revolution agriculture replaces subsistence agriculture. There are two invisible processes of the dispossession of women implicit in such a shift. Firstly, women's role shifts from the

18 J. Bandyopadhyay & M. Moench. 'Basic Needs and Biomass Utilisation' in J. Bandyopadhyay, et al., India's Environment; Dehradun: Natraj, 1987.

ecological category of being soil-builders and primary producers of farm productivity to the economic category of subsidiary workers and wage earners on an agricultural assembly line. Agarwal has observed that between 1961 and 1981, the percentage of women agricultural labourers rose from 25.6 percent to 49.6 percent.[19] This doubling, over two decades, of women's dependence on wage labour is related to the erosion of their independent access to land and land use. Women's traditional control over land was not in terms of ownership but rights to land use. With these decisions now being made by centrally controlled state policy, in tune with corporate demands, women's control over agriculture has been eroded, even as their work burden has increased. That they are losing control over land as a means of production is noted by Mies[20] who draws evidence from the fact that the number of female cultivators dropped by 52 percent between 1961 and 1971, while the number of female agricultural labourers rose by 43 percent. Whereas until 1961, the proportion of women among cultivators had been between 289-498 per 1000 men, this ratio fell steeply between 1961 and 1971 to a mere 135 women to 1000 men. Similarly, the female ratio among agricultural labourers had been relatively stable since 1901, but between 1961 and 1971 it dropped from 819 women per 1000 men to 498 women per 1000 men, a decline of about 40 percent. Women's marginalisation and gender polarisation is further aggravated by the fact that there is a male/female differential in wage earnings, with women generally being paid between half or one-third less than male agricultural labour. Table 4 indicates the shifts in women's visible agricultural work.

The displacement of women cultivators and small peasants is not accidental to the green revolution. Bruce Jennings of Hawaii University has shown how Rockefeller scientists straightforwardly addressed the problem of a 'top-down' versus a 'bottom-up' strategy: 'The plan presented assumes that most rapid progress can be made by starting at the top and expanding downward'.[21] They argued that the 'deficiencies' of Third World farmers made it futile to begin at the bottom. 'Building on the best' was the slogan of the green revolution, and the 'best' was the richest

19 Bina Agarwal, 'Neither Sustenance Nor Sustainability: Agricultural Strategies, Ecological Degradation and Indian Women in Poverty', in *Structures of Patriarchy*, Delhi: Kali for Women, 1988.

20 Maria Mies, 'Capitalism and Subsistence :Rural Women in India', in *Development*, Vol. 4, 1984.

21 B.D. Jennings & K.O. Edmund, 'Science and Authority in International Agricultural Research', Bulletin of Concerned Asian Scholars, Vol. 14, October/December 1982.

TABLE 4

Women engaged in agriculture, 1951-1981

Year	Cultivators		Agricultural labourers	
	No. of workers (millions)	% of total female workers	No. of workers (millions)	% of total female workers
1951	18.4	45.42	12.7	31.37
1961	31.9	55.32	14.2	24.61
1971	9.2	29.73	15.8	50.99
1981	15.2	33.03	20.95	45.57

Source : Report of the Committee on the Status of Women in India, 1975, a'
Census of India, 1981.

farmers of the richest regions. As Anderson and Morrison have observed, the green revolution was 'a development policy made to order for the better-off peasant cultivator in the existing high yield areas'.[22] Excluding the poorer regions and poorer classes was an explicit, not a tacit, bias of the green revolution. In 1959, when a Ford Foundation mission of thirteen North American agronomists came on a mission to India, they rejected the alternative of simultaneous agricultural development in all of India's 550,000 villages. Instead, they advised subsidisation of technical inputs in those areas that were well-irrigated. Thus in the mid-sixties, India's New Agricultural Strategy to promote new seed varieties ended up concentrating on already privileged farmers, who in green revolution language became 'progressive' farmers. The rest were forced to move backward for lack of land, money, access to credit and political influence and were marginalised in their role as food producers.[23] Bhalla tells us that in both HYV wheat and HYV rice areas, 'the distribution of operated land has shifted in favour of big farmers'.[24] Kelkar, who has studied the effects of the green revolution in three villages in Etawah district, observes that the new technology excludes women and marginalises them. According to her, 'With the cultivation of cash crops entirely for the market, women have no decision-making power regarding the

22 R. Anderson & B.M. Morrison, *Science, Politics and the Agricultural Revolution in Asia*, Boulder: Westview, 1982, p. 6.

23 F.M. Lappe &]. Collins, *Food First*, London: Abacus, 1980, p. 104.

24 G.S. Bhalla, *Changing Structure of Agriculture in Haryana: A Study of the Impact of the Green Revolution*, Chandigarh, Punjab University, 1972.

requirement of grain at home. Economic principles are paramount when such decisions are made by men. Women with no control over expenditure or marketing lost authority at home. This has been the natural consequence of displacement from the spheres of work and market'.[25]

The masculinist equation of economic value and cash flows creates a split between the market economy controlled by men, and the survival economy supported by women. Commercialisation leads to increased burdens on women for producing survival and decreased valuation of their work on the market. This devaluation, combined with increased work burdens, reduces women's entitlement to food, nutrition, and even life itself. As women carry more burdens for society, they are increasingly seen as becoming a burden on society, and can be dispensed with, through discrimination, dowry deaths, and femicide.

The violence to women that arises from this epistemological and economic reductionism of agricultural maldevelopment takes place in two ways. The myth that chemicals and machines can replace the life in food and the life of the soil, dispenses with the productive role of women in conservation and in food production and processing. Work and labour that go into maintaining essential ecological processes on the farm and conserving nutrition in food are not registered on the linear scale of inputs and outputs that come from and feed distant markets. Commoditisation of food production thus either destroys the basis of women's work or devalues it. With the decline in the perceived or real productivity of women is associated a decline in their status in society and within the household. In the heart of the green revolution region of Punjab, the food

TABLE 5

Nutritional status of male and female children

	Normal nutrition		70-80% of expected weight		Less than 70% of expected weight	
	M	F	M %	F	M	F
Privileged	86	70	10	11	4	13
Under-privileged	43	26	43	24	14	50

25 Govind Kelkar, 'The Impact of the Green Revolution on Women's Work Participation and Sex Roles', paper presented at a seminar on Rural Development and Women, Mahabaleshwar, 1981.

abundance for the market has not been translated into nutrition for the girl child within the house. A study done in 1978 in Ludhiana district of Punjab[26] shows that the percentage of female children who were under-nourished was higher than that of undernourished male children within the same economic group.

A classic study by Srilata Batliwala[27] was the first attempt made at cal-culating the time and energy expenditure by men, women, and children in work in agricultural contexts. The study concluded that 'if we disag-gregate human energy, the contribution of men, women, and children is 31, 53, and 16 percent respectively (as percentages of total human hours per household per day)'. As discussed, with the commercialisation of the agricultural economy, women's work increases, but the very processes of maldevelopment which increase women's work in producing sustenance, decrease the value of women's work because it is linked to sustenance, not profits. Women are therefore paid less and fed less at the same time that increased work burdens call for higher wages and incomes and more food.

Lower food entitlements, associated with increased work burdens, is only the first and most immediate impact of the commercialisation of agriculture on women. Violence against women related to dowry issues has been found to be highest in the green revolution region of northwest India and is part of the general violence that is becoming endemic to Punjab. The green revolution as a breeding ground for the civil unrest and violence in the state has been analysed by me in a study done for the UNU.[28] As Bina Agarwal observes, 'the northwestern states of Punjab and Haryana rank amongst the highest in terms of the adoption of new green revolution technology. ... However, it is precisely the northwestern regions where discrimination against females is most noted, both his-torically and in the recent period'.[29] This region was also the first to turn amniocentesis into a modern form of female foeticide, by allowing the selective abortion of female foetuses. Between 1978 and 1983, 78,000 fe-male foetuses had been aborted after sex determination tests. The first sex determination clinic was set up in Amritsar in Punjab. People are

26 C. Sathyamala, *et al.*, *Taking Sides*, Madras: Asian Network for Innovative Training Trust, 1986, p. 146.

27 Srilata Batliwala, 'Rural Energy Scarcity and Nutrition', in *Economic and Political Weekly*, February 27, 1982.

28 Vandana Shiva, 'Violence and Natural Resource Conflict: A Case Study of Punjab', Report for the UNU, Tokyo, 1987.

29 Bina Agarwal, *op.cit.*

willing to pay up to Rs. 5,000 to be able to get rid of the 'dispensable sex'. As the menace of dowry spreads across the country, and across classes, the dispensability of the girl child also increases. About 84 percent of gynaecologists currently perform amniocentesis in Bombay and see it as 'a human service to women who do not want any more daughters'.[30] The costs of a sex determination test, and selective abortion of female foetuses are lower in terms of cash than the thousands of rupees needed for a girl's dowry. And in a world dominated increasingly by capitalist patriarchy, cash is the only measure of worth—of women as of everything else.

The Kallars, a landless community in Tamil Nadu, have, over the last 10 to 15 years, started routinely dispensing with their girl children. The logic of dispensability is linked to the green revolution which, through commercialisation, introduces differential wage labour, on the one hand (with men getting Rs. 13 a day and women getting Rs. 6) and, on the other, creates a demand for dowry which has driven the poverty-stricken community to female infanticide. The dowry system came to the Kallars after the dam on the Vaigai river brought irrigation water into Usilampatti, 25 years ago. With commercial prosperity came the increasing devaluation of women and increased dowry demands, and with increasing dowry demands came female infanticide. In each of the more than 300 Kallar villages in Usilampatti taluk, with populations ranging from 500 to 1,500, 20 to 50 girl babies have been killed in the last five years in the face of the excruciatingly cruel dowry problem. Underlying infanticide is dowry, and underlying them both is the green revolution in Usilampatti.[31]

The 'success' of the green revolution in India has often been contrasted to the failure of agriculture in Africa. The successful spread of the green revolution has also deepened the sex-bias against women. As Amartya Sen points out, the sex ratio has been falling systematically over the decades in India and is lower than that for Africa. In 1980 the sex ratio for Africa was 1.015 while that for India was 0.931. Sen calculates the number of women we could expect if the African sex ratio were to hold here. 'At the African ratio, there would have been nearly 30 million more women in India than actually live today'.[32] Contrary to received views that modernisation would liberate women from old discrimination and domination, the modernisation of agriculture in India is deepening old prejudices

30 R.P. Ravindra, *The Scarcer Half*, Bombay: CED, 1986.

31 S.H. Venkatramani. 'Female Infanticide: Born to Die', in *India Today*, June 15, 1986.

32 Amartya Sen, 'Africa and India: What Do We Learn from Each Other?' paper presented at the Eighth Economic Congress, New Delhi, 1986.

and introducing new biases and violence. The assumption of the substitutability and dispensability of nature and women that results from the dichotomies and dualisms of economic and scientific reductionism is the underlying cause for the desertification and death of soils on the one hand, and the deprivation, devaluation, and death of women on the other.

We have arrived at a major crisis in the very nature of the way we produce food that is impoverishing the land that is the primary capital for food production, as well as the people for whom food should be an entitlement and a right through their participation in food production. The green revolution approach has converted a recycling, self-renewing food system into a production line with hybrids and chemicals as inputs, and food commodities as outputs. Nature's food chains have been broken as multinational corporate 'food chains' gain control over the production and distribution of food.

Miracle seeds: breeding out the feminine principle

Seeds are the first link in the food chain. For five thousand years, peasants have produced their own seeds, selecting, storing and replanting, and letting nature take its course in the food chain. The feminine principle has been conserved through the conservation of seeds by women in their work in food and grain storage. With the preservation of genetic diversity and the self-renewability of food crops has been associated the control by women and Third World peasants on germ plasm, the source of all plant wealth. All this changed with the green revolution. At its heart lie new varieties of miracle seeds which have totally transformed the nature of food production and control over food systems: The 'miracle' seeds for which Borlaug got a Nobel Prize and which rapidly spread across the Third World, also sowed the seeds of a new commercialisation of agriculture. Borlaug ushered in an era of corporate control on food production by creating a technology by which multinationals acquired control over seeds, and hence over the entire food system. The green revolution commercialised and privatised seeds, removing control of plant genetic resources from Third World peasant women and giving it over to western male technocrats in CIMMYT, IRRI and multinational seed corporations.[33]

Women have acted as custodians of the common genetic heritage through the storage and preservation of grain. In a study of rural women

33 D. Morgan, *Merchants of Grain*, New York: Viking, 1979, p. 237.

of Nepal, it was found that seed selection is primarily a female responsibility. In 60.4 percent of the cases, women alone decided what type of seed to use, while men decided in only 20.7 percent. As to who actually performs the task of seed selection in cases where the family decides to use their own seeds, this work is done by women alone in 81.2 percent of the households, by both sexes in eight percent and by men alone in only 10.8 percent of the households. Throughout India, even in years of scarcity, grain for seed was conserved in every household, so that the cycle of food production was not interrupted by loss of seed. The peasant women of India have carefully maintained the genetic base of food production over thousands of years. This common wealth, which had evolved over millennia, was defined as 'primitive cultivars' by the masculinist view of seeds, which saw its own new products as 'advanced' varieties.[34] The masculinist breeding strategy of the green revolution was a strategy of breeding out the feminine principle by the destruction of the self-reproducing character and genetic diversity of seeds. The death of the feminine principle in plant breeding was the beginning of seeds becoming a source of profits and control. The hybrid 'miracle' seeds are a commercial miracle, because farmers have to buy new supplies of them every year: they do not reproduce themselves.[35] Grains from hybrids do not produce seeds that duplicate the same result because hybrids do not pass on their vigour to the next generation. With hybridisation, seeds could no more be viewed as a source of plant life, producing sustenance through food and nutrition: they were now a source of private profit only.

The myth of the miracle seeds

These new varieties of seeds have also been called high yielding varieties (HYV); the term is a misnomer, however, as pointed out by Ingrid Palmer in her fifteen nation study of the impact of the new seeds on agriculture.[36] 'Miracle' seeds are not high yielding in and of themselves; their distinguishing feature is that they are highly responsive to heavy inputs of irrigation and chemical fertilizers. It is therefore more appropriate to call them 'high-responsive varieties' (HRVs), because without the ideal inputs,

---

34 P.R. Mooney, *The Law of the Seed, in Development Dialogue*, Uppsala, Dag Hammerskjold Foundation, 1983.

35 D. Morgan, *op.cit.* p. 237.

36 In Lappe & Collins, *op.cit.*

their yield is extremely low. Traditional crop varieties, characterised by tall and thin straw, typically convert heavy doses of fertilizer into overall growth of the plant, rather than increasing grain yield alone. Commonly, the excessive growth of the plant causes the stalk to break, 'lodging' the grain on the ground, which results in heavy crop losses. The main characteristics of the 'miracle' seeds or high yielding varieties which started the process of the green revolution, was to avoid lodging by biologically engineering dwarf varieties through hybridisation. The important feature of these new varieties is not that they are particularly productive in themselves but that they can absorb three or four times the amount of fertilizer that traditional varieties do and convert it into grain, provided proportionately heavy and frequent irrigation applications are also available. In the context of higher inputs, the HYV seeds are resource-wasteful. Besides the heavy demands made on water and fertilizer, the new seeds have a high vulnerability to pests and diseases. The green revolution has been based on breeding crops which are 'impressively uniform genetically and impressively vulnerable'.[37] Uniformity is intrinsic to centralised seed production, which on the one hand displaces mixed cropping patterns and gives rise to monocultures, and on the other displaces genetic diversity in crops by the introduction of highly uniform hybrids. When compared to the cropping systems they displace, the hybrids are not 'high yielding' or 'improved' at all. In the context of genetic diversity, they are clearly inferior to the multitudinous strains of locally adapted varieties of crops. In 1968-69, in Pakistan for example, the yield of Mexican dwarf wheat declined by about 20 percent because of a two-thirds reduction in rainfall. The locally adapted varieties, however, were not adversely affected by the weather changes. In fact, their yields increased by 11 percent.[38]

The lower drought and pest resistance of new sorghum strains has led to severe crop failure, as observed in Dharwar district of Karnataka during a study undertaken for the United Nations University by the author.[39] Prior to 1965-66, indigenous sorghum varieties were cultivated with pulses like *madike**, *avare (Dolichos lablab)*, *togare (Cajanus indicus)*, *hesaru (Phascolus mungo)* and oilseeds like niger. A drought-resistant

37 J. Doyle, *Altered Harvest*, New York: Viking, 1985, p. 14.

38 Lappe & Collins, *op .cit.*

39 J. Bandyopadhyay, S.T.S. Reddy, et al., *High Yielding Varieties and Drought Vulnerability*, Dehradun: Research Foundation for Science, Technology and Natural Resource Policy, 1986.
*Possibly horsegram (*Dolichos biflorus*).

crop called *save (Panicrion miliare)* was also grown as an insurance against crop failure, since it is a quick-growing crop of three months duration which gives good yields of grain and straw even in low rainfall years, which can be considered famine years.

In the sixties, 'high yielding' sorghum was introduced into the area under irrigated conditions. The HYV being susceptible to pests needed pesticide spraying, which destroyed the pest-predator balance in neighbouring fields of indigenous varieties, which were now attacked by a new pest called midge. The midge reappeared year after year and the indigenous variety was wiped out by 1975-76. In Kurugund village, for example, the area under traditional varieties was 839.12 acres in 1960-65, 973.84 in 1970-71 and just four acres in 1975-76. In 1980-81 no area was sown with traditional varieties. Since sorghum is the main food-crop of the region, farmers were compelled to plant HYVS. In 1970-71 the area under HYVs was 99.06 acres; in 1980-81 it rose to 835 acres, but from 1982-83 the area started decreasing again: in 1982-83 it was 832.24, and by 1985-86 it was down to 460.15. The displacement of indigenous varieties has caused a severe reduction in fodder which has reduced the livestock population and therefore also the return of fertility to the soil, blocking the only mechanism for soil moisture conservation in rainfed land. The violence to animals by denying their right to food in order to apparently increase man's food supply is turned into violence to the soil as the producer of food, and ultimately boomerangs as violence to man himself through food scarcity. The yield of the HYVs which was seven to eight quintals per acre is down to less than four due to a complex web of ecological instability inherent in the HYV monoculture; high vulnerability to rainfall decrease and high pest and weed incidence are all associated with the displacement of mixed crops providing a complementary and diverse balance of foods for man and animal.

In the context of diverse outputs from the farm, the HYVs were not really high yielding even under the best conditions. They appeared high yielding because a whole system of cropping that provided diverse foods to man, animals, and the earth was reduced to the output of a single crop. The mixed crop of sorghum with green gram, black gram, niger, which are the source of protein in rural South India, was first reduced to sorghum alone, and then sorghum as a food and fodder crop was reduced to a food-crop alone. The dwarf varieties are necessary to avoid 'lodging' which is inevitable in the tall indigenous varieties with large irrigation and fertilizer inputs. Dwarfing, however, produces short and hard straw which is useless as animal fodder. The 'high yielding' sorghum was thus low yield-ing in the context of fodder production. In the reductionist view, the rest of the cropping system was invisible and was destroyed, even though it provided higher total outputs of food for people, animals, and soil, and even though it provided a sustainable strategy for growing food. When sorghum was cultivated as a mixed crop with pulses, the production per acre was 40 kgs of *madike*, 20 kgs of green gram, 10 kgs of black gram and 10 kgs of niger. Once HYV sorghum was introduced it displaced the mixed cropping: for example, in Kurugund in 1970-71 the area under madikewas 105.14 acres; by 1975-76 it was only 23.34. Pulses have either disappeared or have to be cultivated exclusively, putting a new demand on land. The high yield of HYV varieties is a reductionist fiction which is destroying the very capacity of ecosystems and people to produce food. The strategy for creating a fictitious abundance has become a means for creating real scarcity by destroying the quiet ways of nature's work, peasants' work and women's work. The sorghum-pulse intercrop, which the new seeds displaced, is simultaneously a means of maintaining soil fertility, con-trolling pests and disease and reducing vulnerability to rainfall failure. The dramatic visibility of a large sorghum grain manufactured in the lab and research stations, the drama of killing pests by spraying poisons, the obvious flow of water in large irrigation channels create a mind-set which fails to see the few kilograms of nutritious pulses which invisibly fix nitro-gen and provide it to their fellow sorghum plants, or the habitat in mixed crops for predators which keep pests under control, or the fodder for the cow and bullock and the organic matter from crops and animals which give back food to the soil, conserve moisture and keep soil alive. What it cannot see, it does not measure, and hence the new seeds of reductionist science destroy rich and productive farming systems, in total ignorance of what they destroy. Green revolution varieties of seeds were clearly not the best alternative for increasing food production from the point of view of nature, women, and poor peasants. They were useful for corporations that wanted to find new avenues in seeds and fertilizer sales, by displacing women peasants as custodians of seeds and builders of soil fertility, and they were useful for rich farmers wanting to make profits. The interna-tional agencies which financed research on the new seeds also provided the money for their distribution. The impossible task of selling a new va-riety to millions of small peasants who could not afford to buy the seeds was solved by the World Bank, UNDP, FAO, and a host of bilateral aid pro-grammes which began to accord high priority to the distribution of HYV

TABLE 6

Inputs and outputs per acre for traditional and HYV sorghum

INPUTS

	Fertilizer			Seed	
	Organic quantity	Price (Rs.)	Chemical quantity	Price (Rs.)	Price (Rs.)
Indigen-ous	2.00 tonnes	100.00	—	—	50.00
HYV	2.00 tonnes	100.00	15 kg	450.00	150.00

OUTPUTS

	Foodgrain yield		Fodder yield	
	Quantity	Price (Rs.)	Quantity	Price (Rs.)
Indigen-ous	Jowar 5 quintals	750	3.00 tonnes	600.00
	+ Madike 40 kg	120		
	+ Green gram 20 kg	120		
	+ Black gram 15 kg	40		
HYV	Jowar 4 quintals	600	1.00 tonnes	200.00

Whither the

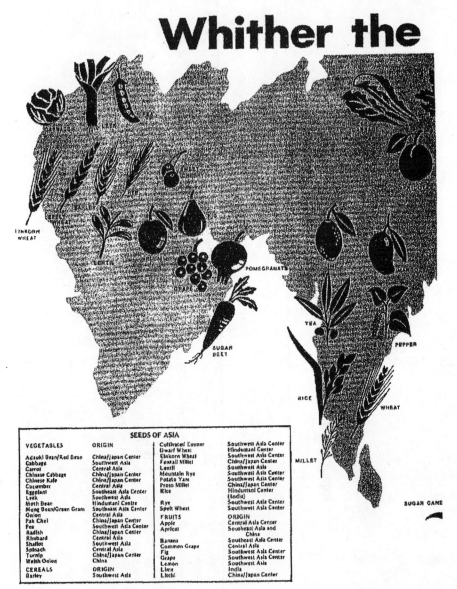

SEEDS OF ASIA

VEGETABLES	ORIGIN		
Adzuki Bean/Red Bean	China/Japan Center	Cultivated Emmer	Southwest Asia Center
Cabbage	Southwest Asia	Dwarf Wheat	Hindustani Center
Carrot	Central Asia	Einkorn Wheat	Southwest Asia Center
Chinese Cabbage	China/Japan Center	Foxtail Millet	China/Japan Center
Chinese Kale	China/Japan Center	Lentil	Southwest Asia
Cucumber	Central Asia	Mountain Rye	Southwest Asia Center
Eggplant	Southeast Asia Center	Potato Yam	Southwest Asia Center
Leek	Southwest Asia	Proso Millet	China/Japan Center
Moth Bean	Hindustani Centre	Rice	Hindustani Center (India)
Mung Bean/Green Gram	Southeast Asia Center	Rye	Southwest Asia Center
Onion	Central Asia	Spelt Wheat	Southwest Asia Center
Pak Choi	China/Japan Center	FRUITS	ORIGIN
Pea	Southwest Asia Center	Apple	Central Asia Center
Radish	China/Japan Center	Apricot	Southeast Asia and China
Rhubarb	Central Asia	Banana	Southeast Asia Center
Shallot	Southwest Asia	Common Grape	Central Asia
Spinach	Central Asia	Fig	Southwest Asia Center
Turnip	China/Japan Center	Grape	Southwest Asia Center
Welsh Onion	China	Lemon	Southwest Asia
CEREALS	ORIGIN	Lime	India
Barley	Southwest Asia	Litchi	China/Japan Center

Source: Balai, No. 7, 1983, Manila.

Seeds of Asia?

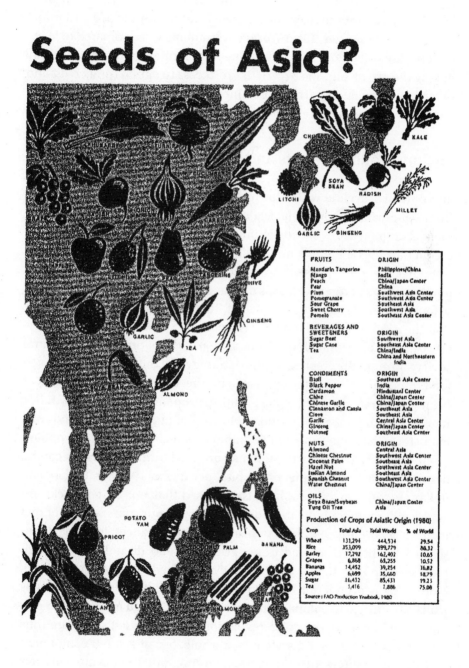

FRUITS	ORIGIN
Mandarin Tangerine	Philippines/China
Mango	India
Peach	China/Japan Center
Pear	China
Plum	Southwest Asia Center
Pomegranate	Southwest Asia Center
Sour Grape	Southeast Asia
Sweet Cherry	Southwest Asia
Pomelo	Southeast Asia Center

BEVERAGES AND SWEETENERS	ORIGIN
Sugar Beet	Southwest Asia
Sugar Cane	Southeast Asia Center
Tea	China/India
	China and Northeastern India

CONDIMENTS	ORIGIN
Basil	Southeast Asia Center
Black Pepper	India
Cardamon	Hindustani Center
Chive	China/Japan Center
Chinese Garlic	China/Japan Center
Cinnamon and Cassia	Southeast Asia
Clove	Southeast Asia
Garlic	Central Asia Center
Ginseng	China/Japan Center
Nutmeg	Southeast Asia Center

NUTS	ORIGIN
Almond	Central Asia
Chinese Chestnut	Southwest Asia Center
Coconut Palm	Southeast Asia
Hazel Nut	Southwest Asia Center
Indian Almond	Southeast Asia
Spanish Chestnut	Southwest Asia Center
Water Chestnut	China/Japan Center

OILS	
Soya Bean/Soybean	China/Japan Center
Tung Oil Tree	Asia

Production of Crops of Asiatic Origin (1980)

Crop	Total Asia	Total World	% of World
Wheat	131,294	444,534	29.54
Rice	353,099	399,779	86.32
Barley	17,292	162,402	10.65
Grapes	6,868	65,255	10.52
Bananas	14,452	39,254	16.82
Apples	6,699	35,660	18.79
Sugar	16,432	85,431	19.23
Tea	1,416	1,886	75.08

Source: FAO Production Yearbook, 1980

seed in their aid programmes. The seed corporations which were increasingly being integrated with chemical companies, could sell seeds to Third World government agencies and let them bear the burden of distribution. With international aid, Third World governments were prepared to heavily subsidise prices and also to force peasant farmers to buy new seed by linking the use of 'improved' varieties to access to agricultural credit and other inputs, including irrigation. Third World peasants did not always choose the new seeds: they were often forced on them.[40]

The myth of high yields and food self-sufficiency

There are two levels at which the matter of food self-sufficiency, based on the green revolution in India, is a myth. At the microlevel, the displacement of crop mixtures of cereals, pulses, and oilseeds by monocultures of commoditised HYV crops undermines food self-sufficiency in a drastic way. First, the small peasant, who does not fit into the credit, purchased inputs and cash crop package, is displaced, losing his or her entitlement to food that food production provided. There is ample evidence available that the green revolution had a class bias and worked against the interests of the small peasant. The dispossession of the poorer sections of rural society through the green revolution strategy and their reduced access to food resources is, in part, responsible for the appearance of surpluses at the macro-level. The surplus, according to prominent economist, V.K.R.V. Rao, is a myth because it is created by lack of purchasing power. While food stocks had shot up from 63 million tonnes in 1966 to 128 million tonnes in 1985, food consumption had dropped from 480 gms per capita, per day in 1965 to 463 gms per capita, per day in 1985. Dr. C Gopalan, India's leading nutritionist, has also stressed that 'our buffer stocks are apparently more an indication of the povery of our masses than of real food surplus'. Large numbers of peasants who produced food for themselves have been displaced from agriculture and do not have enough purchasing power to buy commercially produced and distributed food. Moreover, the production of essential foodgrains like pulses and oilseeds which are critical to balanced food intake has declined in absolute terms under the impact of the green revolution. The increased yields are thus not reflective of the food system as a whole, but of a small component of it that is of interest to the market. Overall, nutrition availability has

40 P.R. Mooney, *op. cit.*

declined. If one also includes the costs to the farm ecosystem in terms of soil degradation, waterlogging, salinity, and desertification, the green revolution has actually reduced productivity, instead of increasing it.

The green revolution has displaced not just seed varieties but entire crops in the Third World. Just as people's seeds were declared 'primitive' and 'inferior' by the green revolution ideology, foodcrops were declared 'marginal', 'inferior', and 'coarse grained'. Only a biased agricultural science rooted in capitalist patriarchy could declare nutritious crops like *ragi* and *jowar* 'inferior'. Peasant women know the nutrition needs of their families and the nutritive content of the crops they grow. Among foodcrops they prefer those with maximum nutrition to those with a value in the market. What have usually been called 'marginal crops' or 'coarse grains' are nature's most productive crops in terms of nutrition. That is why women in Garhwal continue to cultivate *mandua* and women in Karnataka cultivate *ragi* in spite of of all attempts by state policy to shift to cash crops and commercial foodgrains, to which all financial incentives of agricultural 'development' are tied. Table 7 illustrates how what the green revolution has declared 'inferior' grains are actually superior in nutritive content to the so-called 'superior' grains, rice, and wheat.[41] A woman in a Himalayan village once told me, 'Without our *mandua* and *jhangora*, we could not labour as we do. These grains are our source of health and strength'.

The most extreme example of this polarised vision is that of *bathua*, an important green leafy vegetable with very high nutritive value which

TABLE 7

Nutritional content of different foodcrops

	Protein (gms.)	Minerals (100 gms)	Ca (mg)	Fe (100 gms.)
Bajra	11.6	2.3	42	5.0
Ragi	7.3	2.7	344	6.4
Jowar	10.4	1.6	25	5.8
Wheat (milled)	11.8	0.6	23	2.5
Rice (milled)	6.8	0.6	10	3.1

41 C. Gopalan, et al., *Nutritive Values of Indian Foods*, Hyderabad: National Institute of Nutrition, 1981.

grows as an associate of wheat. When women weed the wheat field they do not merely contribute to the productivity of wheat; they actually harvest a rich source of nutrition for their families. However, with intensive chemical fertilizer use bathua becomes a major competitor of wheat and has been declared a 'weed' that is killed with herbicides and weedicides. The food cycle is broken, women are deprived of work, children are deprived of a free source of nutrition. The crops that the green revolution destroys are thus not marginal in the context of nutrition and survival, but in the context of the market and of commodity production of food for profit. The bias against people's seeds and people's crops translates into a bias against women's work in the production of sustenance. Since diversity works against the logic of centralisation and control, genetic diversity must be destroyed. In effect, global agricultural strategies are breeding out those links in the food chain which are of high value to women's work in the survival economy and which have traditionally been under their control. The green revolution in Punjab reduced food values by displacing the traditional cereal-pulse-oilseed mixed cropping patterns and reducing the production of pulses and oilseeds. The rapid spread of HYV rice and wheat took place at the cost of pulses and oilseeds, as shown in Table 8.[42]

TABLE 8
Changes in cropping patterns in Punjab
(percent of cropped area)

	1966-67	1971-72	1976-77	1981-82	1985-86
Wheat	31.09	40.81	41.84	42.05	43.90
Rice	5.50	7.86	10.81	18.31	23.73
Pulses	13.38	6.71	6.28	4.69	3.48
Oilseeds	6.24	5.57	3.98	3.25	2.93

The implications of the centralised control of genetic resources is best illustrated by the case of rice, the staple food for most of Asia. India once used to have four lakh rice varieties. Over the last half century, she has probably grown over 30,000 different varieties of rice. With the green revolution, this genetic diversity is fast being eroded, as uniform populations of hybrids are introduced from IRRI. The International Rice

42 S.S. Johl, *Diversification of Agriculture in Punjab*, a report submitted to the Government of Punjab, 1986.

Research Institute was set up in 1959 by the Rockefeller and Ford Foundations, nine years after the establishment of a premier Indian institute, the Central Rice Research Institute (CRRI) in Cuttack. The Cuttack Institute was working on rice research based on indigenous knowledge and genetic resources, a strategy clearly in conflict with the American controlled strategy of the International Rice Research Institute. The director of CRRI was removed, under international pressure, when he resisted handing over his collection of rice germ plasm to IRRI, as well as the hurried introduction of the HYV rice varieties from IRRI.[43]

The Madhya Pradesh government gave a small stipend to the ex-director of CRRI so that he could continue his work at the Madhya Pradesh Rice Research Institute at Raipur. On this shoestring budget, he conserved 20,000 indigenous rice varieties in situ in India's rice bowl in Chattisgarh.[44] Later the MPRRI, which was doing pioneering work in developing a high yielding strategy based on the decentred knowledge of the Chattisgarh tribals, was also closed down under pressure from the World Bank (which was linked to IRRI through CGIAR) because it had reservations about sending its germ plasm collection to IRRI. While reducing the genetic base in rice farming IRRI is becoming the new monopoly of the world's genetic wealth in rice. As observed by the scientists of the Central Rice Research Institute, 'The introduction of high yielding varieties has brought about a marked change in the status of insect pests like gall midge, brown plant hopper, leaf folder, whore maggot, etc. Most of the high yielding varieties released so far are susceptible to major pests, with a crop loss of 30 to 100 percent. Most of the HYVs used today are derivatives of T(N) or IR-8 and therefore have the dwarfing gene of Dee-geo-woo-gen (DGWG). This narrow genetic base has created alarming uniformity, causing vulnerability to diseases and pests. Most of the released varieties are not suitable for tropical uplands and lowlands, which together constitute about 75 percent of the total rice area of the country.[45] Because of these vulnerabilities, the dwarf varieties brought from IRRI have failed to improve yields in traditional rice growing systems'.[46]

43 R.H. Richaria, 'The Crisis in Rice Research', paper presented at 'The Crisis in Modern Science' Conference, Penang, 1986.

44 Claude Alvares, 'The Great Gene Robbery' in *The Illustrated Weekly of India*, March 23, 1986, p. 9.

45 'Rice Research in India—An Overview', (anon.), CRRI, Cuttack, 1980.

46 Bharat Dogra, 'Empry Stomachs and Packed Godowns', New Delhi, 1987.

With the centralised production and transfer of HYV rice seed has come the transfer of diseases. Virus diseases did not exist in India prior to 1962—they came in with the dwarf varieties from IRRI. Gone is the resistance built on diversity; in its place comes vulnerability. Gone is nature as a source for seeds; in its place come agribusiness and seed corporations. Gone is the decentred local knowledge of millions of tribals and peasants; in its place comes one centralised research institute with largely male, largely white 'experts' who prescribe green revolution rice agriculture to farmers in 111 countries, in uplands and lowlands, in mountains and coastal regions.

The result has been a total undermining of the ecology and economics of rice farming, in particular, and agriculture in general. For equivalent fertilization, the high yielding varieties produce about the same total biomass as traditional rice. They increase the grain yield at the cost of the straw.[47] Thus, while traditional rice produces four to five times as much straw as grain, high yielding rice typically produces a one-to-one ratio of grain to straw. A conversion from traditional to high yielding rice increases the grain available but decreases the straw. The scarcity in straw ultimately reduces biomass availability for fodder and mulch, leading to a breakdown in nutrient recycling.

The IRRI strategy was quite clearly not the best for the rice farmers of Asia. Variety IR-8, released in 1966, suffered serious attacks of bacterial blight in 1968-69. In 1970-71 the rice tungro virus destroyed IR-8 crops throughout the Philippines. The IR-20 which replaced IR-8 in 1971-72 was bred with resistance against bacterial blight and the tungro virus. By 1973 outbreaks of brown plant hopper and grassy stunt virus had destroyed IR-20 in most Philippine provinces. This was superseded by IR-26 in 1974-75, which was attacked by a new strain of the plant hopper. By 1976, another variety, IR-36, was introduced which was threatened by new diseases-ragged stunt and witted stunt.[48]

Indigenous varieties do not have these pest problems, nor is their pest resistance obtained at the cost of yields. The tribals of Chattisgarh breed varieties with normal yields as high as those of HYV under ideal conditions. This strategy gains an advantage because rice strains are adapted to the local environment, they maintain a wide base in genetic diversity and rice farmers of the region use such breeding technologies

47 F. Denton, 'Rice is More than a Dietary Staple: A Study of Its Non-Food Uses', *Ceres*, Vol. 13, No. 3, May-June 1985.

48 R.H. Richaria quoted in Claude Alvares, *op.cit.*

themselves. As Richaria points out, 'The rice farmers are sleeping giants, but they have been tamed by modern science to tell them that their centuries old experience and knowledge are no good. That is not correct. Existence of thousands of rice varieties in India, prior to 1900 when Mendelism was rediscovered, is a testimony to the knowledge and experience which has descended down the generations'.

Bayliss-Smith,[49] in his review of twenty-two rice growing systems, has observed that the green revolution is not the only way of raising yields. Wet rice has the capacity of more and more intensification, a process called 'involution' by Geertz.[50] Such strategies include examples such as double-cropping of rice with broad beans in organically manured fields in Yunnan in China which gives two to three times the yield of green revolution grains. The western model propagated by IRRI was clearly not the only alternative, and it was not the best. It was power, profits and control, not yields, that made global corporate and international aid interests opt for the 'miracle' seeds which made peasants dependent on internationally produced seeds and chemicals. Other alternatives would have left control with women and peasants, and would have kept people fed, but would not have generated profits. As Lappe and Collins observe, the green revolution was a political imperative. 'Historically, the green revolution represented a choice to breed seed varieties that produce high yields under optimum conditions. It was a choice not to start by developing seeds better able to withstand drought or pests. It was a choice not to concentrate first on improving traditional methods of increasing yields, such as mixed cropping. It was a choice not to develop technology that was productive, labour-intensive, and independent of foreign input supply. It was a choice not to concentrate on reinforcing the balanced, traditional diets of grain plus legumes'.[51]

The failures of the green revolution are now apparent both to farmers and to those in global think-tanks. Farmers have stopped using 'miracle' seeds. In Kerala, women rice farmers are reported to have said, 'When we sowed only government approved varieties we had a loss'.[52] In Philippines,

49 T.P. Bayliss-Smith 'Energy Use, Food Production and Welfare: Perspectives on the Efficiency of Agricultural Systems' in G.A. Harrison (ed.), *Energy and Effort*, Basingstoke: Taylor and Francis, 1982.

50 C. Geertz, *Agricultural Innovation: The Process of Ecological Change in Indonesia*, Berkeley: University of California Press, 1963.

51 Lappe & Collins, *op.cit.* p. 114.

52 K. Saradamoni, *op.cit.*

rice farmers called the IRRI seeds 'seeds of imperialism',[53] and in Negros, they are shifting again to traditional seeds as a basis of agriculture which is ecological and equitable. As a visitor to Negros observed, 'The "green revolution" of the '70s made a mockery of two beautiful words. But in Negros we had the feeling that we were seeing the beginning of a genuine green revolution; that is genuinely green and genuinely revolutionary'.[54] As the myth of the miracle seed gets exposed, international agencies are talking of going 'beyond the green revolution'.[55] The post-green revolution era could be based on a recovery of the feminine principle in agriculture consisting of a recovery of genetic diversity, self-renewability, and self-sufficiency in food production, with control in the hands of those who provide sustenance. It could, however, also involve a more rapid breeding out of the feminine principle by deepening trends towards uniformity and vulnerability, and transferring the control of seeds and crops from the hands of women and peasants into the hands of corporate giants.

From the green revolution to biotechnology

Seeds and chemicals have been the two most important inputs for the green revolution. With the biotechnology revolution, these inputs will get fully integrated, as multinational chemical companies start taking over the business of plant breeding and entire university research programmes. The integration of corporate interests will further break down the cycles of nature,[56] and delink women from the food chain.

Biotechnologies are making the hitherto hidden convergences between knowledge, power, and profits explicit. The frontiers of genetic engineering research are not being innocently charted in institutions of learning; they are being worked on in 350 firms ranging from large multinationals to small biotech companies. Biotechnology corporations have merged with seed companies which are also producers of fertilizers and pesticides. The new seeds will be engineered within the old corporate control of Dow, Du Pont, Eli Lilly, Exxon, Merck, Monsanto, Pfizer,

53 Claude Alvares, *op.cit.*

54 D. Lummins, 'Starving in Sugar-land: A Visit to Negros', in *AMPO, Japan–Asia Quarterly Review*, Vol. 18, No. 1, 1986.

55 E. Wolfe, *Beyond the Green Revolution*, Washington: World Watch Paper No. 73, October 1986.

56 P.R. Mooney, *op.cit.*; and H. Hobbelink, *New Hope or False Promise: Biotechnology and Third World Agriculture*, Brussels: ICDA 1987; and Doyle, *op.cit.*

Upjohn, etc. The new, smaller biotechnology corporations will sooner or later merge with the large multinationals, because biologists active in the industrialisation and commercialisation of their research will find it best for profits. A corporate assessment is that at the turn of the century only five multinationals will survive as integrated seed and chemical corporations. Scientists accept that in the future, goals of biotechnology research will be for profit not for public interest.[57]

No more will the separation of science and profits work as a patriarchal fiction because the universities, the modern intellectual 'commons' are being totally 'corporatised' and privatised. Companies are buying up scientists and entire departments and programmes with multimillion-dollar, multi-year contracts.[58]

Biotechnology is more explicitly integrating the corporate food chain with agribusiness and chemical multinationals, breeding crops to suit the needs of the food processing and pesticide industries. This has already started to happen in India, with a biotech nology prescription to solve the problems created by the green revolution in Punjab. A proposal has been submitted to set up a biotechnology research centre for seeds, tied up with a component of exporting processed fruits and vegetables as a collaboration between Pepsico, the U.S. multinational, Tata, and Punjab AgroIndustries Corporation.[59] A pro-Pepsi commentator has called it 'a catalyst for the next agricultural revolution'.[60] Why has it become important to have a second green revolution so soon after the first? And does the second revolution not aggravate the ecological, economic, and political vulnerabilities that the first introduced? In less than two decades, the farmers of Punjab have found that the miracle seeds were not such a miracle after all. Over the years yields and profit margins on rice and wheat in Punjab have stagnated or fallen and are creating an imperative for diversification. The reduced diversity of the genetic base and of cropping patterns is the cause of the ecological and economic problems of green revolution farming in Punjab. The response required to manoeuvre this ecological cul-de-sac is to recover the genetic diversity of living resources

57 S.H. Wittwer, 'The New Agriculture: A View of the Twenty-first Century', in J.W. Rosenblum, *Agriculture in the 21st Century*, New York: Wiley Interscience, 1983, p. 352.

58 M. Kenney, *Bio-technology: The University-Industrial Complex*, New Haven: Yale University Press, 1986.

59 'PAB Refers Pepsico Tie-up Move to Form Ministry', Bombay: *Economic Times*, September 11, 1986.

60 Prem Shankar Jha, 'Punjab: Programme for Peace', *Times of India*, December 11, 1986.

in agriculture, to maintain the health of soils, to use water more prudently and to minimise the risk of pests and diseases. The new call for diversification does not however spring from an ecological basis but from corporate perceptions of commodities. The 'diversification' of Punjab agriculture has been distorted to mean a shift away from staple foodcrop production towards export-oriented production, on an even narrower and more unstable genetic base than the green revolution. The Pepsi project has been floated in this corporate context of 'diversification'; it indicates new political and economic control of living resources, new ecological vulnerabilities, new levels of genetic erosion and new sources of dispossession and dislocation for women and marginal communities. It is a significant watershed in Indian agricultural and land use policy because it introduces new dimensions in the politics of food and of genetic resources, simultaneously threatening food production, food entitlements and the erosion of genetic diversity, and transferring the control of our land and genetic wealth to multinational companies.

The Pepsi project is aimed primarily at producing and processing fruits and vegetables for export. In this, it is a departure from the green revolution which focussed on commercial wheat and rice production for the satisfaction of domestic needs. The project envisages exports of Rs. 55 crores in the first year alone. About 74 percent of the total outlay of Rs. 22 crores on the project is in the processed food sector which will utilise one lakh tonnes of fruit and vegetables. These will be grown on land that now grows cereals. If, as a catalyst, Pepsi triggers off the large-scale transfer of land from staple foods to cash crops for export, who will grow the food? There is, of course, a dependency prescription that countries like India should stop producing food and should buy it from the U.S. Apart from the fact that politically, such dependence violates basic concepts of food security, economically, too, it is invalid because not only do cash crops produce no food, they do not produce much cash either over time. As Lloyd Timberlake states in the context of Africa's food crisis, 'The main drawback to cash crops is that over the past decade they have produced less and less cash.' As the area under crop commodities for export grows, prices fall and returns decline instead of increasing. As a showpiece, the Pepsi project is less portentious than as a catalyst, because in its latter aspect it will put India on the path to debt, dispossession and agricultural decline, such that have been created in Africa and Latin America. Clairmonte and Cavanagh observe—'The outcome, like a Greek tragedy, is ineluctable. Third World countries are literally being driven to market fatter and fatter volumes of commodities at lower and lower prices on the global market in return for higher priced goods and services imports'.[61]

The cash crop export strategy has been tried elsewhere and is a sure prescription for food scarcity and spiralling debt burdens. Africa's food crisis and hunger and famine are linked directly to the underdevelopment of her food production by cash crop development. As Africa invested more heavily in cash crops, food production declined. Scarce resources have been diverted to cash crops, undermining the cultivation of food and causing major ecological instability. According to the Earth Resources Institute's report, *Agribusiness in Africa*,[62] as recently as 1970 she was producing enough food to feed herself. By 1984, 140 million Africans out of a total of 531 million were fed with grain from abroad, because by the end of the 1970s, the economies of many African nations were tied to export-oriented cash crop production. Dependence on single crop commodities for export is in large measure at the root of Africa's ecological, economic and human crises. That for women cash crops bring about a new marginalisation, has already been established in the last section. In spite of of the failure of an export-oriented strategy as a solution to the food crisis and the problem of hunger, the biotechnology revolution is being sold as the new answer to food abundance. And as the last miracle is buried, talk of the promise and power of the new miracles of biotechnologies and genetic engineering is increasingly being heard. The Pepsi project too, promotes biotechnologies which will engineer fruit and vegetable seeds to make them more appropriate for processing, and Pepsico has already integrated its seed and processing business with biotechnologies like clonal propagation and tissue culture.

The 'greatest biological revolution of all time' might well turn out to be the most effective triage against the biology of nature and women, in its response to the profit motive through breeding 'super' plants, 'super' trees, and 'super' seeds. The superiority, of course, will be determined by the reductionist mind, and 'superiority' and 'inferiority' will be new dualisms—cultural creations of a biotechnology based on criteria of profitability alone. The ultimate ecological and cultural impact of this new reductionism will be the annihilation of diversity and sustainability in nature and of basic human needs and rights, as a direct consequence.

61 F.F. Clairmonte & J.L Cavanagh, 'Third World Debt: The Approaching Holocaust', *Economic and Political Weekly*, Vol. 21, No. 31.

62 B. Dinham & C. Hines, *Agribusiness in Africa*, London: Earth Resources Research, 1985.

We do not need genetic engineering to put nitrogen-fixing genes on maize and millet when women and peasants, for centuries, have used the more ecological option of intercropping maize with nitrogen-fixing beans, and millet with nitrogen-fixing pulses. It is not that nature is inadequate, only that corporations cannot make profits without manipulating nature. Transferring nitrogen-fixing genes to cereals becomes a source of profit even as it threatens the source of life held in nature's seeds. And even as masculinist technologies destroy seeds as sources of life, genetic engineering and biotechnologies are held up as the solution to genetic erosion. But such confidence is highly misplaced, as Miguel Mota points out:

> To 'make' new varieties, breeders have to look for the desired genes, which may exist in an old variety or in wild plants. If such material is not available the difficulties may not be overcome because genetics, despite all the wonders it is now capable of doing, is not yet capable of 'making' a gene 'by measure'. We can recombine genes, transfer genes from the cells of a species to cells of a very different species, we can mutate genes, we can even 'multiply' a gene in vitro. Some of today's genetics would be considered wild science fiction 20 years ago. But we do not know how to build up a gene to make wheat resistant to $-5\,^{\circ}$ C. below the present maximum resistance or to make it with three times more lysine in its flour. If we don't have these genes somewhere—maybe in an insignificant weed or a very old variety—we just cannot make a wheat with those characteristics.[63]

Because of the fact that the germ plasm of the world lies in the forests and fields of the Third World, either as old cultivated varieties of crops, or in the wild, the conservation of genetic resources lies in the hands of Third World women, tribals, and peasants. As in all other attempts to protect the sources of life and to conserve the feminine principle, women peasants will probably again take the lead in the politics of seeds.

The death of soils

The fertility of the earth is contained in the thin layer of topsoil which supports all plant life, and which is, in turn, protected by plants. The women of Chipko often describe their struggle as one aimed at protecting this 'skin of the earth' which, when it is peeled off through erosion or dam-

63 M. Mota quoted in Mooney, *op.cit.* p. 19.

aged through loss of nutrients and moisture, leaves the earth wounded and diseased. Women tribals of Orissa sang Mati Devta Dharam Devta (the soil is our goddess, the soil is our faith) when they kissed the earth before being dragged away by the police in their struggle against the ruination of their sacred Gandhamardhan hill.[64]

Today, the soils of India are dying, and the most fertile among them are dying because of the violence of green revolution technologies. The carefully evolved soil building strategies of women's work in organic agriculture have been disrupted overnight by western scientific arrogance which sees fertilizer factories as the only source of soil nutrients, and dams and large scale irrigation as the only source of plant moisture. As a study from Nepal states, 'reports from field observations made by project researches indicate that in all the communities where chemical fertilizer is in common use, it is men who decide on and apply them, while women have almost the complete responsibility for preparation and application of organic manure'. The important role of women in organic agriculture has already been discussed. Here we will focus on how organic practises build and protect soils.

TABLE 9
Fertilizer application by sex

		Male	Female	Both	Total
Organic	(No)	43	251	547	841
	(%)	5.1	29.9	65.	100
Chemical	(No)	65	22	2	89
	(%)	73.0	24.7	2.3	100
Mixture	(No)	109	144	107	360
	(%)	30.3	40.0	29.0	100
Total	(No)	217	417	656	1290
	(%)	16.8	32.3	50.9	100

Soil-building strategies of traditional agriculture

Soil erosion is a major problem in India, and is more prevalent where mixed crops have been replaced by monocultures. As the International Institute

64 Sunderlal Bahuguna, 'Mali Devta, Dharma Devta: A Report on the Save Gandhmardhan Campaign', mimeo, 1986.

for Tropical Agriculture has shown, soil erosion and run-off losses are proportionately less from mixed as compared with sole cropping systems.[65]

TABLE 10
**Soil loss and run-off with monoculture (cassava)
and mixed cropping (cassava with maize)**

Slope	Soil loss (tonnes/ha/annum)		Run-off (%)	
	Monoculture	Mixed cropping	Monoculture	Mixed cropping
1	2.7	2.5	18	14
5	87.4	49.9	43	33
10	125.1	85.5	20	18
15	221.1	137.3	30	19

Mixed cropping, especially with leguminous associates of cereals,
also enhances soil fertility through nitrogen fixing. The mixing of cereals
and pulses, as is the traditional practise in India, tends to help both crops
and soils. Traditional cropping patterns are always based on production
of organic matter as food and nutrition for the soil, either directly, or
through animals. Crop residues and animal waste are recycled carefully
to maintain soil fertility and prevent soil erosion. Table 11 shows how soil
erosion is linked to the organic matter content of soils.[66]

TABLE 11
**Effect of mulch rate on run-off and soil loss
on uncropped land (rainfall = 61.1 mm)**

Mulch rate (tonnes/ha)	Run-off (%)	Soil loss (tonnes/ha)
0	50.0	4.83
2	19.7	2.48
4	8.0	0.52
6	1.2	0.05

65 R. Lal, 'Soil Conserving versus Soil-Degrading Crops and Soil Management for Erosion
Control' in D.]. Greenland & R Lal (eds.), *Soil Conservation and Management in the Humid
Tropics*, New York: John Wiley and Sons, 1977.

66 R. Lal, *op. cit.*

Mixed cropping and organic manuring also reduce the risk of crop failure through reducing vulnerability to drought and pests. In arid zones where vegetative growth both in forests as well as farms is entirely dependent on recharge of soil moisture, organic matter or humus enhances the water retentivity of soils by two to five times. This mechanism of conserving water as soil moisture is of vital importance in the tropics where rainfall is seasonal and has to be effectively stored in the soil to support plant growth during the arid periods. Conserving soil moisture is an insurance against desertification in arid climates.[67] The All India Coordinated Project on Dryland Farming has shown that mulch was responsible for increased food productivity in dry land farming.[68]

TABLE 12

Vertical mulching and sorghum yields/grain yield (kg/ha)

Interval of vertical mulch	'72-'73	'73-'74	'74-'75	'75-'76	'77-'78
4 m	400	1690	1780	1250	1540
8 m	280	1610	1770	1120	1902
Control	20	1120	1100	1080	1470

Besides the technology of water conservation in soil through organic matter, intercropping is another technology for avoiding crop failure in rainfed farming. Sole-cropped sorghum has been found to fail once in eight years and pigeon-pea once in five years, but a sorghum-pigeon-pea intercrop fails only once in 36 years in experiments carried out by the Project on Dryland Farming.

Green revolution: a recipe for desertification

The crisis of desertification and the death of soils has been the result of the following aspects of the green revolution policy: *(a)* introduction of large scale monocultures and uniform cropping patterns; *(b)* high nutrient uptake and low organic nutrient returns to soil by the new hybrid varieties of crops; and *(c)* high water demand and low water conservation

67 V.A. Kovda, *Land Aridisation and Drought Control*, Boulder: Westview, 1980.

68 J. Venkateswarlu, 'Improving the Management of Black Cotton Soils', ICRISAT, 1981.

functions of the new hybrid and cash crop cultivation. There has, consequently, been increased soil and nutrient loss, water-logging, salinisation, and drought and desertification.

It has been the assumption of the green revolution that the nutrient
loss and deficit can be made up by the one-time use of non-renewable
inputs of potash, phosphorous and nitrates as chemical fertilizers. Phosphorous and potash derived from geological deposits, and petroleum-
derived nitrogen are a non-renewable input, the extraction and processing
of which have their own negative externalities. Western reductionist
thinking has led most analysts to see only the possibilities of supplying
nutrients for intensive food production systems from virgin sources. The
narrowness of this vision has thus led us to plan and rely on development
solutions which are non-sustainable. Such a model based on dramatic increases in the use of virgin nutrients which have markedly escalating costs
and finite reserves is clearly non-sustainable. Howard has called this the
NPK mentality, the roots of which according to him lie in the Great War.
'The feature of the manuring of the west is the use of artificial manures.
The factories engaged during the Great War in the fixation of atmospheric
nitrogen for the manufacture of explosives had to find other markets; the
use of nitrogenous fertilizers in agriculture increased, until today the majority of farmers and market gardeners base their manurial programme
on the cheapest forms of nitrogen (N), phosphorus (P), and potassium (K)
on the market. What may be conveniently described as the NPK mentality
dominates farming alike in the experimental stations and the countryside.
Vested interests, entrenched in a time of national emergency, have gained
a stranglehold'.[69]

The experience of the green revolution in Punjab clearly demon-
strates that the chemical approach to soil fertility has its limits. Increased
NPK applications are not able to maintain productivity, and the Punjab
Agriculture University's research has shown that organic inputs are necessary to maintain yields.[70] Green manure has been found to increase
yields of crops such as mustard and pigeon-pea as shown in Tables 13
and 14.

The organic route to soil fertility which was excluded by the chemical route of the green revolution is in conflict with the latter because it
changes the very basis of categories of productivity and yield. In the reductionist paradigm there is a bias to see straw production as 'waste' and

69 Howard, *op.cit*
70 Report from the Department of Soils, Ludhiana: Punjab Agricultural University, 1986.

TABLE 13

Impact of green manuring on grain yield of mustard (t/ha).

N-applied (kg/ba)	Without green manuring	With green manuring	Response to green manuring
0	0.46	0.76	0.30
50	0.58	1.06	0.48
100	0.74	0.16	0.42
150	0.88	1.21	0.33
Mean	0.67	1.05	0.38

TABLE 14

Impact of green manuring on grain yield of pigeon-pea (t/ha)

N-applied (kg/ba)	Without green manuring	With green manuring	Response to green manuring
0	0.34	0.97	0.63
30	0.74	1.11	0.37
45	0.86	1.33	0.47
60	0.94	1.42	0.48
Mean	0.72	1.21	0.49

hence to engineer crops to reduce the straw-grain ratio. Similarly, green manure crops which were not sold but used to recycle nutrients in the field were seen as 'waste' in the commercial context but are now emerging as productive in the ecological context. Conflicts over concepts of fertility are conflicts over concepts of productivity, based either on the inclusion or exclusion of the feminine principle. The crisis of the green revolution is the conflict of interest created in each individual farmer between producing biomass for maintaining the nutrient cycle, and producing biomass to sell on the market. The ecological and feminine imperative demands that the former not be neglected, but the masculinist definition of 'rationality' and 'progressiveness' as profit maximisation forces the farmers to act against the ecological option. If, however, rationality is defined as sustainable resource use, the green revolution is no longer a miracle and its 'improvements' at the scientific and economic levels disappear. In the holistic perspective the indigenous agricultural technologies, aimed primarily at managing and maintaining the nutrient cycle, emerge as superior to the green revolution option because they provide food to the soil and to society. The problem with the green revolution has been that each component of the food production system has been seen in isolation, and the solution to the production problem has been seen as providing chemical nutrients to the soil from fertilizer factories. The Punjab experience shows that chemicals can never be a substitute for the organic production of nutrients.

Diseases of micro-nutrient deficiency and toxicity[71]

After a few years of bumper harvests with the green revolution in Punjab, crop failures were reported at a large number of sites, despite liberal applications of NPK fertilizer. The new threat came from micro-nutrient deficiency caused by rapid and continuous removal of the micro-nutrient by high yielding varieties. Intensive multiple cropping is drawing out micro-nutrients from soils at a very rapid rate creating micro-nutrient deficiency of zinc, iron, copper, manganese, magnesium, molybdenum, boron, and other trace elements. These deficiencies do not occur with organic manuring because organic matter contains and renews all these trace elements, in balance, while chemical NPK does not.

Zinc deficiency is the most widespread of all micro-nutrient deficiencies. Over half of the 8,706 soil samples from Punjab exhibited zinc deficiency, which has reduced yields of rice, wheat and maize by up to 3.9 tonnes, 1.98 tonnes and 3.4 tonnes per ha, respectively. Consumption of zinc sulphate rose from zero in 1969–70 to nearly 15,000 tonnes in 1984–85. Iron deficiency has been reported from Punjab, Haryana, Andhra Pradesh, Bihar, Gujarat, and Tamil Nadu, and is threatening yields of rice, wheat, groundnut, sugarcane, etc. Manganese is another micro-nutrient which has become deficient in Punjab soils. Sulphur deficiency, which was earlier noticed only in oilseed and pulse crops, has now been seen in cereals like wheat as well.

The disturbance of the nutrient balance in the soil takes place through either depletion of trace elements or their excess. The green revolution has also resulted in soil toxicity by introducing excess quantities of trace elements in ecosystems. Fluorine toxicity has been introduced with irrigation by the Nagarjuna Sagar project. Twenty-six million hectares of India's lands are affected by aluminium toxicity. In Hoshiarpur district of Punjab, boron, iron, molybdenum, and selenium toxicity has

71 Report from the Department of Soils, *op. cit.*

built up with green revolution practices and is posing a threat to crop production as well as animal health.

A non-sustainable agriculture has depleted the soil of its organic matter and nutrients, and has introduced hazards of toxicity in their place, besides of course introducing the nitrate pollution of water systems through chemical fertilizers, and the pesticide pollution of entire ecosystems. These are ecological imbalances created by the nutrient demands of the high-yielding varieties. There is a second group of problems created in fertile soils which arise from the high water demands of these varieties and the spread of intensive irrigation to meet these demands.

Waterlogged and saline deserts

Green revolution varieties and cropping patterns need much more water than indigenous varieties and traditional crops. High yielding varieties of wheat, for example, need about three times as much irrigation as traditional varieties. Further, multiple cropping necessitates irrigation throughout the year; while such cropping based on short duration varieties should have increased agricultural productivity it has, instead, created waterlogged or salt-laden deserts. Intensive irrigation has introduced more water into ecosystems than the natural drainage capacity of soils or topographies allow. This causes a rise in the water table and consequent waterlogging. Water-logging reduces soil aeration, leads to anaerobic conditions, restricts root growth and can severely affect plant growth. It is the obverse of desertification through aridisation. Black cotton soils are the most vulnerable to water-logging because of their high water retentivity. This natural quality has made them fertile under rainfed or prudent irrigation conditions. The same quality has turned them into deserts by inappropriate irrigation and cultivation practices. Closely related to the problem of water-logging is the creation of salinity—the salt poisoning of arable lands. In regions of scarce rainfall, the earth contains a large amount of unleached salts. Irrigating soils in such zones brings the salt to the surface, because as the irrigation water evaporates, it leaves a whitish residue of salt behind. This salinisation destroyed Mesopotamian agriculture. Today, salt infestation, which includes salinity and alkalinity, threatens one-third of the world's irrigated lands. The salt-affected soils in India are estimated to be about seven mhs.; Table 15 gives the extent of lands destroyed by salinity and alkalinity in various regions.[72]

72 D.R. Bhumbla, *Salinity in India*, Kamal: Central Soil Salinity Research Institute, 1977.

Several areas in the state of Punjab[73] are affected by water-logging and salinity. It is estimated that about 2.86 lakh hectares have a water table depth of less than 1.5 metres even in the dry and hot month of June. The water table further rises by 0.5 to 1.2 metres during the monsoons. These areas are normally subjected to waterlogging, the degree

TABLE 15

Areas of salinity

Broad group	States in which found	Approximate area (million ha)
Coastal salt-affected soils		
In arid regions	Gujarat	0.714
In deltaic and humid regions	West Bengal, Orissa, Andhra Pradesh, Tamil Nadu	1.394
Acid soils	Kerala	0.016
Salt-affected soils of the medium and dddp black soil regions	Karnataka, Madhya Pradesh, Andhra Pradesh, Maharashtra	1.420
Salt-affected soils of the arid and semi-arid regions	Gujarat, Rajasthan, Punjab Haryana, Uttar Pradesh	1.000
Sodic soils of the Indo-Gangetic plain	Haryana, Punjab, Uttar Pradesh, Bihar, Rajasthan Madhya Pradesh	2.500
	Total	7.044

TABLE 16

Distribution of waterlogged areas in different districts of Punjab (water table less than 1.5 m, June 1983)

District	Waterlogged area (lakh hectares)	Percentage in each
Faridkot	1.12	39.16
Ferozepur	1.02	35.66
Bhatinda	0.32	11.19
Sangrur	0.09	3.15
Amritsar	0.08	2.80
Hoshiarpur	0.07	2.45
Gurdaspur	0.06	2.10
Jalandhar	0.05	1.75
Ludhiana	0.04	1.40
Ropar	0.005	0.17
Patiala	0.005	0.17
Total = 2.86 lakh hectares		

73 G.S. Hira & V.V.N. Murty, 'An Appraisal of the Water-logging Problems in Punjab, Ludhiana: PAU, 1985.

depending upon the topography of the area. The water table depth in different regions of Punjab, and the distribution of waterlogged areas in different districts of Punjab are given in Table 16. As indicated in the Table, the major problem of water-logging is in the south-west districts of Punjab, i.e., Faridkot, Ferozepur, and Bhatinda. Faridkot and Feroze-pur districts alone have about a metre depth of 2.14 and are affected by salinity and sodicity. Bhatinda is the next badly affected district, where it has been estimated that about 0.7 lakhs hectares are severely salt-affected and produce either no or poor crop yields.

Large parts of the state of Karnataka have also lost fertile land through water-logging and salinisation caused by excessive irrigation and seep-age from reservoirs and canals.[74] 2,400 ha of land are waterlogged in the command area out of 75,974 ha irrigated in the Malaprabha project. Two thousand ha of land have become waterlogged out of the 1,43,417 ha in the Ghatprabha project. In the Tungabhadra project, 33,000 ha are water-logged out of 36,300,000 ha. Hydrographs of wells have indicated that the average rate of rise in the water table due to irrigation is 13 cm per year.

Areas around Yellapura, Genekenal, and a few other villages have be-come swamps. Extensive development of saline crusts (2 to 4 cm thick) due to water-logging has taken place in soils near Kurugodu, Bailur, Go-tur, Lakshmipura, and Sangankal. With the building of large dams and large irrigation works to support the green revolution, prosperous peas-ants have been turned into paupers overnight. Instead of paying them compensation, the government has come to collect 'betterment levy'—a tax meant to recover the capital costs on irrigation projects. In the early '80s, farmers in the command areas of the Ghatprabha and Malaprabha projects refused to pay the tax because their land had been destroyed by water-logging. Peasants, including women, were fired at and some killed, during this early movement to protect their soils and their rights. A slogan used by the peasants during that resistance was: 'Who gives you food? What do you give in return?' which showed up the bankruptcy of an agricultural development which has neglected the rights of soils and of peasants, the primary producers of food.

In North India, a movement called 'Mitti Bachao Abhiyan' (Save the Soil Campaign)[75] has grown out of farmers' resistance to the water-logging

74 Ramprasad & K. Malhotra, 'Water-logging in the Irrigated Areas of Kamataka', *State of the Environment: Karnataka, 1985-86*, Department of Environment, Kamataka, 1986, pp. 31-45.

75 A Mishra, *Mitti Bacbao* (Hindi), New Delhi: Gandhi Peace Foundation, 1981.

TABLE 17
Rise of water table in the Tungabhadra command area

Village	Period of observation	Decrease in depth of water table (m)		Net rise in water table (m)	Average rise m/year
		from	to		
Paddy & sugarcane area					
Kamalapur	Apr 77 – May 81	2.60	2.05	0.55	0.14
Siruguppe	Jun 78 – Jun 81	1.90	1.40	0.50	0.16
Kurugodu					
Well No. 1	Jun 77 – Dec 80	1.10	0.75	0.35	0.10
Well No. 2	May 77 – May 80	0.80	0.60	0.20	0.07
Chellur					
Well No. 1	May 79 – May 81	1.60	1.20	0.40	0.20
Well No. 2	May 77 – May 81	1.15	0.95	0.20	0.05
Well No. 3	May 77 – May 80	1.65	1.35	0.30	0.10
Dry-cum-wet crops area					
Lakshmipura	Apr 74 – June 80	2.45	1.75	0.70	0.12
Sidharagadda	Aug 78 – Jul 81	6.60	5.45	1.15	0.29*
Effects due to canal seepage					
Venkatapura	Jul 74 – Jul 80	1.70	1.50	0.20	0.03
Somanhal	May 77 – Apr 81	2.50	1.90	0.60	0.15

* In addition to dry-cum-wet irrigation, seepage from the nearby pond has contributed to the increased rate of rise in water tables.

caused by the Tawa dam in Hoshangabad in the Narmada Valley System. Before the dam, Hoshangabad produced rich quantities of rainfed cereals like wheat and sorghum, oilseeds like sesame and linseed, pulses like pigeon-pea, moong, black beans, and lentil. These crops maintained soil fertility, provided staple foods and produced marketable surpluses. Irrigation has destroyed soils through water-logging, displaced foodcrops, and even destroyed markets. Soyabean has been introduced in place of old crops, and while the official agencies claim that it has brought untold profits to farmers, they fail to mention that the displacement of oilseeds and pulses has meant a loss of nine crore rupees in Hoshangabad district alone. Irrigation has made it impossible to cultivate these rainfed crops. A woman from Byavra village which is waterlogged, says, 'Our house used to be filled with food grains like the Narmada river is filled with water. Today we have no food at all.'

The Narmada river is now to have 30 major dams, 135 medium dams and 3,000 small dams to be built over the next 50 years, at a cost of tens of billions of dollars, displacing two million people for the submergence.

But given the experience of Tawa, farmers in the command area will also be displaced eventually, because their soils will be killed through water-logging or salinisation.

While the green revolution is creating waterlogged and saline deserts in the command areas of large irrigation projects, it is simultaneously causing water depletion in other regions both by damming and diverting rivers as well as by over-exploiting ground water. The high nutrient and water demands for green revolution varieties are a principal cause for the death and desertification of agricultural land in the Third World. The solution to the problems of nutrient imbalance, water-logging, and salinisation within the green revolution paradigm are neither cost-effective nor sustainable. Even the prosperous farmers of Punjab cannot afford the Rs. 16,000 per ha that is needed for introducing tile drains to drain excess irrigation water; nor can they afford micro-nutrient costs in addition to the already exhorbitant costs of NPK fertilizer. Micronutrient treatment carries the hazard of building up soil toxicity: the solution of flushing out salts with inputs of additional water needs too much money and too much water, both of which are scarce.

Groundwater mining and the creation of dry deserts

The water-intensive pattern of the green revolution has created water famine and land aridisation in dry zones where irrigation is being done from groundwater. Cash crop cultivation of sugarcane, grapes, and oranges has left most of the soils of Maharashtra thirsty for water. The shallow wells used for protective irrigation of crops like sorghum have dried up due to over-exploitation of deeper wells through energised pumping for cash crops. Groundwater mining has created an aquifer drought; water tables in large parts of the country have fallen from depths of 10-30 ft. to 300-400 ft., making even drinking water inaccessible to village communities. With the drying up of water sources, the soil too is dying, and each year's crop failure leaves it more impoverished and arid. The life of water and soils has been traded for a few years of cash.

Respecting the rights of the soil

We have had two decades of large-scale and rapid destruction of fertile agricultural soils in India as a result of the very processes which attempted to increase agricultural productivity. We have also had failed attempts at 'technological fixes' to the problem of dying soils from the very agencies which designed the green revolution technologies. The solution to the crisis of dying soils cannot lie in the hands of those who first created the problem, who look only to the market, not to the life of the soil or the work of women as soil builders. The healing and recovery of soils will not emerge by continuing to cling to the market as an organising principle for agriculture. Recovery lies in rediscovering natural ways of renewal and learning, once again, to see that the soil has a right to a share of her produce in order to renew herself. Respecting that right is critical to satisfying our needs.

Under the assumption that nature is inefficient, we are rapidly undermining her productivity. The death of soils is just one among many of the expressions of the arrogance which forces us to work against nature's productivity rather than build on it. There is a common misperception that a concern for nature's rights is to ignore people's rights, and that the sustainable use of soils goes against the demands for food for the hungry. Yet it is not satisfying the needs of the poor that has killed fertile soils through desertification and disease. Water-logging and salinity, micro-nutrient deficiency, toxicity, and the depletion of organic matter are direct and inevitable consequences of a philosophy of agriculture guided by the modern patriarchal principle of profit-maximisation. The recovery of soils can only take place through a philosophy which sees soil fertility, not cash, as agricultural capital, which sees women, not fertilizer factories, as nutrient suppliers, and which puts nature and human needs, not markets, at the centre of sustainable agriculture and land use. If soils and people are to live, we must stop converting soil fertility into cash and productive lands into deserts. Today, as western experts again flock to the Third World in search of instant solutions to the problem of dying soils, they often blame the victims—the woman, the tribal, the peasant. They forget that the 'Dust Bowl' technology for the manufacture of deserts from fertile soils was first mastered in the colonisation of native Indian lands in North America by men of European culture, with European techniques—the intensive use of artificial fertilizers, extensive practice of monoculturing, and intensive and extensive mechanisation which turned the fertile grasslands of Oklahoma into a desert in less than thirty years. As Hyams observes:

> Today it would probably be possible to turn the soil fertility of an area
> as large as the Dust Bowl into some other form of wealth, or into cash,
> in about ten years, with the aid of the enormously powerful machinery

now available for soil fertility mining.... When, between 1889 and 1900, thousands of farmers were settling Oklahoma, it must have seemed to them that they were founding a new agricultural civilization which might endure as long as Egypt. The grandsons, and even the sons of these settlers who so swiftly became a disease of their soil, trekked from their ruined farmsteads, their buried or uprooted crops, their dead soil, with the dust of their own making in their eyes and hair, the barren sand of a once fertile plain gritting between their teeth.... The pitiful procession passed westward, an object of disgust—the God-dam'd Ok-ies. But these God-dam'd Okies were the scapegoats of a generation, and the God who had damned them was perhaps, after all, a Goddess, her name Ceres, Demeter, Maia, or something older and more terrible. And what she damned them for was their corruption, their fundamental ignorance of the nature of her world, their defiance of the laws of cooperation and return which are the basis of life on this planet.[76]

Since then, western patriarchy's highly energy-intensive, chemical-intensive, water-intensive, and capital-intensive agricultural techniques for creating deserts out of fertile soils in less than one or two decades has spread rapidly across the Third World as agricultural development, accelerated by the green revolution and financed by international development and aid agencies.

The recovery of the soil as a living system needs the recovery of the feminine principle in agriculture, and with it a spirit of respect and care for the earth as caring and protective.

Pesticides: poisoning the web of life

With the green revolution, the very production of food is often a threat to life. The new seeds of this kind of agriculture are highly vulnerable to pests, and require a heavy use of pesticides to ensure 'pest control' and 'plant protection'. Like much else in the language—and claims—of the green revolution, these too, are exaggerated and falsified. Pesticides, far from controlling pests, are actually prescriptions for fostering them, and because they create new mutants and increase vulnerability to old ones, they expose plants to ever new hazards.

I have often walked with women through the terraced fields of Garhwal which are a mosaic of diversity. On that diversity is based

76 E. Hyams, *Soil and Civilization*, London: Thames and Hudson, 1952, p. 150.

plant protection, through the maintenance of pest-predator cycles and through building up the resistance of crops to pests and disease. When I ask the women peasants of Garhwal if they have pest problems, they laugh and reply, 'Pests? What is that?' The absence of pest damage in ecologically sound cropping patterns and the evolution of pest resistant strains is in stark contrast to the new pest hazards which are part of the green revolution package of hybrid monocultures. We have already given instances of the vulnerability to pests in the new rice and sorghum varieties. *Ragi (Elusiene coracaua)* is an example of another crop which has been converted from a totally pest-free to a pest-prone one through green revolution technology.

The farce of 'improved' varieties

Ragi is one of India's staple coarse grains. Introduced from the Horn of Africa more than 40 centuries ago, it has provided a balanced diet to Indian peasants over millennia, and is a genuine 'miracle' crop—very hardy and drought resistant. Even under unfavourable conditions the crop maintains its growth, and is remarkably free from fungus and pest attacks. It was, until recently, stored in underground pits by women in their houses because it can keep for decades. All these qualities have made it an excellent crop for food security in drought-prone regions. It has been found that the protein of *ragi* is as biologically complete as that of milk. Writing in 1886, Church noted that *ragi* 'is a fairly productive rainyweather crop for light soils, and may be grown almost upon stones and gravel. It yields from five to six maunds of grain per acre upon the hills, 12 to 14 maunds in the plains, if carefully cultivated and weeded'.[77]

Traditional *ragi* cultivation has been based on wide genetic diversity. *Hullubili, guddabili, karigidda, jenumudde, madayanagiri, hasarukambi, doddaragbiliragi, balepatte, karimurakabi, majjige, rudragade, jade shankara*—these are only some of the varieties that have been grown in Karnataka.[78] All have shared a diversity of properties of being highly nutritive, highly productive, pest resistant, and drought resistant. Yet the crisis mind could not resist trying to 'improve' *ragi*, and in its attempt to do so, it introduced pests in a pest-free crop, and drought vulnerability in a drought resistant one.

77 A.H. Church, *Food Grains of India*, (Reprint), New Delhi: Ajay Book Service, 1983, p. 89.

78 A.K. Yegna Narayan Aiyer, *Field Crops of India*, Bangalore: Bangalore Press, 1982.

New varieties of *ragi* were introduced in South India in the 1960s under the All-India Co-ordinated Millet Improvement programme.[79] Table 18 gives the comparative performance of indigenous and HYV *ragi* during 1976-77 and 1977-78

TABLE 18

Performance of indigenous and high yielding *ragi*

	Indigenous ragi		HYV ragi	
	1976-77	1977-78	1976-77	1977-78
Area (ha)	132,439	125,259	53,078	90,531
Production (mt)	124,176	149,983	60,133	129,396
Yield (kg/ha)	938	1,197	1,138	1,429
Average	1,022		1,283	

The HYV performance in grain does not excel that of indigenous varieties significantly. In straw and fodder performance, the yields are lower. In fact, under stable cropping, as in Church's data, indigenous varieties had yields as high as those of HYV.

The new INDAF varieties are not drought resistant. If rainfall is scanty or absent during critical stages of growth, the expected yield is never reached. Again, they are amenable to certain pests and diseases and if not sprayed regularly with pesticides, are liable to crop failure. Plant protection chemicals are sprayed two to five times for irrigated and one to two times for dry *ragi*. In Dharmapuri district in Tamil Nadu, for example, local varieties are preferred because of their 'guaranteed yield' and lower costs. The additional fertilizer and pesticide cost per ha. of HYV *ragi* is Rs. 250 approximately, and is barely offset in the best years by slightly higher yields. In years of rainfall fluctuation or pest damage, the yield and income from HYV *ragi* are much lower than that from local varieties. With the HYV package, which includes pesticides, are thus sown the seeds of famine. The choice, as an expert of the British Agrochemicals Association has stated, is not between pesticides or famine: 'The effect of not spraying tropical crops would of course be disastrous, and the resulting famine would be the greatest the world has ever

79 S. Girriapa, 'Role of Ragi in Dry Area Development', SEC, mimeo, 1980.

known'.[80] Sustainable farming systems that maintain high productivity are possible only through natural means of plant protection. Cropping systems which are ecologically unstable create pest problems and encourage crop failure. Pesticides aggravate this instability, and their poisons work against the basic biological productivity and living principles of crop production. Ironically, this collapse in biological productivity is the result of a violent pursuit of increased productivity, indifferent to nature's checks and balances.

Fostering pests with pesticides

Violence was part of the very context of discovery of pesticides during World War I. The manufacture of explosives had a direct spin-off effect on the development of synthetic insecticides. The tear gas, chloropicrin, was found to be insecticidal in 1916 and thus changed from a wartime product to a peace time one. DDT's discovery was the culmination of a research effort motivated purely by commercial concerns, but the compound's adoption was inextricably enmeshed in the politics of war.[81] Pesticides were born as 'devastating weapons in man's war against his own kind'. Organophosphates, of which parathion and malathion are the most widely used, are aimed at destroying the nervous system, 'whether the victim is an insect or a warm-blooded animal'.[82]

The context for the creation of pesticides was war. The metaphor for pesticide use in agriculture was also war. This is how the introduction to a textbook on pest-management reads:

> The war against pests is a continuing one that man must fight to ensure his survival. Pests (in particular insects) are our major competitors on earth and for the hundreds of thousands of years of our existence they have kept our numbers low and, on occasions, have threatened extinction. Throughout the ages man has lived at a bare subsistence level because of the onslaught of pests and the diseases they carry. It is only in comparatively recent times that this picture has begun to alter as, in certain parts of the world, we have gradually gained the upper hand over pests.
>
> The war story described some of the battles that have been fought and the continuing guerilla warfare, the type of enemies we are facing

80 Hessayan, *op. cit.*

81 J.H. Perkins, *Insects, Experts and the Insecticide Crisis*, New York: Plenum, 1982, p. 5.

82 Rachel Carson, *Silent Spring*, London: Penguin, 1983, p. 42.

and some of their manoeuvres for survival; the weapons we have at our command ranging from the rather crude ones of the 'bow and arrow' age of pest control to the sophisticated weapons of the present day, including a look into the future of some 'secret weapons' that are in the trial stages; the gains that have been made; and some of the devastation which is a concomitant of war.[83]

But the 'war' with pests is unnecessary. The most effective pest control mechanism is built into the ecology of crops, partly by ensuring balanced pest-predator relationships through crop diversity and partly by building up resistance in plants. Organic manuring is now being shown to be critical to such a building up of resistance; women have thus been invisible plant protectors through their work in organic manuring.

Reductionism fails to see the ecology of pests as well as that of pesticides because it is based on invisible, subtle balances within the plant and its environment. It therefore simplistically reduces the management of pests to the violent business of war with poisons. It also fails to recognise that pests have natural enemies with the unique property of regulating pest populations. In de Bach's view, 'The philosophy of pest control by chemicals has been to achieve the highest kill possible, and percent mortality has been the main yardstick in the early screening of new chemicals in the lab. Such an objective, the highest kill possible, combined with ignorance of or disregard for, on-target insects and mites is guaranteed to be the quickest road to upsets, resurgences, and the development of resistance to pesticides'.[84]

De Bach's research on DDT-induced pest increase showed that these increases could be anywhere from thirty-six fold to over twelve hundredfold. The aggravation of the problem is directly related to the violence unleashed on the natural enemies of pests. Reductionism, which fails to perceive the natural balance, also fails to anticipate and predict what will happen when that balance is disturbed.

The introduction of pesticides is largely a function of exaggerated claims of the damage prevented by western male science and industry. It is also a function of the visibility of the effect of pesticides. Natural enemies work quietly, invisibly; 'the effects of chemical pesticides, on the other hand, are highly visible. They act quickly, multitudes of dead bugs

---

83 W.W. Fletcher, *The Pest War*, Oxford: Basil Blackwell, 1974, p. l.

84 De Bach, *Biological Control by Natural Enemies*, London: Cambridge University Press, 1974.

are an impressive sight and a good selling point'.[85] The drama of violence becomes the distorted and misguided criterion for cognitive strength. The myth of the cognitive superiority and success of a modern reductionist patriarchal science of death is founded on this illegitimate translation of violence as a sign of effectiveness. The strategy of overkill breeds pest outbreaks, it does not regulate or control them. Why does the myth that modern science controls nature, persist, when it actually creates a nature that is completely out of control? Violence is not an indicator of control; its use is a sign that the system is becoming uncontrollable.

The mystification of violence as control runs through the western patriarchal scientific process, beginning with the 'scientific' and 'controlled' experiment. Experiments on the effectiveness of pesticides are not real-life experiments, comparing the natural and chemical control of pests. The caricature of the potential natural or biological control is an untreated test-plot surrounded by plots located with different materials, dosages and intervals of application of poisons. The untreated plot therefore receives chemicals from its surroundings and also suffers from the effect of earlier spraying of the larger field. The natural enemies on this sample plot are thus destroyed, as are natural controls. Pests tend to explode on this check-plot and pesticide plots therefore show a greater amount of damage prevented!

Yet, in spite of of its complete failure in solving the problem of pest control and of so much destruction and violence against nature and man, pesticide sales go up, not down. The use of pesticides is ensured through state agricultural policy, pesticide subsidies, and propaganda. It continues because they are 'ecological narcotics',[86] their use ultimately becoming a habit. Continued pesticide use can render a potentially more effective biological control ineffective by destroying the pest-predator equation. The market for pesticides grows in spite of of their ineffectiveness because they destroy the ecological basis of any alternative system of pest management, because it does not have a potential for profit-making. Natural enemies, not available on the market, are a common and free resource, but because they are specific to a particular species they have a limited market. Chemical pesticides by contrast, are chosen for their 'broad-spectrum' capabilities so as to have a large market potential, thus forging a strong link between science, violence, and profits.

---

85 R.C. Oelaf, *Organic Agriculture*, New Jersey: Allanheld, Osmunand Co., 1978, p. 81.
86 Oelaf, *op. cit.*, p. 60.

Nonviolent pest control: learning from nature, women, and peasants

Nonviolent ways of controlling pests have always existed. As Howard noted half a century ago, 'Nature has never found it necessary to design the equivalent of the spraying machine and the poison spray for the control of insect and fungus pests. It is true that all kinds of diseases are to be found here and there among the plants and animals of the forest, but these never assume large proportions. The principle followed is that plants and animals can very well protect themselves even when such things as parasites are to be found in their midst. Nature's rule in these matters is to live and let live'.[87] Howard believed that the cultivators of the east had a lot to teach the western expert about disease and pest control and to get western reductionism out of the vicious and violent circle of 'discovering more and more new pests and devising more and more poison sprays to destroy them'. When Howard came to Pusa in 1905 as the Imperial Economic Botanist to the Government of India, he found that crops grown by cultivators in the neighbourhood of Pusa were free of pests and needed no insecticides and fungicides.

> I decided that I could not do better than watch the operations of these peasants and acquire their traditional knowledge as rapidly as possible. For the time being, therefore, I regarded them as my professors of agriculture. Another group of instructors were obviously the insects and fungi themselves. The methods of the cultivators, if followed, would result in crops practically free from disease, the insects and fungi would be useful for pointing out unsuitable varieties and methods of farming inappropriate to the locality.

At the end of five years of tuition under his new professors—'the peasants and the pests'—Howard had learnt

> ... how to grow healthy crops, practically free from disease, without the slightest help from mycologists, entomologists, bacteriologists, agricultural chemists, statisticians, clearinghouses of information, artificial manures, spraying machines, insecticides, fungicides, germicides, and all the other expensive paraphernalia of the modern experiment station.[88]

87 Howard, *op. cit.*
88 Howard, *op. cit.*

Howard could teach the world sustainable farming because he had the humility to learn it first from practising peasants and nature herself. He found that the most effective way to control pests is the nonviolent method based on the feminine principle, by building pest resistance in the plant, rather than by attacking pests. 'Nature has provided a marvellous piece of machinery for conferring disease resistance on the crop. This machinery is only active in soil rich in humus; it is inactive or absent in infertile land and in similar soils manured with chemicals'.[89] A feminine, nonviolent perspective on agriculture would thus need to take organic manuring, largely carried out by women, as work in pest management and plant protection while contributing to soil fertility and soil moisture conservation at the same time.

The crisis mind is, of course, now talking of engineering pest resistance into plants with biotechnology. This view, however, fails to see that pest resistance is an ecological state, not an engineered one. As Chabousson comments, 'The gene, the vector of heredity, can only operate as a function of the environment. Thus it is useless improving the resistance of a plant to such and such a disease if that 'genetic' immunity is going to be impaired by applying a pesticide aimed at some other pest'.[90]

The traditional (or what the reductionist world view has labelled 'unscientific') system of food production has managed pest control by a series of measures which include building up plant resistance, practising rotational and mixed cropping, and providing habitats for pest-predators in farms, trees, and hedgerows. These practices created a stable local ecology and economy. Under ecologically stable conditions, a balance was achieved between plants and their pests through natural competition, selection, and predator-prey relationships. Women are generally found to be important sources of traditional knowledge about essential ecological processes and relationships between plants. For example, the Kayape Indian women of the Amazon basin have a ritual in which they paint their faces with ground ant parts in the maize festival. The principal theme of the festival is the celebration of the little red ant as the guardian of the fields and a friend of the women. Apparently meaningless from the reductionist point of view, Posey points out that,

89 Howard, *op. cit.*

90 F. Chabousson, 'How Pesticides Increase Pests', *Ecologist*, Vol. 16, No. 1, 1986, pp. 29-36.

the myth begins to make sense when we understand the co-evolution-
ary complex of maize, beans, manioc and this ant. Manioc produces
an extra floral nectar that attracts the ants to the young manioc plant.
The ants use their mandibles to make their way to the nectar, cutting
away any bean vines that would prevent the new, fragile manioc stems
from growing. The twining bean vines are therefore kept from climbing
on the manioc and are left with the maize plants as their natural trellis.
The maize can shoot up undamaged by the bean vines, while the bean
plant itself furnishes valuable nitrogen needed by the maize. The ants
are the natural manipulator of nature and facilitate the horticultural
activities of the women.[91]

'Scientific' farming which saw the red ants as 'pests', upset this balance and created favourable conditions for the spread of disease. Organic fertilizer which builds up plant resistance to disease was replaced
by chemical fertilizers which decreased plant resistance to pests. Since
many pests are specific to particular plants, replacing crop rotation by
the planting of the same crop year after year often encourages pest build-
ups. Substitution of mixed crops by monocultures also makes the crop
more prone to pest outbreaks. Mechanisation of farming leads to the destruction of hedgerows and farm trees and thus destroys the habitat for
some pest predators. Birds and trees are other invisible workers in pest
control. The Dutch elm disease which has killed the tree in large parts
of America and Europe has been traced to the annihilation of the pred-
ator birds which fed on the bark beetle, which in turn is responsible for
spreading the fungus which causes Dutch elm disease. As the curator of
birds at the Milwaukee Public Museum said, 'The greatest enemy of insect
life is other predatory insects, birds and some small mammals, but DDT
kills indiscriminately, including nature's own safeguards or policemen ...
In the name of progress are we to become victims of our own diabolical
means of insect control to provide temporary comfort, only to lose out
to destroying insects later on? By what means will we control new pests
which will attack remaining tree species after the elms are gone, when
nature's safeguards (the birds) have been wiped out by poison?'[92]
The cows which provide humus, the birds which feed on insects, the
trees which provide food for cows and homes for birds, these are members of the earth-family on which permanent pest control strategies need

91 D.A. Posey, 'Indigenous Ecological Knowledge and Development of the Amazon', in E.
F. Moran (ed.), *The Dilemma of Amazonian Development*, Boulder: Westview, 1983, p. 234.
92 Perkins, *op. cit.*

Sacred Cow vs Milk machine

Source : C. Sivaramamurti, Approach to Nature in Indian Art and Thought New Delhi - Kanak Publications 1980.

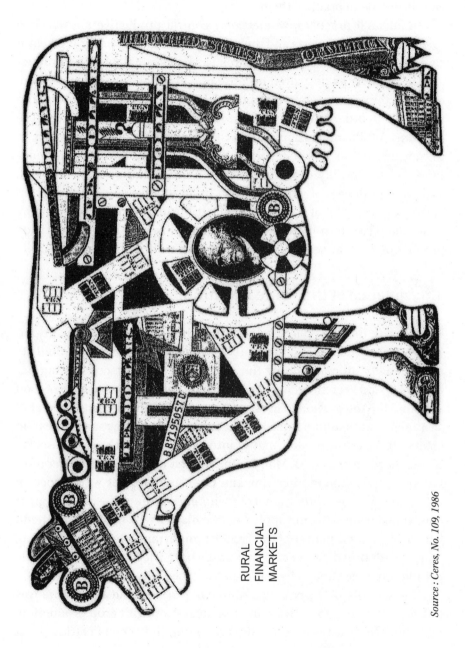

RURAL
FINANCIAL
MARKETS

Source : Ceres, No. 109, 1986

to be built. Nonviolent alternatives exist, but it needs a feminine and ecological perception to see them, and feminine priorities of sustaining and
enhancing life to practice them.

In all such practises, women play central productive and creative
roles. They are the experts and the controllers of food security and health
care systems. Their work and nature's work in sustainable food production today is being destroyed because of a new death-based knowledge
and development system, which puts violent modern man at war with the
web of life in order to make profits and gain control over nature and the
economy. While integration at the ecological level is being destroyed, at
the corporate level it is being perpetuated. Nature and women, as main-
tainers of soil fertility, protectors of plants and managers of pest control,
and as reproducers of genetic wealth in all its diversity, are being displaced by a handful of multi-national agribusiness corporations run by
a handful of western males who control fertilizer production, pesticide
production and the seed industry, and hence control the food chain.[93]

The violence of the white revolution

Ecologically the cow has been central to Indian civilization. Both materially and conceptually the world of Indian agriculture has built its
sustainability on maintaining the integrity of the cow, considering her
inviolable and sacred, seeing her as the mother of the prosperity of food
systems. The integration of livestock with farming has been the secret of
sustainable agriculture. Livestock perform a critical function in the food
chain by converting organic matter into a form that can be easily used by
plants. According to K.M. Munshi, India's first agriculture minister after
independence, 'The mother cow and the Nandi are not worshipped in
vain. They are the primeval agents who enrich the soil—nature's great
land transformers—who supply organic matter which, after treatment,
becomes nutrient matter of the greatest importance. In India, tradition,
religious sentiment, and economic needs have tried to maintain a cattle
population large enough to maintain the cycle, only if we know it'.[94]

The sanctity of the cow as a source of prosperity in agriculture was
linked to the need for conserving its integration with crop production.
By using crop wastes and uncultivated land, indigenous cattle do not

93 Rachel Carson, *op. cit.*, p. 108.
94 K.M. Munshi, *op.cit.*

compete with man for food; rather, they provide organic fertilizer for fields and thus enhance food productivity. Within the sacredness of the cow therefore, lies this ecological rationale and conservation impera-tive. The work of the cow as a source of fertilizer through cowdung en-ergy, nutrition, and leather, was linked to the work of women in feeding and milking cows, in collecting cowdung, in nurturing them in ill health. Women have thus been the primary experts in animal husbandry as well as the food processors in the traditional dairy industry, making curds and butter, ghee and buttermilk. Their contribution to the Indian economy through their work with cattle has been very significant. An attempt was made in 1932 to estimate the monetary contribution of Indian cattle to the Indian economy:

> The actual and potential value of cattle products is very great. Milk and milk products may be valued at about three hundred crores. This is roughly equivalent to the value of India's total output of rice, and is three to four times the value of the output of wheat. India is also the largest exporter of hides and skins in the British Empire, her yearly out-put of this group of products being valued at about roughly forty crores of rupees, or more than the value of the total Indian production of sugar. Cattle labour also represents an important contribution of livestock to Indian agriculture, the monetary value calculated on the basis of culti-vation costs being estimated at between three hundred to five hundred crores of rupees. The value of cattle as a means of raising the fertility of the soil cannot be readily computed. One estimate places the cash value of cattle manure at two hundred and seventy crores of rupees.[95]

It should be noted that two-thirds and more of the power require-ments of Indian villages are met by some 80 million work animals of which 70 million are the male progeny of what the western masculinist perspective sees as 'useless' low milk-yielding cows. It has been calcu-lated that to replace animal power in agriculture, India would have to spend about a thousand million U.S. dollars annually on petrol. Indian cattle excrete 700 million tonnes a year of recoverable manure: half of this is used as fuel, liberating the thermal equivalent of 27 million tonnes of kerosene, 35 million tonnes of coal or 68 million tonnes of wood, all of which are scarce resources in India; the remaining half is used as fertil-izer. As for other livestock produce, it may be sufficient to mention that

95 N. Wright, *Report on the Development of the Cattle and Dairy Industries in India*, Simla, Government of India Press, 1937.

the export of hides, skins, etc. brings in 150 million dollars annually into the national coffers. With limited resources, indigenous cattle produce a multiplicity of uses'.[96]

In India, cattle use 29 percent of the organic matter provided to them, 22 percent of the energy, and three percent of the protein, in contrast to nine, seven, and five percent respectively in the intensive cattle industry in the U.S. Indian cattle provide food in excess of the edible food consumed, in contrast to the U.S. where six times as much edible food is fed to cattle as is obtained from them.[97]

TABLE 19

Inputs and useful outputs from U.S. cattle and Indian cattle and buffalo (1972)

Inputs and outputs	Matter (10^{10} kg)		Energy (10^{12} calories)		Protein (10^9 kg)	
	U.S.	India	U.S.	India	U.S.	India
Inputs						
Edible by man	11.9	0.68	38.8	1.7	16.0	2.1
Inedible by man	22.2	40.00	88.0	120.5	25.1	33.3
Total	34.1	40.68	126.8	122.2	41.1	35.4
Outputs						
Work	.	.	.	6.50	.	.
Milk	1.12	0.51	5.04	2.09	2.06	0.88
Meat	0.90	0.50	4.40	2.23	0.17	0.11
Hides	0.11	0.07	.	.	.	.
Manure	0.87	10.81	.	16.16	.	.
Total	3.00	11.89	9.44	26.98	2.23	0.99
Efficiency (%)	9	29	7	22	5	3

Source: Reprinted from 'Agriculture: A Sacred Cow,' by Bruce Leon, *Environment*, Vol. 17, No. 9, p. 38. (1975), Scientists' Institute for Public Information.

Yet this highly efficient food system, based on the multiple uses of cattle, has been dismantled in the name of efficiency and 'development' by the reductionist strategies of the green and white revolutions splitting and dichotomising an integrated system of crop production and animal husbandry, necessary for maintaining each other sustainably. With the green and white revolutions, competition replaces complementarity,

96 Shanti George, *Operation Flood*, Delhi: Oxford University Press, 1985, p. 31.

97 Shanti George, *op. cit.*

linearity replaces cyclical processes, high inputs replace low inputs, and single-commodity outputs replace multi-dimensional uses. A shift is consequently made from technologies which strengthen life-sustaining eco-processes to anti-life technologies which disrupt them. Since it is women who are partners with nature in maintaining the cyclical and sustainable flows of fertility between crops and cattle, the disruption of nature's work and women's work goes hand in hand. The separation of crop production from animal husbandry destroys the ecological processes of sustainable farming, by eroding its organic matter base. Women's work in the organic integrity between livestock and crops is also destroyed with this separation. The green revolution shifts the fertilizer base of agriculture from renewable and sustainable organic inputs to non-renewable, non-sustainable, chemical ones, making both cattle, and women's work with cattle, dispensable to the production of food grain. The white revolution, aping the inefficient and wasteful animal husbandry and dairying practices of the west, destroys the civilizational base of the world's most evolved dairy culture, and displaces women from their role in the dairy processing industry.

The green revolution has emerged as an enemy to the white, as the high yielding crop varieties have reduced straw production, and their by-products are unpalatable to livestock; they are thus useless as fodder. Further, hybrid crops deprive the soil of nutrients, creating deficiencies in fodder and disease in livestock. The white revolution, in turn, instead of viewing livestock as ecologically integrated with crops has reduced the cow to a mere milk machine. As Shanti George observes, 'The trouble is that when dairy planners look at the cow, they see just her udder; though there is much more to her. They equate cattle only with milk, and do not consider other livestock produce—draught power, dung for fertilizer and fuel, hides, skins, horn and hooves'.[98]

Milk in India has been only one of the many products of the interdependence between agriculture and animal husbandry. This is why India has bred dual purpose cattle, optimising both the draught power and milk output, and maintaining a complementarity between different productive processes and between the needs of humans and animals. The relationship in India between agriculture and animal husbandry has evolved over centuries to be mutually enriching. Cattle are primarily viewed as agents of production in the food system; only secondarily are they viewed as producing consumable items. By making the subsidiary

98 Shanti George, *op.cit.*, p. 30.

function primary and exclusive, the white revolution threatens to damage the delicate balance between soils and animals which has conserved productivity over centuries. As cautioned by the Royal Commission and by the ICAR, 'If milk production is unduly pushed up, it may cause deterioration in the draught quality of the cattle and indirectly affect the entire basis of agriculture in India'.[99]

Hybridisation as genetic violence

The white revolution came from the west to 'improve' dairying practises in that part of the world which had placed the cow at its ecological centre. The feminine principle was embodied in the cow, and was based on relatedness and integration within the agrarian system on the one hand, and genetic diversity on the other. India has produced some of the world's best tropical cattle breeds—among them the Sahiwal, the Red Sindhi, Rathi, Tharparhar, Hariana, Ongole, Kankreji, and Gir. These were carefully evolved over centuries to suit the diverse ecological needs of the country.

> It may perhaps have taken many thousands of years for our forefathers to evolve the best dairy and draught breeds for the tropics ... who could be kept under a tree in hot summer, who could drink village pond water, could stand up to fly and mosquito nuisance and tropical disease, and who could live on grazing and monsoonic grass or on roughages ... which are available as agricultural by products.[100]

The centuries-old breeding strategies were evolved and maintained by indigenous experts, who were 'scientific' breeders, although they did not have university degrees behind their names or present papers at workshops . These invisible scientists were women and men of nomadic communities based in the dry interior regions where cultivation pressures were low and access to natural pasture high. The specialised skills and knowledge of these breeding castes are not, however, a component of the 'science' of the white revolution. Dairy scientists now are the western educated males of urban India, in whose perspective these erstwhile specialist breeders are hardly thought to be either scientists or professionals, and who do not see India's cattle as genetically evolved through

99 Shanti George, *op. cit.*, p. 59.
100 *Ibid.*, p. 118.

careful selection. They homogenise their genetic diversity in the name of 'development', to create a high risk and fragmented animal husbandry strategy. The pure indigenous breeds are replaced by homogenised hybrids of the Zebu cow with exotic strains like the Jersey, Holstein, Friesian, Red Dane, and Brown Swiss, to improve the Zebu's dairy productivity. Like much else in reductionist development, this strategy is highly inappropriate to Indian agriculture because, as Harris has pointed out, 'If the main economic function of the Zebu cow is to breed male traction animals, then there is no point in comparing her with specialised American dairy animals, whose main function is to produce milk'.[101]

Shanti George wryly comments, 'When the milk produced by Danish and Indian cows is compared, it might be instructive to ask how the work performance of the Danish bull measures up to that of his Indian counterpart'.[102] The 'improvement' of Indian cattle through cross-breeding with exotic strains is as fictitious as the high yields of hybrid seeds. Hybridisation in cattle and crops, when guided by reductionist principles, creates a fiction of growth and a reality of fragmentation, disruption, and destruction. Ecologically, this violates the integrity of systems and species; economically, it creates scarcity by destroying critical functions and outputs of ecosystems. The breakdown of the integrated nutrient cycle in the farm is one aspect: the breakdown of the cattle system itself is another.

Indigenous breeds, evolved over centuries, are specially adapted to the Indian climate. They have extra epidermal area for increased heat tolerance, light skin colour for comfort in sunlight, long ears and tails to keep insects away, a hump to store muscular fat. Cross-breeding with exotics breeds out these adaptation strategies. Tropical nature is no longer habitat but hazard. Temperate straws make cross-breeds strangers to the Indian climate, leading to depressed yields. As Singh points out, large-scale cross-breeding is feasible only 'if the agro-climatic conditions of January to March can be maintained throughout the year'.[103] This means that either hybrid cows live in airconditioned housing and animal husbandry as a livelihood option no longer exists for the poorest communities, or that the maladaptation of cattle in the heat of summer and the humidity of the monsoons is an inevitable handicap.

101 Shanti George, *op. cit.*, p. 39.

102 *Ibid.*, p. 37.

103 Shanti George, *op. cit.*, p. 107.

With climatic maladaptation, the innate disease resistance of indigenous stock is drastically lowered. The simple act of taking a cow out
to graze, a standard mode of milch-stock nutrition in villages, is fraught
with hazards in the case of a cross-bred that will pick up ticks and fleas
and consequent illnesses. Not only are hybrids more vulnerable to disease, they have imported new ailments such as viral pneumonia, bovine
rhinotractitis, malignant catehral fever, bovine viral diarrhoea, tubercu-
losis, and ephemeral fever.[104]

Like hybrid crops, hybrid cattle also demand resource-intensive inputs. For each intensively reared cross-bred cow, about two million cal-
ories of food may be lost per year ... enough for the annual food supply
of two persons. The unhybridised cattle live on agricultural by-products
and waste. Cross-breds, however, like hybrid crops, respond only to intensive inputs like green fodder and concentrated feeds, which puts new
pressures on land. According to Shanti George,

> There is only one thing amiss with the cross-bred cow: she is in the
> wrong country. Wrong not so much in terms of agro-climatic circum-
> stances, since there are such things as airconditioners and vaccines, as
> from the viewpoint of the milch-stock owners of this country, the large
> majority of whom cannot provide adequate basic nutrition and health
> care for their children, let alone expensive equivalents for hybrid live-
> stock. In many parts of India, indeed, it must be more comfortable to be
> a large holder's cross-bred cow than to be a small farmer's child. We are
> told, for example, that while most rural Indians have to drink from the
> pond, crossbred cows get clean water. In the Anand region that boasts
> the most elaborate and efficient veterinary system in India, they say it
> is easier to get a doctor for a sick animal than for a sick human being.[105]

The white revolution is an excellent example of reductionism. It has
reduced the cow to a milk machine, and milk merely into a commodity
for sale, not an essential nutritive product which should be consumed
in rural areas. The capitalist shift from need to markets is related to a
capitalist patriarchal shift from household dairy processing to factory
processing and from high labour inputs to high capital inputs. This shift
has displaced women's work and their control on income from milk produce. The major indigenous dairy products are ghee, its byproduct, buttermilk, curds, cottage cheese, and *khoya* which can be made in every

104 *Ibid.*, p. 108
105 Shanti George. *op.cit.*, p. 112.

rural kitchen and preserved without refrigeration. The National Commission on Agriculture estimates that 45 percent of India's milk is consumed in liquid form, 39 percent converted to ghee and five percent processed into *khoya*. And while ghee is sold, nutritious buttermilk remains for local consumption. The white revolution propaganda would have us believe that before the EEC and World Bank aided dairy development, India had no dairy industry and no trade in milk products. It declared that the traditional dairy industry, controlled by women, was a 'vast inefficient structure of traditional milk production and marketing'.[106] Records however show that ghee processed by rural women travels better than the milk processed in expensive dairy plants.

The white revolution has thus diverted milk from basic rural needs to dairy foods for the elite, modelled on western consumption patterns, such as butter, cheese, and dried skimmed milk and chocolates. Seventy percent of milk procured by dairy plants in India is manufactured into these products, consumed by only two percent of the population. Expensive methods of collection, chilling, transportation, processing, testing, packaging, and advertising are employed for the manufacture and marketing of luxury dairy products by government, cooperative, and private sector factories. These are used mainly by the affluent, either directly or indirectly through such products as ice-cream, biscuits, chocolates, etc. The economic reductionism inherent in the white revolution logic of seeing cows as producers of milk as a commodity, has various levels of violence against women and children built in. Rural women are violated by the negation of their role as animal husbandry experts and dairy food producers. Churning the curd for making ghee and buttermilk has been a symbol of this productivity. The white revolution removed this churning from the domain of women's work to an imported dairy processing plant run by men, thus simultaneously diverting nutrition away from rural to urban areas.

The white revolution, by turning milk into a commodity, has totally deprived rural children of their access to dairy nutrition. In villages not affected by its strategy, people continue to sell ghee and retain buttermilk for local consumption while in the white revolution villages they sell fluid milk and retain nothing for self-consumption. The marketing of ghee does not entail an anguished choice between money and nutrition, because buttermilk, which retains the nutritive part of the milk, is consumed in villages and given away free to the poor. By contrast, with

106 *Ibid.*, p. 120.

the marketing of fresh milk, rural producers are faced with the 'painful choice of feeding milk to dairies like Amul or to their children'. Villages in Gujarat, the home of the white revolution, have very serious nutritional deficiencies. In children below five years, there is a high incidence of protein-calorie malnutrition since adequate quantities of milk are not available as a weaning food.[107] Urban children are also violated nutritionally, because what is a 'value added' process for the dairy industry is a 'value annihilation' process from the point of view of nutrition. The divorce between food-value and profit-value applies as much to dairy products as it does to other foods processed by modern industry. Products that generate high profits, such as baby foods and chocolates, are health hazards, not sources of nutrition.

Fragmentation of nature : integration of markets

Just as the green revolution replaced local ecological integration by commercial integration at the level of global markets and the manufacture of pesticides, fertilizers, and seeds, the white revolution has replaced local ecological linkages between fodder, cattle and food with global commercial linkages between trade in cattlefeed and in milk products and substitutes. While livestock genes are imported from the north countries to fragment the integrity of India's indigenous genetic resources in livestock, and western dairy technologies and equipment are imported to violate the integrity of women's and nature's work in dairying and agriculture, a further violation to land and food systems is induced by the export of cattle-feed.

The white revolution has a major oilseeds component. Its policy of 'demand-led marketing' makes the flow of milk and cattle-feed follow purchasing power instead of need, threatening the very basic rights of children to nutrition. Soya bean, cultivated largely for cattle-feed for the north, is being spread throughout the south under oilseeds programmes, displacing traditional staple food crops integrated with soil and nutrition patterns. Soya was discovered as a 'miracle bean' by western agribusiness. Grain trading multinationals like Gargill, Continental and Bunge which, with Louis Dreyfus and Andre Garnac, control 50 percent of the world grain trade, also control the soya trade now, especially as

107 Shanti George, *op.cit.,* p. 261.

inputs for the cattle-feed industry.[108] The nice thing with soya in the corporate perspective is that unlike traditional oilseeds and beans, it needs industrial processing and is eminently suitable for feeding factories instead of stomachs. It cannot be processed locally by women, like traditional oilseeds whose oilcake made very important cattle-feed. Hungry stomachs and malnutritioned children are however the justification for the large scale spread of overcoming edible oil scarcity. However, replacing traditional oilseeds by soya bean, an introduced crop, is once again based on the myth of productivity increase. The average oil recovery from soya bean is only 144 kg/ha, against 175 kg/ha from mustard seed and 150 kg/ha from groundnut. As an oilseed, soya bean is quite clearly unproductive. The hidden agenda for the spread of soya bean is not the production of oil but of oilcake for export. De-oiled cake recovery is as much as 655 kg in the case of soya bean, against 325 kg for mustard seed and 200 kg for groundnut. In less than a decade the production of soya bean has reached 11 lakh tonnes in India.[109] As late as 1976 the cultivation of soya bean was insignificant. By 1982-83 it was 3.58 lakh tonnes and by 1990, it is expected to reach 30 lakh tonnes. India exports 1.5 million tonnes of oilcake as cattle-feed, 50 percent of it to the EEC. Exports of oilcake tripled in 1986.[110] Global dairying interests are thus putting European dairy cattle in direct competition with Indian people for the produce from India's land through development projects like the white revolution, which are ostensibly aimed at improving the availability of food and nutrition to people in India. Food entitlements are going down through the disruption of crop and livestock links on the farm, through milk export from rural areas and through feed exports from the country. The absurdity and violence of disintegration at the local ecosystem level and integration at the global commodity trade level is apparent when the cattle in the EEC countries are annihilated for 'overproduction'.[111] The cattle of both regions are thus rendered dispensable by a reductionist logic of dairy development controlled by transnational business interests. Indigenous cattle are bred out for being 'inferior' and European and American cattle are killed for producing surplus. The cow which was transformed into a milk machine by reductionist logic is next destroyed by the full unfolding

108 'Soja Sover', *Milieudefensie*, Amsterdam, 1982.
109 'Can Soya Replace Traditional Oilseeds?' *The Times of India*, May 24, 1985.
110 'Oilcakes Export up by 60 percent', *Indian Express*, September 5, 1985.
111 'U.S. Cows Face Penalty for Plenty', *Indian Express*, March 29, 1986.

of that logic. With the cow go the small people whose prosperity was linked to the cow—the small dairy producer in the North as much as the small livestock owner in India. And as the old generation of biological reductionism in turning the cow into a dispensable milk machine runs into trouble worldwide, the new miracle of biotechnologies and genetic engineering is sold to further increase the milk output of cows, and further threaten the livelihood of the small producer. Multinationals like Elanco (a subsidiary of Eli Lilly), Cynamid, Monsanto, and Upjohn are all rushing to put BST, bovine somatrophin, on the market in spite of of controversy and anxiety about its ecological impact.[112] Somatrophins are proteins which tell the body what to do with the energy generated from food. BST producing genes have been inserted into the DNA of bacteria through genetic engineering, and the growth hormone is now being produced in commercial quantities by drug multinationals. When injected daily into cows, BST diverts energy to milk production. One of the problems not yet overcome is that there is a chance that cows may get emaciated if too much energy is diverted to produce milk. A second problem is that, as in all other 'miracles' of modern science in agriculture, the gain in milk production is conditional on a number of other factors such as industrial feed and computerised feeding equipment and programmes.[113] Just as, in the first phase of the white revolution, women were displaced from the processing sector and their control over milk, removed, so with genetic engineering, they are being marginalised in their role of caring for cows. This activity is now in the hands of men and machines.

The inherent violence of the white revolution as reductionism in livestock management lies in the manner in which it treats the needs of small people throughout the world as dispensable, and living resources merely as raw material for commodity production, dispensable in the logic of the market if they produce the wrong thing in the wrong quantity. The same global commoditisation processes which render Indian cattle 'unproductive' (even when, in multidimensional terms, they are highly productive) simultaneously dispense with European cattle for being overproductive. This annihilation of livestock in its diversity is linked to the annihilation of knowledge of the protection and conservation of living resources as sources of life. This is replaced by the need to protect the profits of rich farmers and increase the control of agribusinesses.

112 'Buttercup Goes on Hormones', *The Economist*, May 9, 1987.

113 B. Kueen, 'Biocow' in *The Ram's Horn*: Newsletter of the Nutrition Policy Institute, Toronto, No. 40, May 1987.

The needs of people are replaced by the needs of multinational aid and business. It is in order to reverse this anti-life logic that the feminine principle needs to be recovered. When peasant women in India resist the sale of milk, as in the hill areas of Garhwal, saying it is not a commodity; when they resist the shift from staple foods like millets and pulses to soya bean or cash crop cultivation; or when European women organise to move the butter and food mountains;[114] or peasants in Portugal's highlands refuse to kill their cows to maintain EEC market prices, the feminine principle is stirring towards life-conserving, life-enhancing perceptions and actions.[115]

The recovery of the feminine principle in dairying involves the recovery of the integrity of the cow, and the rejection of the 'sacredness' of a violent science. It involves the recovery of the integration of dairying with farming, and of rebuilding the relatedness of soils and animals. It involves the recovery of the diversity that such integration with nature's processes involves, and to place at the centre of concern in food and nutrition systems, the needs of the earth, the animals, the people. It means that invisible workers, like women and their cows, be put at the centre of an integrated and ecologically sound food production process. It is they who satisfy basic sustenance needs and maintain the integrity of ecosystems and living beings and constitute the only viable response to the violent forces of disruption and breakdown that masculinist science and development have unleashed as 'progress'. The feminist agenda for food is the recovery of the feminine principle in food production so that sustainability and diversity, and patterns of equitable distribution are ensured. Equity rooted in diversity arid in self-generated development is nowhere more conspicuous than in food —as are the injustice, violence, and external patriarchal control arising from uniformity and reductionism.

As producers of sustenance, rural women have always been in the lead in struggles related to the right to food. During the Tebhaga uprising in Bengal, following the great famine, women had formed the Nari Bahini to protect their right to food by resisting the exploitative takeover of 50 percent of the farm produce by the jotedars. The Tebhaga movement was a demand for a two-third share for those who produced the food, and its

114 Reported by Danielle Grunberg of Women for Peace at the END Convention, Coventry, July 1987.

115 Reported by Maria Lourdes at the meeting of the Committee for a Just World Peace, Yokohama, December 1986.

slogan was 'Pran debo, dhan debo na' (we will give up our lives, not our rice).[116] In the new context where the jotedar has been replaced by multi-national and international aid agencies, and where exploitation involves not just robbing the peasant, but also nature, the productive base of the peasant, it will again be rural women who will protect the sources of life by protecting the sanctity of seeds, soils, and cattle. The right to food is today inextricably linked to the right of nature to conserve her ability to produce food sustainably. The partnership between women and nature for a recovery of the organic base of sustenance is crucial for making that right a reality for all.

It is in this sense that ecological movements spearheaded by rural women create sane alternatives not just for women, but for society as a whole. The struggles of the Chipko women of Garhwal to conserve an organic system of food production based on conserving trees, soils, water, cattle, and genetic diversity, are struggles that challenge the gender and class-based ideologies of exclusion with trans-gender, declassed ideologies of inclusion.

---

116 Peter Custers, *Women in the Tebhaga Uprising*, Calcutta: Noya Prokash, 1987.

CHAPTER SIX

Women and the Vanishing Waters

The disappearing source

The drying up of India, like that of Africa, is a man-made rather than a natural disaster. The issue of water, and water scarcity, has been the most dominant one in the '80s as far as struggles for survival in the subcontinent are concerned. The manufacture of drought and desertification is an outcome of reductionist knowledge and modes of development which violate cycles of life in rivers, in the soil, in mountains. Rivers are drying up because their catchments have been mined, deforested, or over-cultivated to generate revenue and profits. Groundwater is drying up because it has been over-exploited to feed cash crops. Village after village is being robbed of its lifeline, its sources of drinking water, and the number of villages facing water famine is in direct proportion to the number of 'schemes' implemented by government agencies to 'develop' water. Since women are the water providers, disappearing water sources have meant new burdens and new drudgery for them. Each river and spring and well drying up means longer walks for women for collecting water, and implies more work and less survival options. In Uttar Pradesh, Rajasthan, Gujarat, Madhya Pradesh, Maharashtra, Karnataka, Andhra Pradesh, and Tamil Nadu, most villages are facing new water scarcities created by maldevelopment and a reductionist science.

In Uttar Pradesh, as many as 43 out of 57 districts were reeling under an acute drinking water famine in 1983. The crisis is clearly man-made: in the '60s, the number of villages with drinking water problems was 17,000—in 1972 it went up to 35,000. New schemes were implemented to bring water to 34,144 of the villages, which should have left only 856 villages with water problems. But 1985 saw 25,000 new villages facing acute scarcity; the schemes failed because water sources had dried up.[1]

The worst hit regions of U.P. are Banda, Hamirpur, Jhansi, Allahabad, Mirzapur, Varanasi, Ballia, Jaunpur, and the hill districts. Sources of potable water are drying up everywhere, and because of this, handpumps and piped water supply schemes are becoming useless. In Banda, trains have been used to provide water; in Hamirpur, bullock-carts are being used, while women now have to walk for 15-20 miles to fetch water.[2]

In the hill districts of U.P. 2,300 out of 2,700 projects which were implemented for drinking water supply have failed because the sources have dried up.[3] How this translates into a burden for women is evident from the fact that no woman is willing to marry a man from Dharchula because of the water scarcity in Dharchula district.[4] The Chipko message that forests produce water, is becoming a truism as continuing deforestation is leading to increased scarcity of water in the hills. Madhya Pradesh, the forested heartland of India, was famous for water at every step. It lost 18 lakh ha. of forests from 1975 to 1982. Whenever afforestation has been undertaken it has made the situation worse because species like eucalyptus further deplete water resources. Today Madhya Pradesh is trapped in an irreversible depletion of water resources: most of its rivers, ponds, wells, and springs have dried up. In 1985, an official memorandum to the Central government stated that all 45 districts were in the grip of an unprecedented crisis: 'If adequate steps to provide drinking water facilities are not taken immediately, it can be said without exaggeration that a large population will have no water to drink at all.' In towns, the water scarcity is leading to violence. In May 1985 hundreds of people, including policemen, were hurt in clashes over water in Jabalpur. Sagar is without water, because the Debus river which provides it with drinking water dried up

1 'Water Crisis Hits Most U.P. Areas', *Hindustan Times*, June 13, 1983.

2 'Acute Water Crisis Grips Uttar Pradesh', *Indian Express*, May 19, 1984.

3 'Serious Water Crisis in U.P. Hill Districts', *Indian Express*, June 15, 1984.

4 'No Water, No Wife', *Indian Express*, July 6, 1984.

for the first time in 1985. Water was sold for Rs. 10 a drum, and people are keeping their drinking water, supplied under police protection, under lock and key. As the Superintendent of Police stated, 'We had to post policemen with each water tanker and lorry because of frequent cases of quarrels, assaults on drivers, and attempts to snatch water'.[5] The Malwa region, once known for its abundance of water, is today dry, both above and below ground. While, earlier, water was normally struck at 80 ft., it is now difficult to find even after drilling 300 ft. below ground. As a result of the over-exploitation of groundwater, the number of villages whose water sources have dried up increases every year. Even those villages where the problem is supposed to have been tackled by new schemes are experiencing a recurrence of drinking watr shortages. In 1980, out of 70,000 villages of the region, 36,420 reported water shortage; in 1982, this number rose to 50,000 and in 1985 it was 64,565. In other words, nearly all the villages of the state suffer from a water crisis. Commercial exploitation of forests, over-exploitation of ground water for commercial agriculture and inappropriate afforestation are the major reasons identified for the water crisis.[6] Metereologically, neither Madhya Pradesh nor neighbouring Orissa are arid zones. Desertification and dessication in these regions has been manufactured by maldevelopment. Kalahandi in Orissa is a glaring example: 30 years ago it was an unending stretch of lush green forests, rich in teak and sal which provided a livelihood to the tribal population. Today, 830 out of its 2,842 villages are desertified. One hundred and ninety villages have been deserted, with some people migrating to cities, others into forests where edible roots and fruits help them survive. Nowapura subdivision which was, until recently, densely forested is today a stretch of parched land. A systematic exploitation of its forest resources has left the region barren and dry. Each year Kalahandi faces more acute water scarcity which in turn leads to scarcity of food, employment, and means of livelihood. The Adivasis, Harijans, and other poor people who were supported by forest resources have started fleeing their parched houses. According to one estimate 40,000 people have left the district over the last few years to escape starvation. Those who stay behind are largely women and children, and they are the worst victims of scarcity conditions. In

5 'Sagar Crying Out For Water', *Indian Express*, June 16, 1986 and 'Drought in M.P. Leaves Trail of Misery', *Indian Express*, June 19, 1985.

6 'Alarming Fall in M.P. Water Resources', *Indian Express*, June 23, 1985.

the summer of 1985, four children and two women died of starvation in Kamna block. Panasi Punji, a 35-year-old shepherd woman in Amrapali village in Kalahandi, is an example of how women are special victims of desertification. Panasi's husband left her to search for work; initially, she supported her children and her 14-year-old sister-in-law, Vanita, by working on people's farms. With increasing water scarcity, agricultural employment also came to an end. Finally, Panasi survived for a little longer by selling Vanita to a rich farmer who paid her Rs. 50.[7]

Gujarat's biggest problem today is drinking water. For the first time in the history of the state, the shortage of drinking water has assumed alarming proportions because most of the wells, ponds, and dams have gone dry. The number of villages declared as 'no source' villages has been increasing with each passing year, in spite of of an expenditure of Rs. 400 crores on drinking water supply schemes. At the end of the Fifth Plan, 3,844 villages had drinking water problems. But surprisingly, in the first year of the Seventh Plan, the number of no-source villages shot up to more than 6,000. In 1985, the figure went up to 8,000 and in 1986, 12,250 villages out of a total of 18,000 were without water. In 1985–86, potable water was being supplied to Gujarat by special trains, tankers, camels, and bullock-carts. The government's crash programme in 1985–86 to provide drinking water, estimated to have cost nearly Rs. 86 crore, has left the problem as acute as ever. New sources have dried up, and the 4,000-tubewells dug have run dry. The government is now ready to spend another Rs. 93 crores on long distance transfer and on more tubewells. Gujarat also has a World Bank aided water supply project of Rs. 136 crores, but both technology inputs and financial inputs are failing in providing water in the face of the depletion of water sources themselves.[8]

The cause of the water crisis and the failure of solutions both arise from reductionist science and maldevelopment working against the logic of the water cycle, and hence violating the integrity of water flows which allows rivers, streams, and wells to regenerate themselves. The arrogance of these anti-nature and anti-women development programmes lies in their belief that they create water and have the power to 'augment' it. They fail to recognise that humans, like all living things, are participants in the water

7 'A Drought-hit People', *Times of India*, July 26, 1986; 'Stage-show and Survival Struggle', *Indian Express*, June 26, 1985; 'Severe Scarcity Conditions in Orissa', *Times of India*, July 3, 1986; 'Plight of Women', *Indian Express*, July 28, 1986; 'Stir in Orissa over Water Shortage', *Indian Express*, April 21, 1985.

8 'Gujarat in for Acute Water Famine', *Times of India*, December 20, 1986; 'Solutions that Hold no Water', *Times of India*, December 8, 1986.

cycle and can survive sustainably only through that participation. Working against it, assuming one is controlling and augmenting water while over-exploiting or disrupting it, amounts at one point to a breakdown of the cycle of life. That is why in water management, it is imperative to think and act ecologically, to 'think like a river' and to flow with the nature of water.[9] All attempts that have violated the logic of the water's natural flow in renewing itself have ended up worsening the problem of water scarcity. Water circulates from seas to clouds, to land and rivers, to lakes and to underground streams, and ultimately returns to the oceans, generating life wherever it goes. It is a renewable resource by virtue of this endless cyclic flow between sea, air, and land. Despite what engineers like to think, water cannot be 'augmented' or 'built'. It can be diverted and redistributed and it can be wasted, but the availability of water on earth is united and limited by the water cycle. Since it is volatile, and since most of its flow is invisible, in and below the soil, it is rarely seen as being the element that places the strictest limits on sustainable use. Used within these limits, water can be available forever in all its forms and abundance; stretched beyond these limits, it disappears and dries up. Over-exploitation for a few decades or even a few years can destroy sources that have supported life over centuries. Violence to the water cycle is probably the worst but most invisible form of violence because it simultaneously threatens the survival of all.

Dominant approaches to water utilisation and management are reductionist and fail to perceive the cyclical nature of water flows. They linearise and commoditise thinking about water as a resource and create an illusion of producing abundance while manufacturing scarcity. The submersion of catchments and the diversion of surface water by large dams; the depletion of groundwater caused by diverting river flows as well as by over-exploitation made possible by energised pumping and tubewells; and the overuse of water by surface cultivation of water intensive crops and trees are some major causes for the drying up of water systems. Yet the crisis mind proposes an extension of the disease as the cure—its solution to desertification is more dams, more tubewells, more water intensive cultivation on the one hand, and more technology intensive solutions to the drinking water crisis on the other. Nature's natural flow is further violated, destroying the feminine principle and sustaining power of water, and destroying women's knowledge and productivity in providing sustenance.

9 D. Worster, 'Thinking Like a River', in W. Jackson, et al. (eds.), *Meeting the Expectations of the Land*, San Francisco: Northpoint Press, 1984, p. 57.

Dams as violence to the river

India is a riparian civilisation. The temples of ancient India have often
been temples dedicated to rivers and their sources, and one of the best
descriptions of the vital ecoprocesses of the water cycle is the story of
the mighty river Ganga, roaring down the Himalayan slopes with no one
to hold the Earth together in the face of her might. Brahma, the creator
of the universe according to Indian mythology, was deeply concerned
about the ecological problem of the descent of Ganga from the heavens
to the Earth. He said,

Ganga, whose waves in swarga flow
Is daughter of the Lord of Snow
Win Shiva, that his aid be lent
To hold her in her mid-descent
For earth alone will never bear
These torrents travelled from the upper air.[10]

The above metaphor is a description of the hydrological problem
associated with the descent of mighty rivers like the Ganga, which are
fed by seasonal and powerful monsoonic rains. Reiger, the eminent Himalayan ecologist, describes the material rationality of the myth in the
following words:

In the scriptures a realisation is there that if all the waters which de-
scend upon the mountain were to beat down upon the naked earth,
then earth would never bear the torrents.... In Shiva's hair we have a
very well known physical device which breaks the force of the water
coming down ... the vegetation of the mountains.[11]

A Chipko song by Ghanshyam 'Shailani', inspired by a Garhwali
woman, talks of the natural broadleaved forests of oak-rhododendron
on mountain tops, inviting the rain and yielding water from their roots.
Rivers have thus been perceived and used in the total integration of their
relationship with rainfall, mountains, forests, land, and sea. Natural forests in catchments have been viewed as the best mechanism for water
control and flood control in Indian thought. Catchment forests of rivers
and streams have therefore always been treated as sacred.

10 H.C. Reiger, 'Whose Himalaya? A Study in Geopiery', in T. Singh, (ed.), *Studies in
Himalayan Ecology and Development Strategies*, New Delhi: The English Book Store,
1980, p. 2.
11 *Ibid.*

Rapidly, however, the temples of ancient India, dedicated to the river goddesses, were substituted by dams, the temples of modern India, dedicated to capitalist farmers and industrialists, built and managed by engineers trained in patriarchal, western paradigms of water management. Water management has been transformed from the management of an integrated water cycle by those who participate in it, particularly women, into the exploitation of water with dams, reservoirs, and canals by experts and technocrats in remote places, with masculinist minds. These engineering and technological feats are part of the Baconian vision of substituting sacred rivers with inert, passive water resources which can be managed and exploited by scientific man in the service of profit. The desacralisation of rivers and their sources has removed all constraints from the overuse and abuse of water. Projects of controlling the rivers, of damming and diverting them against their logic and flow to increase water availability and provide 'dependable' water supplies have proved to be self-defeating. The illusion of abundance created by dams has been created by ignoring the abundance provided by nature. The role of the river in recharging water sources throughout its course, and in its distributive role in taking water from high-rainfall catchments through diverse ecosystems has been ignored. When dams are built by submerging large areas of forested catchments, and river waters are diverted from the river course into canals, four types of violence are perpetrated on the river's water cycle:

1. Deforestation in the catchment reduces rainfall and hence reduces river discharges and turns perennial flows into seasonal flows.

2. Diversion of water from its natural course and natural irrigation zones to engineered 'command' areas leads to problems of waterlogging and salinity.

3. Diversion of water from its natural course prevents the river from recharging groundwater sources downstream.

4. Reduced inflows of fresh water into the sea disturb the fresh water-sea water balance and lead to salinity ingress and sea erosion.

Violence is not intrinsic to the use of river waters for human needs. It is a particular characteristic of gigantic river valley projects which work *against*, and not *with*, the logic of the river. These projects are based on reductionist assumptions which relate water use not to nature's processes but to the processes of revenue and profit generation. Impounding rivers and streams for irrigation is not in itself an example of modern western technology. The ancient anicuts on the Kaveri and Krishna rivers in South India are examples of how riparian societies in India used river water to increase benefits to man without violence to the river. In the indigenous system, water storage, and distribution were based on nature's logic, and worked in harmony with nature's cycles. Among these nonviolent irrigation systems was the major tank system of Mysore. Major Sankey, one of the first British engineers who came to Mysore observed that 'to such an extent has the principle of storage been followed that it would require some ingenuity to discover a site within this great area suitable for a new tank. While restorations are of course feasible, any absolutely new work of this description would, within this area, almost certainly be found to cut off the supply of another, lower down the same basin'.[12] These tank systems constructed over centuries also endured over centuries. Their management was based on local participation with women and men desilting the tank-beds and repairing the breaches during February, March, and April. On Bhim Ekadashi day, villagers imitated the epic hero, Bhim, by collective desilting of field channels. Though observed as a religious festival, it had the effect of preventing water-logging.[13] Small tanks in the village were replenished by women who carried water from the river.

The sophisticated engineering sense, built on an ecological sense that provided the foundation for irrigation in India, has been commented on again and again by famous British engineers who learnt water management from indigenous techniques. Major Arthur Cotton, credited as the 'founder' of modern irrigation programmes, wrote in 1874:

> There are multitudes of old native works in various parts of India.... These are noble works, and show both boldness and engineering talent. They have stood for hundreds of years.... When I first arrived in India, the contempt with which the natives justifiably spoke of us on account of this neglect of material improvements was very striking; they used to say we were a kind of civilized savages, wonderfully expert about fighting, but so inferior to their great men that we would not even keep in repair the works they had constructed, much less even imitate them in extending the system.[14]

12 B.V. Krishna Murthy, *Eco-development in Southern Mysore*, New Delhi: Dept. of Environment, p. 30, 1983, p. 7.

13 K.M. Munshi, *Land Management in India*, New Delhi: Ministry of Agriculture, 1952.

14 N. Sengupta, 'Irrigation: Traditional vs. Modern,' Madras: Institute of Development Studies, 1985, p. 17.

The East India Company which took control of the Kaveri delta in 1799 was unable to check the rising river bed. Company officials struggled for a quarter century; finally, using indigenous technology, Cotton was able to solve the problem by renovating the Grand Anicut. As he wrote later:

> It was from them (the native Indians) we learnt how to secure a foundation in loose sand of unmeasured depth....The Madras river irrigations executed by our engineers have been from the first the greatest financial success of any engineering works in the world, solely because we learnt from them....With this lesson about foundations, we built bridges, weirs, aqueducts and every kind of hydraulic work....We are thus deeply indebted to the native engineers.[15]

Throughout the country, irrigation works, big and small, protected agriculture in the dry season. Persian wheels and counterpoise lifts, rope and bucket lifts and water ladders used renewable human and animal energy and kept water use within the limits of renewability. So adequate were these diverse irrigation systems that when the agriculture policy was being formulated in independent India, the only task considered for irrigation was restoration and repair of old works.[16] With independence, the project to build a modern India got a new impetus. Dam-building took the form of an epidemic, with large structures being built for flood control, irrigation, and power generation.

River valley projects are considered the usual solution to meeting the water needs of agriculture, for controlling floods or mitigating drought. More than 1,554 large dams have been built in India during the past three decades. It is estimated that about 79 mha metre of water can be used annually from the surface in Indian rivers, but less than 25 mha metres is actually utilised. The obvious answer so far has been to provide storage capacity in large reservoirs behind huge and costly dams. Between 1951 and 1980, India has spent Rs. 75,100 million on major or medium irrigation dams. Yet the return from this large investment has been far less than anticipated. In fact, where irrigated lands should yield at least five tonnes of grain per ha, in India yield has remained at 1.7 tonnes per ha. The annual losses from irrigation projects caused by unexpectedly low water availability, heavy siltation, reducing storage capacity, water-logging, etc., now amount to Rs. 4,270 million. The Kabini project in

15 *Ibid.*, p. 18.
16 K.M. Munshi, *op.cit.*, p. 9.

Karnataka is a good example of how water development projects can themselves become the cause of disruption of the hydrological cycle and destruction of water resources in the basin. It has a submersion area of 6,000 acres, but it entailed the clear-felling of 30,000 acres of primeval forest in the catchments to rehabilitate displaced villages. As a consequence, the local rainfall fell from 60 inches to 45 inches, and high siltation rates have already drastically reduced the life of the project. In the command area, large areas of well developed coconut gardens and paddy fields have been laid waste through water-logging and salinity within two years of irrigation from the project. The story of the Kabini project is a classic case of how the water crisis is being created by the very projects aimed at increasing water availability or stabilising water flows.[17]

The damming of two of India's most sacred rivers, the Ganga and the Narmada, have been seriously resisted by women, peasants, and tribals whose sacred sites will be destroyed and whose life-support systems are being disrupted. But the people of Narmada Valley, resisting dislocation and displacement from the Sardar Sarovar and Narmada Sagar dams,[18] or the people of Tehri, resisting the Tehri dam,[19] do not merely struggle to preserve their homeland. Their resistance is against the destruction of entire civilizations and ways of life in the very process of dam building which involves the large scale dislocation of peoples and river systems. As the women of Tehri state on the site where they have been protesting daily for nearly two decades, 'Tehri Dam is a symbol of total destruction'. (Tehri dam *sampurna vinash ka pratik hai*).

The reductionist mind which sees 'environment' as passive and fragmented has viewed the 'recovery' of ecological balance merely as a matter of creating plantations in the command. However the destruction of forests in the catchments cannot be restored by planting trees elsewhere because catchments are where rain falls most bountifully, and catchment forests contribute to the overall precipitation and its conservation. Research by the United Nations University has established that 75 percent of rainfall in rainforest regions is contributed by the rainforest itself. Moist forests in the tropics create rain and conserve it for perennial discharge. Destroying the rainforest implies decreasing the available

17 B. Prabhakar, 'Social Forestry Dissertation', Dehradun: Forest Research Institute, 1983.

18 'The Narmada Project,' *Kalpavriksha*, New Delhi, 1988; Medha Patkar, 'Development or Destruction? A Case of Sardar Sarovar Project on the Narmada River,' paper, 1987.

19 *The Tehri Dam: A Prescription for Disaster*, New Delhi: INTACH, 1987.

rainfall. Plantations somewhere else cannot recover these biospheric functions because they are not ecologically equivalent to the catchment forest—for one they are man-made plantations and not forests, for another, they are in the command and not in the catchments.

Most rivers in India have been used for irrigation, over centuries. Irrigation systems were created like the 'round river', taking off from the river to nurture agriculture, and going back to the river to recharge it. Modern irrigation, overpowered by the masculinist trend of the large and spectacular and by the principle of overpowering the river, has created systems that work against nature's own drainage. On the one hand, this leads to a destruction of irrigated agriculture in the river valley and turns skilled farmers into unskilled 'refugees'. The Soliga, displaced from Kabini, were originally irrigated-paddy cultivators; today they are ignorant dryland farmers. The Soliga women complain about how they are now captives of pesticide firms and banks which come to give them new 'expertise' for cash crop cultivation. The peasants uprooted by the Srisailam dam lost irrigated land along the Krishna and are today living in abject poverty.[20] Probably they too, like the Santhal in Bengal, created songs about dams that caused their destruction:

> *Which company came to my land to open a karkhana?*
> *It awakened its name in the rivers and the ponds*
> *calling itself the DVC*?*
> *It throws earth, dug by a machine, into the river.*
> *It has cut the mountain and made a bridge.*
> *The water runs beneath.*
> *Roads are coming, they are giving us electricity,*
> *having opened the karkhana.*
> *The praja all question them.*
> *Then ask what this name belongs to.*
> *When evening falls they give paper notes as pay.*
> *Where will I keep these paper notes?*
> *They dissolve in the water.*
> *In every house there is a well which gives water*
> *for brinjal and cabbage.*
> *Every house is bounded by walls which make it look*
> *like a palace*
> *This Santhal tongue of ours has been destroyed in the district.*

20 *Lokayan Bulletin*, Reports on Displacement by Srisailam Dam.

* Damodar Valley Corporation. (A song sung in the Purulia District of West Bengal.)

You came and made this a bloody burning ghat,
calling yourself the DVC.[21]

Every major new dam in modern India has displaced people from fertile river valleys, both upstream and downstream of the dam, and has left fertile alluvial soils submerged or barren. This destruction of irrigation potential is never accounted for in new irrigation projects.

The new command areas created have topographies, soils, climates which were never intended to manage large water inputs. Water-logging and salinity are therefore the result. The water cycle can be destabilised by adding more water to an ecosystem than the natural drainage potential of that system. This leads to desertification through water-logging and salinisation of land. Desertification of this kind is also a form of water abuse rather than water use. It is associated with large irrigation projects and water intensive cultivation patterns. About 25 percent of the irrigated land in the U.S. suffers from salinisation and water-logging. In India 10 mha of canal-irrigated land have become waterlogged and another 25 mha are threatened with salinity. Land gets waterlogged when the water table is within 1.5 to 2.1 metres below the ground surface. The water table goes up if water is added to a basin faster than it can drain out. Certain types of soils and topography are most vulnerable to waterlogging. The rich alluvial plains of Punjab and Haryana suffer seriously from desertification induced by the introduction of excessive irrigation water to make green revolution farming possible. Heavy water-logging and salinity threaten three southern districts of Punjab, viz., Faridkot, Ferozepur and Bhatinda. In Haryana, in nearly 6,80,000 hectares of land the water table is within a depth of three metres and in another 3,00,000 hectares it is approaching this level.[22] A 10-year Rs. 800 crore phased programme aided by the world financial institutions to save the heartland of the state from the scourge of rising saline groundwater has been planned by the Haryana Minor Irrigation and Tubewell Corporation.[23] When this cost is added to the cost of supplying irrigation water, water intensive cropping patterns will not emerge as more productive than rainfed ones. Just as, in the case of desertification due to water depletion, the cause is mistakenly identified as drought, in the case of desertification due to water-logging, the

21 Quoted in Shiv Viswanathan, 'From the Annals of a Lab. State', *Lokayan Bulletin*, Vol. 3, No: 4/5, p. 39.

22 'The High Cost of Irrigation', *Indian Express*, Nov. 4, 1986.

23 'Rising Saline Groundwater in Haryana', *Economic Times*, October 13, 1984.

cause is mistakenly identified as absence of adequate surface and subsur-
face drainage. The engineering solution offered by the reductionist mind
is capital intensive, artificial drainage works—some including trench-
ing machines which have to be imported. A simpler ecological solution,
which recovers the productivity of soils and women as food producers, is
a shift in cropping patterns, away from thirsty cash crops to water prudent staple foods so that less water is introduced into the system and the
threat of water-logging is immediately emoved. Intensive irrigation which
requires intensive drainage works is a counterproductive strategy and results in the abuse of water resources.

Black cotton soils are extra prone to water-logging, while they are
highly productive in a sustainable manner under rainfed conditions.[24]
Such soils have a natural advantage for being rainfed because they have
a high water-holding capacity and are very retentive of moisture. They
are considered the most fertile and are suited for dry cultivation. Cotton, jowar, bajra, and wheat grow principally with underground moisture
alone. The retentive nature of the soil, especially when it has much depth
in addition makes possible the dry cultivation of several crops which
are ordinarily grown only under irrigation in other soils. It is because
the natural productivity of black cotton soils is being destroyed through
irrigation and consequent water-logging that farmers in these regions
have been resisting the government's irrigation policy. The Mitti Bachao
Abhiyan (Save the Soil Movement) in Tawa and the Ryot Sangha resistance in Malaprabha Ghatprabha (Karnataka) are signals of how productive rainfed land has been laid waste by irrigation. Visveshwara, the 19th
century scientific genius of Mysore, had categorically ruled out irrigation
schemes for black cotton soil regions while building large dams for Mysore State. Yet the reductionist mind continues to build these and large canal networks, threatening ecological stability everywhere. It is predicted
that the massive irrigation project in Rajasthan, the Indira Gandhi Canal,
will render more than 30 percent of the 15 lakh hectares of command
into waterlogged and saline wastelands.[25]

Taking water in large canals to arid regions to 'make the desert bloom'
has been a particularly favourite masculinist project. In regions of scarce
rainfall, the earth contains a large amount of unleached salts; pouring
excessive water into these canals brings the salts to the surface, and also
leaches them to other water sources. As the irrigation water evaporates,

24 J.S. Kanwar, *Rainwater Management*, Hyderabad: ICRISAT, 1983.

25 'Indira Gandhi Canal to Create More Problems', *Times of India*, January 16, 1987.

it leaves a whitish residue of salt behind. Finally, more water is used to flush away salt left by earlier irrigation. The cure to the problem of water scarcity as created by the crisis mind demands more water and more energy—a cure that at some point becomes even worse than the illness. The reductionist mind-set treats the river as a linear, not a circular flow, and is indifferent to the diversity of soils and topography. Its engineering feats continue to be ecological failures because it thinks against the logic of the river. This violence to the river is a sporadic act, ill-considered, and destructive. As Worster points out, 'The natural river has been regarded by a succession of planners as an unruly dangerous beast that must be tamed and disciplined by modern science and its commodities'.[26] It is this mentality that is tapped in an advertisement for cement which says, 'The river is furious, but the dam will hold. The cement is Vikram'. Yet we know that dams do not always hold. The Koyna and Morvi disasters are witness to the vulnerability of the 'invulnerable' projects of modern man, whose reductionist mind, in tearing nature apart, reduces her capacity to renew herself and support life.

This engineering logic, by taking water away to where it does not belong, creates wet and salt-laden deserts. In addition, dams also divert water away from where it belongs in nature's logic, and leave entire regions with dry river beds and wells. The perennial river is not merely a surface flow, it also renews water below the ground. The diversion of rivers results in the depletion and drying up of groundwater. Nowhere have I seen this more clearly than in Maharashtra where the damming up of the Yarala river led to a drying up of the river downstream as well as the drying up of all the wells the river used to recharge. It was an old woman who quietly said to me, 'They do not see the huge water reservoir nature provides below the ground. They do not see nature's work and our work in distributing water. All they can see is the structures they build'.

The masculinist mind, by wanting to tame and control every river in ignorance of nature's ways, is in fact sowing the seeds of large scale desertification and famine. The Ethiopian famine which has killed nearly one million people and affected eight million, is not merely related to the failure of rainfall. It is more closely linked with the damming of the Awash river. Before the construction of dams, more than 1,50,000 people were supported by agriculture in the Awash Valley. The building of a series of dams on the Awash with World Bank funds to provide water to the sugarcane, cotton, and banana plantations of rich Ethiopians and Dutch, Italian, Israeli, and British firms dried up the lands downstream

26 D. Worster, *op. cit.*, p. 34.

and flooded the lands upstream, uprooting more than 20,000 people. The Afar, the traditional pastoralists of Awash Valley, were pushed up the fragile slopes, which their herds turned bare in the struggle for survival. The 1972 drought killed 30 percent of the Afar tribe. How many other rivers must have run dry, how many millions of acres of land in other regions been turned into desert because the reductionist vision failed to see the invisible flows of water when it dammed and diverted the rivers? How many peasants must be left with parched fields because engineers and planners take their water away to produce cash crops and commodities? The links between new capital and technology intensive irrigation works and cash crop farming have already been discussed. The example of emerging femicide trends in Tamil Nadu (discussed earlier in the section on Food) shows that the devaluation of the work of the river is associated with the devaluation of the work of women, and both arise from the commoditisation of the economy which forces violence on nature and women. Rivers, instead of being seen as sources of life, become sources of cash. In Worster's words the river ends up becoming an assembly line, rolling increasingly toward the goal of unlimited production. The irrigated factory drinks the region dry. The premium on visibility and dramatic impact, and ecological blindness towards the water cycle have facilitated the commercialisation of land and water use. 'Engineers enjoy the challenge of designing irrigation schemes, particularly when they are on a large scale, and therefore speak of water "wasted" when it runs into the sea; if it runs into the sea through a good dam site or a desert they become almost uncontrollable'.[27] But the water flowing into the sea is not waste: it is a crucial link in the water cycle. With the link broken, the ecological balance of land and oceans, fresh water and sea water, also gets disrupted. Saline water starts intruding inwards, sea water starts swallowing the beaches and eroding the coast. Marine life is depleted, deprived of nutrients that rivers bring. In the lower Indus, fishing as a livelihood has come to an end because all the water in the lean period is extracted for irrigation. In the Nile Basin, the building of the Aswan High Dam has led to a disruption of fisheries, caused by the loss of 18,000 metric tons of Nile nutrients per year.[28] Rivers imprisoned in dams and wasted by giant hydraulic systems are prevented from performing the

27 Carruthers Clark, *The Economics of Irrigation*, Liverpool: English Language Book Society, p. 184.

28 'The Seven Deadly Sins of Egypt's Aswan High Dam,' in E. Goldsmith & N. Hildyard, *The Social and Environmental Effects of Large Dams*, Cornwall: Wadebridge Ecological Centre, 1986, Vol. II p. 181.

multi-dimensional functions of maintaining the diversity of life throughout the basin. Dams create dead rivers, and dead rivers cannot support
life. A song by Daya Pawar, sung by Dalit women in Maharashtra captures
the anti-life force of the dammed river which irrigates commodity crops
like sugarcane, while women and children thirst for drinking water.

> *As I build this dam*
> *I bury my life.*
> *The dawn breaks*
> *There is no flour in the grinding stone.*
>
> *I collect yesterday's husk for today's meal*
> *The sun rises*
> *And my spirit sinks.*
> *Hiding my baby under a basket*
> *And hiding my tears*
> *I go to build the dam*
>
> *The dam is ready*
> *It feeds their sugarcane fields*
> *Making the crop lush and juicy.*
> *But I walk miles through forests*
> *In search of a drop of drinking water*
> *I water the vegetation with drops of my sweat*
> *As dry leaves fall and fill my parched yard*

Drilling deep and draining dry: the groundwater famine

In regions where life was not sustained by a river, water was provided
sustainably from wells and tanks and ponds. Depending on the local
ecology, rainwater was stored, in diverse systems, in the ground and used
for drinking and protective irrigation. Women of rural India have provided survival over centuries from these tanks and wells. Today, most
tanks and shallow wells are dry because of over-exploitation; the linear
mind saw groundwater as a limitless resource instead of as a critical part
of the water cycle which depends on rainfall for its renewal and can be
sustainably used only when utilised within the limits of its renewability.

Tanks and wells made for a viable and adequate water technology,
accessible to and controlled by all in Malwa, in Maharashtra, in Kolar, in

Kalahandi until about a decade ago. Today all these regions are ravaged by famine, triggered by the mining of groundwater. Kalahandi, which has become India's Ethiopia, is a dead region because all its groundwater has run dry. As late as 1959, the composition of irrigation in the district showed that about 77 percent of the area was irrigated by tanks and 23 percent by shallow wells. Tanks irrigated about 40,000 hectares in 1960-61; by 1976–77 this area had declined to 7,481 hectares. Similarly, the area under wells declined from 3,642 hectares to 1,681 hectares during the same period. The internal insurance measures against drought have thus collapsed, and modern irrigation systems have further increased vulnerability to rainfall failure through over-exploitation.[29]

The water famine in Maharashtra is also a direct result of maldevelopment, the three characteristics of which are evident in the Maharashtra experience of water scarcity. The profit motive diverts water resources from vital sustenance functions to commodity production and calls it development; a reductionist approach facilitates such diversion by creating technologies of over-exploitation and describing sustainable technologies as 'inefficient' and 'primitive', and the combination of reductionism and maldevelopment violates the integrity of the water cycle as well as the integrity of women as water providers.

Traditionally, groundwater extraction in Maharashtra has come mainly from open dugwells. Fifty-nine percent of the state has also been irrigated by groundwater through 9.39 lakhs of open dugwells. Ninety-three percent of Maharashtra is made up of hard rocks consisting of the Deccan Trap. In it recharge is slow because the storage space for groundwater is developed through secondary features like joints, weathering, fissuring, and so on. All these features do not occur in uniform fashion, in depth or lateral extent.[30]

In the Deccan Trap, therefore, there is nothing like a subsoil water table. Water is stored in joints and bedding planes and is recharged locally. This seriously limits the availability and recharge of groundwater, a limit which new technologies of water exploitation have tried to overcome by digging deeper and using more power for the withdrawal of water. The old methods of withdrawal through human energy or animal energy put limits on extraction and were therefore called inefficient. As an expert comments:

29 H. Purohit, R.S. Rao & P.K. Tripathi, *Economic and Political Weekly*, November 2, 1985.

30 P.N. Jagtab, *Planning Groundwater Exploration in the Deccan Trap*, Poona: Groundwater Survey and Development Agency, 1984.

There were 5.42 lakh wells in Maharashtra in 1960-61. This number increased to 8.16 lakh in 1980. The average increase per year during the last two decades was 13,700. It is significant to note that although the number of wells increased by about 51 percent during the 20 years, the area irrigated by them has nearly doubled during the same period of years. This is mainly due to the fact that more and more wells are being fitted with mechanised pumps (oil engines and electric pumpsets), *discarding the outmoded device of draft-like mhots, persian wheels, etc. Mechanisation of draft has increased the utility of wells and has resulted in optimum use of water available for each well.*[31]

However, the illusion of increasing the efficiency of wells and creating abundance through energised pumps has been shortlived. Powerful water-withdrawal technologies have merely led to the over-exploitation and not the optimum use of water. The result is groundwater famine.

Energisation of pumps has mushroomed after the 1972 drought when financial assistance from the World Bank created heavy subsidies for mechanised withdrawal of water. The Bank gave credit for a rapid expansion oftubewells to feed commercial irrigation as well as tide over the water scarcity. As a result, sugarcane cultivation expanded rapidly. In less than a decade, sugarcane fields have converted groundwater into cash, leaving people and staple foodcrops thirsting for water.

The depletion of groundwater is directly linked to the expansion of energised tubewells to irrigate sugarcane. While sugarcane is cultivated on only two-three percent of Maharashtra's irrigated land, it consumes eighty percent of all the irrigation water and eight times more than other irrigated crops. This has necessitated the intensive use of groundwater, leading to a drying up of wells, shallow as well as deep.

Maharashtra is known as the land of the Sugar Barons, where the rich sugarcane lobby controls politics and power. This power, it is now being discovered, has been built on the water resources that provided food and drinking water to rural Maharashtra. As the state reels under a water famine, the sugarcane fields and sugar mills flourish, and the drinking water crisis is repeatedly converted into new mechanisms for augmenting irrigation supplies.

Maharashtra has 77 cooperative sugar factories of which 70 percent are in western Maharashtra. Seventy percent of the villages in these districts supply sugarcane to these factories, using ground water for irrigation. The sugar factories have been actively supporting their shareholders

31 V.B. Hebalkar, *Irrigation by Groundwater in Maharasbtra*, Poona: Groundwater Survey and Development Agency, 1984.

in digging and deepening their borewells. As a result public wells and shallow wells belonging to small farmers have run dry. Table 1 gives the distribution of villages facing water scarcity in western Maharashtra[32] and Table 2 the distribution of sugar factories in the region.[33]

TABLE 1
Distribution of drought-stricken villages in Western Maharashtra

District	No. of villages	No. of villages declared drought-prone	No. of villages and wadis supplied water by tankers & bullock-carts
Ahmednagar	1323	953	160 + 158
Kolhapur	1175	60	51
Pune	1603	687	230 + 510
Sangli	720	339	209
Satara	1440	452	199
Solapur	1104	1104	63
Total	7365	3595	1589 (921 + 668)

TABLE 2
Distribution of co-operative sugar factories in Western Maharashtra

District	No. of co-operative sugar factories	No. of villages in area of operation of sugar coops.	% of these villages to total number of villages in district
Ahmednagar	13	1081	82
Kolhapur	11	1048	89
Pune	7	522	33
Sangli	7	502	70
Satara	7	1057	73
Solapur	8	917	83
Total	53	5127	430

Year	Area under sugarcane (well-irrigated) (hectares)
1961-62	3248
1971-72	6990
1981-82	17612

32 'The Problem in Maharashtra', *Economic Times*, May 17, 1987.
33 *Ibid.*

In the area around one sugar factory alone in Sangli district, sugar-cane cultivation with groundwater irrigation has increased dramatically over two decades, even as water scarcity has grown.[34] Incomes have risen as a result of shifting from rainfed coarse grain production to a water-hungry cash crop. But the costs have been heavy. Manerajree village of Tasgaon taluk in Sangli is among those that have benefited financially in the short run but have lost, materially and ecologically, by the expansion of energised groundwater withdrawal for sugarcane cultivation. All solu-tions provided by the crisis mind are short-lived. A new water scheme with a potential supply of 50,000 litres was commissioned in November 1981 at a cost of Rs. 6.93 lakhs. The source well yield lasted for one year; by November 1982 it ran dry. For increasing yields three bores were taken near the well for 60 metres. The yield from all three, with power pumps, was 50,000 litre/day for 1982 and all bores had gone dry by Novem-ber 1983. Since 1983 there has been a continuous tanker service. More than 2,000 privately owned wells in this sugarcane country have also gone dry.[35]

In the drought of 1972–73, drinking water was not a major problem, and the government spent only Rs. 8 crores on providing it. In 1985–86 on the other hand, the government spent Rs. 150 crores on emergency drinking water supplies and had to employ 6.54 lakh people in relief work. The Groundwater Survey and Development Agency of Maharashtra has found that out of 1481 watersheds in the State, there is over-exploitation of 77 spread over 14 districts. The problem is extremely acute in the five districts of Ahmednagar, Sangli, Jalgaon, Dhule, and Nasik. Abuse of wa-ter for waterintensive cultivation has created severe drinking water and food crises. As the Chief Minister of Maharashtra stated at the last NDC meeting, in the Sixth Plan 17,112 villages were identified as facing drink-ing water problems; of these, 15,302 villages are likely to be covered by the end of this year, leaving 1,810 villages for the ensuing Seventh Five Year Plan. The rapid depletion of groundwater resources has, however, increased the number of problem villages with no source of drinking water to a staggering 23,000 villages. Forty-nine thousand tubewells dug during the decade 1972–83 are dry, and digging deeper, as the Manera-jree experience has shown, is no real solution.

Technological solutions to an ecological problem have clearly been unsuccessful. The basic assumption of water 'development' in a

34 Note from Shetkari Sahkari Sugar Factory, Sangli, Maharashtra, 1984.
35 Note from Environmental Engineering Works in Sangli, 1984.

reductionist perspective is that nature is 'deficient' and people's traditions are 'inefficient' in the use of natural resources. Nature has created different ecozones which have been the basis of diverse cultures and economies. The arid zones have been sustainably used by pastoralism, and the semi-arid zones have been used for dry farming, with protective irrigation coming from water storage and water distribution designed according to nature's logic. The reductionist mind, however, makes intensive irrigation the model, and in trying to introduce uniformity in water use, destroys the diversity of ecozones and disrupts the water cycle. In Maharashtra, the introduction of water intensive sugarcane cultivation has led to a water famine. Land productivity, instead of being improved, has been destroyed. The Sahelian famine has similar contributing factors: development projects in the arid sub-Saharan region assumed that digging wells was the best mechanism for developing pastoralism and pastoralists; in fact, they have undermined it. Since energised wells provide water in excess of what pastoralists are used to, herds are maintained in one place rather than moving from well to well, as traditionally. This has introduced new pressures on the vegetation around the well, and has accelerated the process of desertification. Increasing the 'efficiency' of wells has also increased the vulnerability of the ecosystem by obviating the strategy of distributing grazing pressure, characteristic of nomadic pastoralism. 'Settling' pastoralists has worsened the problem of desertification by violating the limits put on water use by nature's water cycle and bypassing traditions that have evolved over centuries to ensure survival under conditions of low water availability.[36]

There is a tendency to associate rainfall failure with the groundwater famine and to see the lack of rain as the cause for the disappearance of water. Yet rainfall failure cannot lead to the disappearance of groundwater by itself because groundwater storages are the cumulative effect of long periods of percolation and recharge. For instance the deep aquifers under the Sahara are recharged at the rate of 4 Km³/year and their total capacity is 15,000 Km³/year. This means that it would take nearly 4,000 years at the present rate of recharge to fill these formations. Quite clearly, groundwater will not get exhausted merely because rains fail during one year. On the other hand, even with regular rainfall, groundwater depletion can take place if withdrawal exceeds annual recharge. The Rayalseema region of Andhra Pradesh is a good example of how groundwater famine, which was induced by over-exploitation through powerful technologies,

36 Lloyd Timberlake, *Africa in Crisis*, London: Earthscan, 1985.

was blamed on the failure of rainfall. The rainfall in Rayalseema has been between 650-700 mm from 1945 to 1985 as shown in Table 3.[37]

TABLE 3

Average annual rainfall in Rayalseema, 1945-85

Year	Rainfall (in mm)	Year	Rainfall (in mm)
1945	nd	1965	405
1946	1048	1966	977
1947	476	1967	nd
1948	631	1968	601
1949	nd	1969	768
1950	603	1970	649
1951	482	1971	nd
1952	641	1972	946
1953	915	1973	680
1954	774	1974	734
1955	766	1975	nd
1956	774	1976	698
1957	304	1977	885
1958	763	1978	954
1959	557	1979	882
1960	608	1980	402
1961	587	1981	762
1962	806	1982	548
1963	nd	1983	765
1964	737	1984	728
		1985	678

Note: Figures are the average of annual rainfall. Where data for one or more stations are missing, nd is entered above.

Irrigation that violates essential ecological processes can itself become the cause for water scarcity and desertification, especially in arid and semi-arid zones. The hydrological cycle is an essential ecological process which recycles and regenerates water resources. Part of the rainfall received at the surface infiltrates and percolates into the ground and recharges the groundwater. In arid regions, where rainfall itself is

37 K.W. Olsen, 'Manmade Drought in Rayalseema', *Economic and Political Weekly*, Vol. XXII, No. 11, March 14, 1987, pp. 441-443.

low, percolation into the ground is even lower, and sustainable limits for groundwater exploitation are therefore very low. The water-table goes down when the rate of withdrawal of groundwater exceeds the rate of recharge of water through percolation. In order to assure groundwater supply on a continuous basis, withdrawal should be confined to the net natural recharge of the aquifer. If withdrawal exceeds this amount, groundwater mining takes place, and an aquifer drought is created even when no meteorological drought exists. However, ignoring this basic ecological fact, irrigation schemes in arid regions have been expanding rapidly as a strategy for drought-proofing. In Rayalseema region, new borewells and pumpsets are being installed at an alarming rate.

TABLE 4
Number of electric pumpsets

Year	Chitoor District	Anantapur District	Rayalseema	Andhra Pradesh
1968	22,353	10,491	41,769	1,22,321
1974	41,273	20,614	81,992	2,61,968
1969	48,676	26,425	98,402	3,45,396
1984	68,585	39,433	1,44,639	5,82,197
Increase of 1984 over 1968 (%)	207	276	246	376

Source: Handbook of Statistics, Andhra Pradesh, various fiscal years (Bureau of Economics and Statistics, Hyderabad).

Increasing exploitation of groundwater, beyond the limits of renewability, has led to a drying up of wells and tanks. As a study on Rayalseema points out, 'Irrigation has left us with the popular perception that this drought is more severe and more permanent than any past drought. Climatic change is a myth brought on by the novelty of exponential growth in water usage ... the falling water table is evidence of overuse of water, not of climatic change'.[38]

With groundwater mining having created drought in agriculture even when drought does not exist metereologically in Rayalseema, demands are now being made to bring irrigation water to it from the Srisailam dam on the Krishna river, through the Telugu-Ganga Canal, and further plans are afoot to augment the Krishna river supplies from the

38 K.W. Olsen, op. cit.

Polavaram dam on the Godavari. As local water resources are overused and misused everywhere, an infinite regress of demands is made on distant regions. Desertification, which starts as a patchy phenomenon thus spreads everywhere under the impact of non-sustainable water use in agriculture which generates water scarcity. Water, a renewable resource has thus been transformed into a non-renewable resource by overuse and over-exploitation.

The over-exploitation of groundwater rarely takes place for survival needs—it is always associated with the production of cash crops. Women as water providers from wells and tanks are first replaced by men switching on electric pumpsets to irrigate commercial crops, and are subsequently substituted by the government machinery which brings water in trains, tankers, and bullock-carts. Wells and tanks which were the source of water, are now filled with water transported from long distances. Source and sustainer both are transformed into passive receivers by a shortsighted notion of productivity which displaces women, disrupts the water cycle, and threatens the survival base for society as a whole.

Nature's work and women's work in water conservation has usually been ignored by the masculinist paradigm of water management which has replaced community control by privatisation, and water-prudent staple foodcrops by water-thirsty cash crops. Women have had a significant productive role in food cultivation based on water-conserving technologies. They have been central to food production, based on the sustainable use of water, in arid zones. The maldevelopment model which sees agricultural output in terms of cash rather than nutritive value, has undermined the efficient production of nutritive crops like jowar and bajra by seeing them as 'marginal' and 'uneconomic'. Ignoring the economics of food value, of water use, and of women's work, maldevelopment replaces sound and sustainable agriculture by land use that deprives people of food and water, and pushes women out of productive roles. Table 5 shows the productivity of different crops when viewed from the perspective of water conservation; for women, working for sustenance, maximising the production of nutrition while minimising water use, millets are a highly productive food crop.[39]

Women's work in producing staple, water conserving food grains is only one of the many mechanisms for water conservation; their work in

39 S. Girriapa, *Water Use Efficiency in Agriculture*, New Delhi: Oxford and IBH, 1983. p. 49.

TABLE 5
Productivity of food crops per hectare per mm. of water used

	Productivity (kg/ha/mm)
Rice	1.72
Jowar	4.47
Bajra	5.74
Ragi	4.65
Pulses	2.26

adding organic matter to the soil—from crops, from the cowshed, from trees and forests—also contributes critically towards conserving water and preventing desertification.

While water is recognised as a central input in plant productivity, recognition of the fact that the soil is a massive water reservoir and that its capacity is dependent on vegetative cover as well as organic content (which determines the water retentivity of soil), is generally lacking. In arid zones where vegetative growth both in forests as well as farms is entirely dependent on recharge of soil moisture by rain, an extremely important, and the only viable and sustaining, mechanism for water conservation is the addition of organic matter. Organic matter or humus dramatically enhances the water retentivity of soils.[40] This mechanism of conserving water as soil moisture assumes critical importance in the tropics where rainfall is seasonal and has to be effectively stored in the soil to support plant growth in the arid periods. Conserving soil moisture is thus an insurance against desertification in arid climates. Adding organic matter increases soil moisture in situ and contributes significantly to increased food production. The All India Dry Farming Coordinated Project[41] has shown that mulch was responsible forincreased food productivity in dry land farming.

Besides the technology of water conservation in soil through organic matter, intercropping is another safeguard against crop failure in rainfed farming. Evidence exists that sole-cropped sorghum fails once in eight

40 V.A. Kovda, *Land Aridisation and Drought Contra Colorado*: Westview, 1980; M.N. Peat & I.D. Teare, *Crop-Water Relations*, New York: John Wiley, 1983.

41 Venkateswarlu, cited in J. Bandyopadhyay *et al*, *India's Environment: Crises and Responses*, Dehradun: Natraj, 1985.

TABLE 6
Vertical mulching & sorghum yields/grain yield (kg/ha)

Interval of vertical mulch	'72-'73	'73-'74	'74-'75	'75-'76	'77-'78
4m	400	1690	1780	1250	1540
8m	280	1610	1770	1120	1920
Control	20	1120	1100	1080	1470

years and pigeon-pea once in five, but that a sorghum-pigeon-pea inter-crop fails only once in 36 years.[42]

Women's work in traditional agriculture has been an effective partnership with nature which increases water availability for human survival without disrupting the water cycle. This partnership is now being substituted by a partnership between chemicals and masculinist science and industry. Instead of water retentivity and soil fertility being increased by organic matter produced by nature and processed and distributed by women and peasants, National Chemical Labs and Indian Organic Chemicals Limited are manufacturing a chemical polymer called 'Jalshakti'. IOCL has a semi-commercial plant to produce 200 tonnes of Jalshakti per annum, and plans to set up a 5,000 tpa commercial plant with an annual turnover of Rs. 40 crore. The compound costs Rs. 70 per kg.[43] First, organic matter was substituted by chemical fertilizers, now it is being substituted by chemical absorbants. The trend however is the same—a reductionist shift from the multifunctional 'internal resources' of agriculture produced and renewed freely by nature and women and peasants, to the introduction of single-function, external inputs, manufactured in factories and purchased on the market. These external inputs necessarily diminish the strength, vitality, and usefulness of the internal resources controlled and reproduced by women on the farm. Women's work in conserving water is consequently eroded. Sometimes inappropriate afforestation strategies can become the cause of depletion of soil moisture and land aridisation. The large scale introduction of the eucalyptus in India is contributing to such land aridisation, first by its high water uptake ahd second by its insignificant contribution to humus formation. There is no scientific work done yet on the water relations of indigenous tree

42 J.S. Kanwar, *Rainwater Management, op. cit.*

43 'Jalshakti—A Boon to Farming', *Aquaworld*, Vol II, No. 8, August 1987, p. 248.

species but women's wisdom in rural India has a categorisation of species in terms of their water conserving properties: root systems, crown morphology, and physiology which are adapted to the hydrological conditions prevailing in the tropics. Indigenous or naturalised plant species therefore contribute to water conservation in a number of ways.

Today, the two regions with the most successful afforestation programmes, Gujarat and Karnataka, are also the very regions experiencing total water famine.[44] Most movements against eucalyptus cultivation have been movements for water conservation. The women and peasants of the affected villages see the connection between water and vegetation quite clearly. For the reductionist minds guiding afforestation, trees produce only commercial wood, not water, while for women in the ecology movements, trees in drought-prone areas should be planted primarily to produce water. Similarly, for reductionist engineers, dams and canals and pipes produce water, and western trained men are water experts, while for the ecology movements, catchment forests, rocks and rivers and wells produce water, and women who participate daily in the water cycle and provide water to their families are the real water experts.

Women: the water experts

The Doon Valley in the Himalayan foothills receives about 3,000 mm of rainfall only over the three months of the monsoon, but its streams and springs provide water throughout the year. Some water has been stored in the rich humus of the oak forests in the higher reaches, and at lower altitudes in the mixed natural forests of *timla* (*Ficus Roxburghii*), *banj* (*Quercus incana*), *bhimal* (*Grewia oppositifolia*), *semla, dudla* (*Bauhinia retusa* and *Sapium insigue*), *farsu, kol, tun* (*Cedrela toona*), *shisham,* and *haldu* (*Dalbergia sishoo* and *Adina cordifolia*). But most of the water has been stored in the cracks and fissures of the limestone rocks in the Himalayan range. Over millenia, nature had transformed these cracks into a network of storage cavities, through the dissolving of limestone in rainwater. Nature's work had created a massive storage tank in the mountains which fed thousands of springs and hundreds of streams feeding into the mighty Ganga and Yamuna rivers, into which the Valley drains.

A few decades ago, maldevelopment came to the Doon. Mountains were mined for chemical grade limestone, forests were uprooted, debris

44 'Drying Up', *India Today,* July 15, 1985.

was thrown down the slopes, and nature's system of water storage was destroyed. Now, when the rains come, 3,000 mm of water run off the slopes immediately, creating floods carrying topsoil and boulders, eroding river banks and filling up flood plains—after that the land is parched, the streams and rivers dry. In mining the limestone, nature's water reservoir has been mined too; the reductionist mind fails to see the non-commercial economic functions that minerals perform in their linkages with other elements of nature.[45]

Beginning September 16, 1986, rural women in the Doon Valley started a 'Chipko' movement to blockade mining operations in the Nahi-Barkot area. They set up the blockade on the banks of Sinsyaru Khala, the stream which was the lifeline of the village and whose source had been mined for twenty years. When Chamundeyi came to Nahi-Kala seventeen years ago, the forests were rich and dense with *ringal, tun, sinsyaru, gald, chir,* and *banj.** The mine destroyed the forests and with them the water sources. Twelve springs in the vicinity of the mine have gone dry. Two years ago, the perennial waterfall, Mande-ka-Chhara, which originates in Patali-ka-dhar and feeds Sinsyaru Khala, dried up. Mining has killed the forests and streams, the sources of life in the village.

Itwari Devi, the village elder who has guided the local Chipko movement, recalls how Sinsyaru Khala was a narrow perennial stream, full of lush sinsyaru bushes which provided rich fodder to cattle, especially in the summer months. Today it is a wide, barren bed of limestone boulders. The water-mills, the paddy fields, the forests on the river banks—all have been washed away. Women like Itwari Devi who co-habitate with the elements, who participate in nature's cycles, who watch and experience nature's destruction in their everyday lives even while they produce sustenance with nature, have a kind and level of knowledge that no western trained technocrat can have access too. They show the world that rocks are not just minerals to be used as raw material for factories: they are nature's waterworks. This participation in nature is the source of a different kind of knowledge and power, which opposes the knowledge and power that is causing destruction. According to Itwari Devi:

> Shakti (strength) comes to us from these forests and grasslands; we
> watch them grow, year in and year out through their internal shakti,

45 J. Bandyopadhyay, et al., *Doon Valley Ecosystem,* Dehradun: Research Foundation for Science, Technology and Natural Resource Policy, 1984; J. Bandyopadhyay & Vandana Shiva, 'Chipko Comes to Doon Valley', *India Magazine,* June, 1987.

* Botanical names are given where available. In other cases, local names are used.

and we derive our strength from it. We watch our streams renew themselves and we drink their clear and sparkling water—that gives us shakti. We drink fresh milk, we eat ghee, we eat food from our own fields—all this gives us not just nutrition for the body, but a moral strength, that we are our own masters, we control and produce our own wealth. That is why 'primitive', 'backward' women who do not buy their needs from the market but produce them themselves are leading Chipko. Our power is nature's power, our shakti comes from prakriti. Our power against the contractor comes from these inner sources, and is strengthened by his trying to oppress and bully us with his false power of money and muscle. We have offered ourselves, even at the cost of our lives, for a peaceful protest to close this mine, to challenge and oppose the power that the government represents. Each attempt to violate us has strengthened our integrity. They stoned us on March 20 when they returned from the mine. They stoned our children and hit them with iron rods, but they could not destroy our shakti.

Women's knowledge and politics are the basis of the countervailing power of the Chipko movement in Doon Valley and other regions. On November 30, 1986, Chamundeyi was out collecting fodder in the forest when she heard trucks climbing up the mountain to the limestone quarry in the area. The trucks should not have been there, because of the Chipko blockade in the region. The quarry workers had attacked the protestors, removed them from the blockade, and driven their trucks through. Chamundeyi threw her sickle down, raced down the slope, and stood in front of the trucks: she told the drivers that they could go up only over her dead body. After dragging her along for a distance, the trucks turned back.

In late 1987, the people of Nahi-Kala are still protesting because the government has been dragging its feet regarding closing the mine whose lease had expired in 1982. People's direct action to stop the mine from working was an outcome of the government's failure to implement its own laws. The quarry contractor in the meantime tried to take the law into his hands and on March 20, 1987, brought about 200 hired musclemen to attack the villagers. They assaulted the peaceful protestors with stones and iron rods. But the children, women, and men have not withdrawn from the blockade. They are their own leaders, their own decision makers, their own source of strength. The myth that movements are created and sustained by charismatic male leaders from outside is shattered by the ten months of nonviolent struggle in Nahi-Kala in which ordinary women like Itwari Devi and Chamundeyi have provided local leadership through extraordinary strength. Indeed, it is the invisible strength of women like them that is the source of the staying power of Chipko—

a movement which in its two decades of evolution has widened from embracing trees to embracing living mountains and living waters. Each new phase of Chipko is created by invisible women. In 1977 it was Bachni Devi of Advani who created Chipko's ecological slogan: 'What do the forests bear? Soil, water, and pure air'. A decade later in Doon Valley, Chamundeyi inspired the Chipko poet Ghanshyam 'Shailani' to write a new song:

> *A fight for truth has begun*
>
> *At Sinsyari Khala*
>
> *A fight for rights has begun*
>
> *At Malkot Thana*
>
> *Sister, it is a fight to protect*
>
> *Our mountains and forests.*
>
> *They give us life*
>
> *Embrace the life of the living trees and streams*
>
> *Clasp them to your hearts*
>
> *Resist the digging of mountains*
>
> *That brings death to our forests and streams*
>
> *A fight for life has begun*
>
> *At Sinsyaru Khala*

Each Chipko protest has demonstrated the special ecological perceptions of women who work daily in the production of survival. On World Environment Day in 1979, hundreds of women of the Chipko movement collected in Tehri with empty water-pots. They were protesting against the deepening water scarcity but also against the failure of water supply schemes and of a model of science which saw metal pipes and concrete tanks as producers of water, and male engineers and technicians who fitted pipes and designed schemes, as providers of that water. When the district collector came out to hear their grievances, they showed him the empty pots and asked why, if paper plans and metal and concrete could ensure water, their pots were still empty? They said, 'We have come to tell you that nature is the primary source of water, and we are the providers for our families. Unless the mountains are clothed with forests, the springs will not come alive. Unless the springs come alive, the taps will be dry. It is the live springs and not the dry taps which fill our pots. If you want to solve our water problems please plan for water, not for pipes'.

That water is the source for water supply schemes seems to be a simple fact that escapes the reductionist mind. A recent advertisement for plastic pipes proudly proclaims: 'We're putting water on tap for thirsty millions', and goes on to state, 'In Buldana, Maharashtra, drought set off a calamitous scarcity of potable water. Then, within a matter of a few days, a network of Hootalen pipes was laid to rush precious water to parched mouths'. Yet pipes have failed to provide water to Maharashtra because water sources are drying up. Ask any rural woman in Maharashtra and she will tell you that it is not Polyolefins Industries Ltd. or Hoechst of Germany who put water on the tap, but nature. If nature's water cycle is maintained, and water is conserved, water pots are purnakumbhas even without pipes and taps. If nature's cycle has been disrupted and rivers and wells go dry, pipes will also run dry, as region after region with failed water schemes in India is teaching us, the hard way.

The National Master Plan for India for the International Drinking Water Supply Decade[46] (1981–1990) has planned everything except water itself. It has classifications of types of pipes required for the decade programme—263,313 kms of plastic pipes; 221,741 kms of AC pressure pipes; 150,903 kms of GI pipes; 113,645 kms of stoneware pipes; 58,031 kms of cast-iron spun pressure pipes and so on. It has an exact assessment of cement needed for water supply for each state, adding up to 13.4 million tonnes over the decade. It has a projected requirement of 1,05,415 power driven borewells and 88,254 handpumps. It has even assessed the need for 5,415 trucks, 988 tractors, 20,540 motorcycles, and 13,528 cars, jeeps, and mini buses. Energy needs are projected at 2,614 megawatts of electricity, 468,240 metric tonnes of petrol, 816,534 metric tonnes of diesel. But I have looked over and over again at the nearly 200 pages of statistics and not found a single table that talks of how much water is needed during the Drinking Water Decade, or where it will be found. And with the source being forgotten, the providers are also forgotten. 'Manpower' needs are accurately projected: India will need 28,678 engineers, 111 economists, 3,505 accountants, 563 health educators, 661 sanitary chemists and biologists, 15,908 draughtsmen, 47,840 plant operators, 27,769 electricians, 31,235 plumbers, 3,105 drillers, 1,405 lab technicians. Water has disappeared from the water plan and so have the water experts—the women who, in their capacity as participants in the water cycle and as providers of water, are the invisible experts.

46 National Master Plan for India for the International Water Supply Decade, Government of India, 1983.

As in all other cases, maldevelopment in water management is based on an assumption that there is no history of water management before the introduction of management systems run by engineers and technicians trained in western paradigms. It is assumed that societies are deprived of potable water until a masculinist 'scheme' is created to supply it. This ignores the basic fact that it is nature, not water supply schemes, which supplies water, and it ignores the Third World reality in which women, using traditional technologies, treat water and make it potable. As Jahan has observed:

> Water management and water treatment in the western world is a field dominated by men, but in tropical developing countries women were the actual pace-makers for traditional water purification. As far as aid organisations have given any thought at all to the role of women in the context of new water supply projects, they have only been concerned with the time wasted and the hardship endured in fetching water from distant sources. But women are not just victims of the burden of providing water, they have been the source of knowledge and skills for providing safe water, and hence better health for rural areas.[47]

> Traditional technologies are not merely atavism or ethnographic curiosities, but a vital parameter for public health. Unlike heavy chlorination, the plants used by Third World women are both medicinal as well as scented. They improve water quality in many ways. The western colonisation of the Third World destroyed these traditions. The use of herbs was identified as unscientific superstition. This reinforced an exaggerated confidence in costly modern technologies as the only alternative for improvement of water supply, and a mistrust and despising of 'old fashioned methods' of traditional water purification.[48]

Western male consultants who propose water purification technologies for the drinking water needs of households and small communities ih the Third World go for the large, centralised, capital intensive, chemical based treatment plants for filteration and chlorination. Indigenous technologies used by Third World women for purified water are decentralised, low cost, and plant based. As engineers and engineering works replace women's and nature's work as the source of water supply, less people have access even to minimal drinking water. The exclusion of people arises partly from the effect of disruption of the water cycle and

47. S.A. Jahan, 'Traditional Water Purification in Tropical Developing Countries', GTZ, (W. Germany), 1981, p. 13.

48 S.A. Jahan, *op. cit.*, p. 14.

destruction of water resources by water resource 'development' in the maldevelopment paradigm. It also arises because the capital and technological intensity of water schemes increasingly excludes regions and people from participating in and deriving benefit from the projects.

An example of new exclusion is the Technology Mission on Drinking Water of the Government of India, launched in response to the drinking water crisis across the country. While the crisis has hit most villages, the Technology Mission will exclude most and focus only on 50 pilot projects in 10 districts in 10 states over the entire Seventh Plan period. The Plan, itself, thus does not conceive of solving the water crisis as an urgent survival need for all. The technologies being explored do not include safe, participatory technologies over which women have traditionally had control and through which all members of society can have access to safe water. They include high-tech engineering fantasies spun in the labs of the Atomic Energy Commission and the Council of Scientific and Industrial Research.[49] The lakhs of villages whose water sources have dried up recede from the horizon of the Plan. The water problem is reduced further to the Baconian vision of spectacular controlling and overpowering on the basis of experiments in the lab. In Bacon's Solomon's House, one lab had a number of artificial wells and fountains, made in imitation of natural sources and baths. Salt water could be made fresh, for 'we have also pools, of which some do strain fresh water out of salt'.[50] Desalination is the modern realisation of Bacon's fantasy in New Atlantis. It is being propagated as a solution to India's water famine by the Technology Mission on Drinking Water. Our scientists and planners are merely three decades behind America in the 'hysterical endorsement' of the breakthrough in water management provided by desalination. Gilbert White sees the preoccupation with desalination as 'an example of the way in which belief in a single scientific advance may run away with those who espouse it ... a sobering caution for those who would engage in environmental modification on a grand scale, a caution against promising too much too soon, becoming bemused with one answer, against making a public commitment for which there then becomes a political necessity to build support by continuing heavy investment in research which does not fulfil high hopes'.[51]

49 'CSIR Help Sought to Procure Water', *Economic Times*, August 3, 1986; Water Treatment Scheme in 10 Districts,' *Indian Express*, August 2, 1986.

50 Carolyn Merchant, *Women, Nature and the Scientific Revolution*, San Francisco: Harper and Row, 1980, p. 182.

51 Quoted in R.J. Barnet, *The Lean Years*, London: Abacus, 1981, p. 201.

The fragmented and piecemeal approach characteristic of reductionism fails to see that new energy demands, new demands for cement and iron and steel to create manmade structures for the storage and flow of water, ultimately aggravate the water problem because they lead to increased deforestation, increased mining, increased water consumption by power plants and the cement and metallurgical industries. This masculine project becomes an endless spiral of new techniques which demand more water, further diminish and deplete water resources, and change nature's abundance into irreversible scarcity. Deprived of the feminine principle it fails to see that nature's water cycle is a perennial, endless process of desalination. Each year, the sun's energy lifts 500,000 cubic kilometers of water, of which 86 percent is saline water from the oceans. It transforms this salt water into fresh and pours it on the earth. The global water cycle, as a desalination process, annually distills and transfers 38,000 cubic kilometers of water from the oceans to the land. Trees and soil, rocks and sand help in conserving this cyclical flow, refilling streams and rivers above and below the ground, recharging ponds, lakes and wells. The recovery of the feminine principle in water management consists of recovering the stability of the water cycle, and recovering the role of women and poor peasants and tribals as water managers for the use of water for sustenance and not for non-sustainable profits and growth. The recovery of the feminine principle involves the recognition that sustainable availability of water resources is based on participation in the water cycle, not on manipulation or mastery over it. The first step to these nonviolent alternatives involves resistance to the violence against the water cycle perpetrated by the masculine projects of reductionist science and maldevelopment.

Women and nature are first displaced in water conservation as participants in the water cycle and are then displaced in its process of purification and treatment. For centuries, nature's various products and women's knowledge of their properties have provided the basis for making water safe for drinking in every home and village of India. In both the oral and written traditions knowledge of these alternative methods of water treatment is still available. The *Sushruta Samhita* lists seven modes of purifying water, among which is the clarification of muddy water by natural coagulents such as the nuts of the *nirmali* tree (cleaning-nut tree—*Strychnos Potatorium*). The seeds of the nirmali tree are used to clear muddy water by rubbing them on the insides of vessels in which it is stored. Seeds of honge (*Pongamia glabra*) are similarly used. The drumstick tree (*Moringa oleifera*) which provides a very nutritious vegetable, produces seeds which are also used for water purification. (This tree has travelled from India to Africa as a water purifier, and in Sudan, is called the clarifier tree.) *Moringa* seeds inhibit the growth of bacteria and fungi. Since the drumstick is a food, it does not create any risk of toxicity, as chemicals do. Other natural purifiers include *amla* (*Phlanthus emblica*) whose wood is used to clear small rain-ponds in the Indian peninsula. In Kerala, wells are cleared with burnt coconut shells. The *tulsi* (*Ocimun sanctum*) is a water purifier with anti-bacterial and insecticide properties. Copper or brass pots are what Indian women use to bring water from the source, and for storage; unlike plastic which breeds bacteria, they have antiseptic properties. In Ayurvedic medicine, small doses of specially prepared copper powder are an ingredient of medicines used for diarrhoea, cholera, and typhoid. The technologies women have used for water purification are based on locally available natural products and locally and commonly available knowledge. Women working with nature have not only provided alternatives to western patriarchal traditions of water management but also to western patriarchal traditions of health-care based on violence to the ecology of the human

TABLE 7

Natural water purifiers and their use in the treatment of water-related diseases

Species	Symptom	Preparation
Acacia catechu	Diarrhoea	Catechu (resinous extract from the wood)
Moringa oleifera	Gastro-intestinal disorders	tea of pounded seeds
	Diarrhoea	pounded seeds in curdled milk
Pongamia glabra	Intestinal worms; parasitic skin diseases	seeds
Strychnos potatorium	Chronic diarrhoea	Half to one seed rubbed into fine paste with buttermilk (internally)
	Eye infections, boils	powdered seed in honey

body. The *honge*, *nirmali* and drumstick trees are partners with women in the safe and easy cure of everyday illnesses like diarrhoea which can otherwise be fatal.[52]

As Mira Shiva says:

> Diarrhoea is by far the major killer in the developing world. It has been estimated that annually there are over 1,400 million episodes of diarrhoea in children under five years of age in Africa, Asia and Latin America. This results in five to eighteen million childhood deaths per year. In other words, somewhere in the world *every six seconds a child dies of diarrhoea*. One of every ten children born in developing countries dies of diarrhoea before reaching the age of five. Yet the greater tragedy behind this fact is that all or most of these deaths are preventable — not by sophisticated or expensive means, but by simple and cheap home remedies that any woman can learn and use.[53]

52 S.A. Jahan *op.cit.*

53 Mira Shiva, 'A Taste of Tears: Oral Rehydration Therapy in Diarrhoea', New Delhi: Voluntary Health Association of India, 1982, p. 1.

CHAPTER SEVEN

Terra Mater: Reclaiming the Feminine Principle

In December 1987, two prizes were awarded in Stockholm: the Nobel Prize for economics was given to Robert Solow of MIT for his theory of growth based on the dispensability of nature. In Solow's words, 'The world can, in effect, get along without natural resources, so exhaustion is just an event, not a catastrophe'.[1] At the same time, the Alternative Nobel Prize (the popular name for the Right Livelihood Award), instituted 'for vision and work contributing to making life more whole, healing our planet and uplifting humanity', honoured the women of the Chipko movement who, as leaders and activists, had put the life of the forests above their own and, with their actions, had stated that nature is indispensable to survival.[2]

The two prizes dramatically pose the two oppositional world-views grappling with each other. These world-views hold opposing assumptions of the worth and value of different kinds of work and existence. In the world-view personified by the MIT Professor only that counts as knowledge which is produced by male western experts, and only that counts as wealth that such knowledge in turn produces. The economic 'growth' that the masculinist model of progress has sold has been the

1 Solow, quoted in Narendra Singh, 'Robert Solow's Growth Hickonomics', *Economic and Political Weekly*, Vol. XXII, No. 45, Nov. 7, 1987.

2 Press Release of the Right Livelihood Foundation, October 9, 1987, which states, 'The Chipko movement is the result of hundreds of decentralised and locally autonomous initiatives. Its leaders and activists are primarily village women, acting to protect their means of subsistence and their communities.'

growth of money and capital based on the destruction of other kinds of wealth such as the wealth produced by nature and women. In this view, nature in itself has no value, unless controlled and exploited by western masculine science, and women and non-westernised peoples have and produce no value, because they, like nature, have no intrinsic intellectual or economic worth: they are the bearers of ignorance and passivity while western man is the bearer of knowledge and progress.

In the world-view personified by the Chipko women, nature is Prakriti, the creator and source of wealth, and rural women, peasants and tribals who live in, and derive sustenance from nature, have a systematic and deep knowledge of nature's processes of reproducing wealth. Nature and women do not acquire value through domination by modern western man; they lose both through this process of subjugation. The domination of nature by western industrial culture, and the domination of women by western industrial man is part of the same process of devaluation and destruction that has been characterised in masculinist history as the 'enlightenment'. With the Alternative Nobel Prize, part of the world's community is joining the Chipko women in challenging this notion of progress and enlightenment. A decade after the women of Henwal Ghati came with lanterns during the day to show forestry experts 'the light'—that forests produce soil and water and not just timber and revenue—they have been joined by others in challenging the enlightenment symbol of 'light' as the exclusive monopoly of the western expert.[3]

The categories of gendered inequality that the age of enlightenment gave rise to are today being challenged everywhere as the categories of a special project of a narrow group of western, technocratic men which excluded all other groups from the production of intellectual and material wealth while including the excluded people's minds in sharing the myth of seeing nature's destruction and women's subjugation as 'progress'. The reductionist categories of modern western scientific thought were categories that were intrinsically violent and destructive to nature as a producer, and to women as knowers. In this destruction of material and intellectual wealth, reductionist categories in science are dialectically linked to reductionist categories in economics which reduce all value to market value, and register only those activities and processes

3 The social construction of gender and nature as gendered activity during the enlightenment is discussed extensively in Carol MacCormack & Marilyn Strathern (eds.), *Nature, Culture and Gender*, Cambridge: Cambridge University Press, 1987.

that are monetised and involve cash transactions. Reductionist economics assumes that only paid labour produces value. On the one hand this
leads to ignoring man's dependance on the natural world, while on the
other, it provides the ideology of the gender division of labour such that
women's work in producing sustenance is treated as having no economic
value even while it provides the very basis of survival and well-being.
Since poor Third World women provide water, fodder, wood from the free
commons that nature provides, collecting them is not considered work
in reductionist economics. A gendered dichotomy is created between
'productive' and 'non-productive' work, on the basis of money and price
as the only measure of economic worth and wealth.

This ideological divide between 'productive' and 'unproductive' work
based on market criteria very rapidly unfolds into the contemporary economic crises in which wealth is no longer linked to work, or the production of goods and services.

From the production of goods and services, the dynamic edge of economic activity has shifted to paper transactions and speculation. Futures
markets and speculation have begun controlling real producers and consumers such as the poor, and women, tribals and peasants in the Third
World, dispensing with them if they do not 'fit' into the market transactions of artificially created prices. Instead of a sustainable reproduction
of wealth, the global economic system, led by commercial capitalism, has
started to focus on instant wealth creation through speculation at the
cost of the future—and of the poor. The decade of 1973–1982 has seen the
escalation of capital flows from transnational banks and financial institutions to the Third World. This phase of borrowing is at the root of the
contemporary Third World debt crisis. And this borrowing was induced
to recycle the huge amounts of liquidity that the financial system of the
North had built up and could not absorb. The Third World became an
important source for investment at high profitability: profits of the seven
biggest U.S. banks rocketed from 22 percent in 1970 to 55 in 1981, and to
a record 60 percent in the following year. The South was caught in a debt
trap, borrowing merely to pay interests on earlier loans.[4]

The paradoxical nature of the current global integration of the
world's economies through the web of speculation and moneylending,
is that it deals with mythical constructs on computers and electronic
boards, and is able to destroy, instantly, the real economies of entire

4 F.F. Clairmonte & J. Cavanagh, 'Third World Debt: The Approaching Holocaust', in
Economic and Political Weekly, Volume XXI, No. 31, Aug. 2, 1986.

countries through numbers flashing in the financial nerve-centres of the world. There has been a shift from the factory to the financial district, but it is a shift which ties the financial districts intimately to the remotest and smallest farms in the world. During the post-war period, capitalist 'growth' came from industrial expansion; today wealth comes from unproductive and fictitious economic exchange. It is based not on exchange of industrial commodities but on servicing a paper and electronic money system. Real things and real people are merely inputs into what has become essentially a game of buying and selling fictitious goods in the hope of accruing large profits when the price of goods rises or falls in the future. Only about five percent of commodity transactions on futures markets relate to actual delivery of goods. Yet this mythical game is loaded in favour of Northern speculators, who 'gamble not only with the wealth of nations but also with the lives of powerless farmers within those nations'.[5] Wealth from the South is transferred to the North in a new wave which colonises the land and forests of the Third World through commodity prices and futures markets. Entire countries, ecosystems, and communities are vulnerable to instant collapse in this game of speculation, which bids on them and their produce, and then abandons them as waste—wastelands and wasted peoples. As Ruth Sidel has noted in her book, *Women and Children Last*, when the economies of the world, based on the masculinist paradigm of wealth, start to crash, 'women and children will be first—not the first to be saved but the first to fall into the abyss that is poverty'.[6]

The modern creation myth that male western minds propagate is based on the sacrifice of nature, women, and the Third World. It is not merely the impoverishment of these excluded sectors that is the issue in the late twentieth century; it is the very dispensability of nature and non-industrial, non-commercial cultures that is at stake. Only the price on the market counts. That market prices in today's world are totally divorced from real worth matters little.

Consider the simple case of rice, which the Thai women call 'life', because as food, rice is life itself. The 1985 U.S. Farm Bill allowed the U.S. to lower world prices of rice from $8 per hundredweight to less than $4. Thai farmers who brought in 15 percent of the foreign exchange for their country through rice exports were forced to lower prices and increase their volume of production to maintain exports to meet foreign debt

5 Jon Bennet, *The Hunger Machine*, Cambridge: Polity Press, 1987, p. 131.
6 Ruth Sidel, *Women and Children Last*, Harmondsworth: Penguin Books, 1987, p. xv.

obligations. New regions were opened up for rice production for export, displacing forests and forest tribes.[7]

Debt, the debacle in commodity prices, and speculation in the commodities futures markets have become a major source of 'economic growth'. In the U.S., interest payment on the farm debt, which rose 1000 percent in a decade—from $20 billion in the '70s to $225 billion in the '80s—exceeds net farm income. In the South, since 1981, Third World countries have become net capital exporters: soaring from $7 billion in 1981 to $74 billion in 1985. This excludes the TNCs' profit repatriation and capital flights. If all these were added up, the flow of capital from South to North is about $240 billion—a sum four times greater than that of the Marshall Plan, which was repaid with interest to the U.S. Most of these funds are being emptied into speculative ventures so characteristic of the grand casino society. The survival of the poor and the future are being sacrificed to keep the casino running. Resources from the poor have become a major source of inflows and savings to the centre. As Cavanagh observes, 'In terms of scale and sheer magnitude the tribute extracted from the Indian subcontinent (and one of the major sources of financing the eighteenth century industrial revolution) by such nabobs as Warren Hastings and the British East India Company pales in comparison to the current outflows'.[8]

The global economic system is quite evidently non-sustainable and inequitable. Its basis in indebtedness, in living at the cost of the future, cannot but generate crises. Black Monday, when the stock market crashed on Wall Street, could be just the beginning of deeper crises in international trade and finance. Living high on borrowed or stolen wealth is the economic prescription of today's high priests in banks and financial institutions, who see natural resources and the poor as dispensable elements of ecosystems. The Wall Street collapse has shown that this prescription is not only unjust and unethical, it is also unworkable. America, which has provided the model of the affluent consumer society, can no longer work as the norm, because for the women, the workers, and the small farmers of America, prosperity has come to an end and they, too, have become dispensable. The crisis of survival that the categories and concepts of the age of masculinist 'enlightenment' have engendered cannot be overcome from within those categories. When the stock market

---

7 Mark Ritchie & Kevin Ristau, Crisis by Design: A Brief Review of U.S. Farm Policy, League of Rural Voters Education Project, Minneapolis, 1987, p. 7.

8 Clairmonte & Cavanagh, *op. cit.*

crashed on Wall Street it became evident that the deficit financed casino wealth of America was non-sustainable. As John Kenneth Galbraith observed, Reagan's favourite magic of the market was itself writing the last chapter of Reaganomics. Yet all Reagan could say was, 'I've believed this too long to change my mind now'.[9]

The crisis mind can offer no solutions. Those who dare to think of solutions are precisely those who were declared incapable of thinking. Like the women in the Third World, they are clear that the issue is survival, and they have the relevant expertise. 'Rational' man of the modern west is exposed today as a bundle of irrationalities, threatening the very survival of humankind. When we find that those who claimed to carry the light have led us into darkness and those who were declared to be inhabiting the dark recesses of ignorance were actually enlightened, it is but rational to redefine categories and meanings. Recovering the feminine principle as respect for life in nature and society appears to be the only way forward, for men as well as women, in the North as well as the South. The metaphors and concepts of minds deprived of the feminine principle have been based on seeing nature and women as worthless and passive, and finally as dispensable. These ethnocentric categorisations have been universalised, and with their universalisation has been associated the destruction of nature and the subjugation of women. But this dominant mode of organising the world is today being challenged by the very voices it had silenced. These voices, muted through subjugation, are now quietly but firmly suggesting that the western male has produced only one culture, and that there are other ways of structuring the world. Women's struggles for survival through the protection of nature are redefining the meaning of basic categories. They are challenging the central belief of the dominant world-view that nature and women are worthless and waste, that they are obstacles to progress and must be sacrificed.

The two central shifts in thinking that are being induced by women's ecological struggles relate to economic and intellectual worth. The first relates to our understanding of what constitutes knowledge, and who the knowers and producers of intellectual value are. The second involves concepts of wealth and economic value and who the producers of wealth and economic value are. Women producing survival are showing us that nature is the very basis and matrix of economic life through its function in lifesupport and livelihood, and the elements of nature that the dominant view has treated as 'waste' are the basis of sustainability and the

9 Quoted in Lance Morrow, 'Who's in Charge?' *Time*, November 9, 1987, p. 20.

wealth of the poor and the marginal. They are challenging concepts of waste, rubbish and dispensability as the modem west has defined them. They are showing that production of sustenance is basic to survival itself and cannot be deleted from economic calculations; if production of life cannot be reckoned with in money terms, then it is economic models, and not women's work in producing sustenance and life, that must be sacrificed. The intellectual heritage for ecological survival lies with those who are experts in survival. They have the knowledge and experience to extricate us from the ecological cul-de-sac that the western masculinist mind has manoeuvred us into. And while Third World women have privileged access to survival expertise, their knowledge is inclusive, not exclusive. The ecological categories with which they think and act can become the categories of liberation for all, for men as well as for women, for the west as well as the non-west, and for the human as well as the non-human elements of the earth. By elbowing out 'life' from being the central concern in organising human society, the dominant paradigm of knowledge has become a threat to life itself. Third World women are bringing the concern with living and survival back to centre-stage in human history. In recovering the chances for the survival of all life, they are laying the foundations for the recovery of the feminine principle in nature and society, and through it the recovery of the earth as sustainer and provider.

INDEX

About the Author

Photo by Kartikey Shiva

Vandana Shiva is a physicist, world-renowned environmental thinker and activist, and a tireless crusader for economic, food, and gender justice. She is the author and editor of many influential books, including *Making Peace with the Earth, Earth Democracy, Soil Not Oil, Stolen Harvest, Water Wars,* and *Globalization's New Wars.* Dr. Shiva is the recipient of more than twenty international awards, among them the Right Livelihood Award (1993); the John Lennon-Yoko Ono Grant for Peace (2008); The Sydney Peace Prize (2010); and the Calgary Peace Prize (Canada, 2011). In addition, she is a board member of the World Future Council and one of the leaders and board members of the International Forum on Globalization (whose other members include Jerry Mander, Edward Goldsmith, Ralph Nader, and Jeremy Rifkin). She travels frequently to speak at conferences around the world.

About North Atlantic Books

North Atlantic Books (NAB) is a 501(c)(3) nonprofit publisher committed to a bold exploration of the relationships between mind, body, spirit, culture, and nature. Founded in 1974, NAB aims to nurture a holistic view of the arts, sciences, humanities, and healing. To make a donation or to learn more about our books, authors, events, and newsletter, please visit www.northatlanticbooks.com.